Case Studies in
Needs Assessment

Sara Miller McCune founded SAGE Publishing in 1965 to support the dissemination of usable knowledge and educate a global community. SAGE publishes more than 1000 journals and over 800 new books each year, spanning a wide range of subject areas. Our growing selection of library products includes archives, data, case studies and video. SAGE remains majority owned by our founder and after her lifetime will become owned by a charitable trust that secures the company's continued independence.

Los Angeles | London | New Delhi | Singapore | Washington DC | Melbourne

Case Studies in Needs Assessment

Edited by

Darlene F. Russ-Eft

Oregon State University

Catherine M. Sleezer

Employee Training and Performance Improvement Specialists

Los Angeles | London | New Delhi
Singapore | Washington DC | Melbourne

FOR INFORMATION:

SAGE Publications, Inc.
2455 Teller Road
Thousand Oaks, California 91320
E-mail: order@sagepub.com

SAGE Publications India Pvt. Ltd.
B 1/I 1 Mohan Cooperative Industrial Area
Mathura Road, New Delhi 110 044
India

SAGE Publications Ltd.
1 Oliver's Yard
55 City Road
London EC1Y 1SP
United Kingdom

SAGE Publications Asia-Pacific Pte. Ltd.
18 Cross Street #10-10/11/12
China Square Central
Singapore 048423

ISBN: 978-1-5443-4233-7

Acquisitions Editor: Helen Salmon
Editorial Assistant: Megan O'Heffernan
Production Editor: Gagan Mahindra
Copy Editor: Lana Arndt
Typesetter: Hurix Digital
Proofreader: Talia Greenberg
Cover Designer: Dally Verghese
Marketing Manager: Shari Countryman

19 20 21 22 23 10 9 8 7 6 5 4 3 2 1

Table of Contents

Preface

Are you dissatisfied with aspects of the current status quo that are not what they could or should be? If so, do you know how to conduct a needs assessment—in your workplace, volunteer organization, or community—to identify the important needs and to obtain the insights and resources to successfully address the needs? This book offers a wealth of practical insights for conducting needs assessments and addressing the identified needs.

While we could find many resources that describe how needs assessments *should* be conducted, we could not find any current books on needs assessment cases that describe how needs assessments *are* conducted. Written in plain English, this book contains 20 needs assessment cases, and each describes how practitioners assessed real-life gaps between the current and desired conditions.

The book contains a collection of needs assessment cases. You will find cases conducted by external consultants, internal employees, students, experts, and individuals and teams. You will also find cases written for evaluation, training, education, health care, career development, leadership development, community development, policy development, strategic planning, and more.

Some cases are set in the United States; some are set in other countries. The contexts for the cases include multinational organizations, government agencies, communities, volunteer organizations, health care, higher education, and more. The data collection, analysis methods, and reporting approaches varied across the cases.

Learning to conduct needs assessments is like learning to drive motor vehicles. Both efforts involve acquiring *what knowledge* and developing *how-to knowledge*. Novice drivers acquire what knowledge by reviewing a Driver's Education manual, often while sitting in a high school classroom. What knowledge includes the rules of the road, road signs, and so forth. Novice drivers often develop how-to knowledge while practice driving with a coach, driving instructor, or trusted family member. A few new drivers tackle the how-to knowledge by jumping into the driver seat and taking off—thus, creating white knuckle experiences, fender benders, and hazards for other drivers on the road.

Novice needs assessors (i.e., analysts) often learn what knowledge from textbooks and instructor presentations. Examples of what knowledge include definitions, tools such as logic models and design thinking, approaches to needs assessment, and strategies for collecting and analyzing data. However, developing the how-to knowledge required to successfully conduct needs assessments can be much more difficult than learning to operate motor vehicles. Why? Because behaviors such as braking and steering vary little across automobile makes and models. By contrast, the practice of needs assessment varies greatly across contexts. For example, an analyst who is experienced working with for-profit businesses can struggle when working with a government agency, and vice versa. In addition, needs assessments are often intense, leaving experienced coach analysts immersed with little time to assist novices.

The cases in this book allow you to ride along with practitioners as they describe implementing needs assessments. Learning how-to knowledge from other practitioners is not as exciting as jumping feet first into conducting a needs assessment in a real-life situation. However, it can help you avoid creating accidents, unnecessary tensions and costs, and serious professional and organization problems.

Consider also the value of saving time, gaining credibility, and producing more useful results that you can obtain by using the tricks of the trade that the practitioners so graciously shared in the cases. For example, check out how Cumberland saved time when scheduling interviews, how Silverstein engaged decision makers in analyzing data, and how Engle and Altschuld visually presented needs assessment results to community members. These are only a few of the many examples shared in the cases.

The tricks of the trade that the book's practitioners shared can sharpen thinking and practice and make the difference between success and taking a wrong turn that causes a needs assessment project to fail. Finally, the cases provide a powerful tool for reflection because they allow you to digest the activities of needs assessments at your own pace.

Details on the Case Studies

The identification and selection of the case studies was not completely random. Rather, we used our professional networks to locate practitioners and scholar-practitioners who were likely to be able to contribute a case study. The professional organizations that we contacted included (a) the Academy of Human Resource Development; (b) the Needs Assessment Topical Interest Group of the American Evaluation Association (AEA); and (c) the Business, Leadership, and Performance of AEA. In addition, we contacted some former students from our respective academic institutions. Finally, upon seeing that there were no job and task analysis cases, we contacted the Human Resources Research Organization (HumRRO), given their reputation for work in this area.

The cases were then grouped into the following categories:

- Knowledge and skills assessment
- Job and task analysis
- Competency assessment
- Strategic needs assessment
- Complex needs assessment

Each case describes

- The background for the needs assessment
- The organization's profile

- What led to the needs assessment
- The focus and the boundaries for the effort
- How the needs assessment was conducted (including data collection and analysis—reporting)
- The needs assessment results and how they were used
- What influenced the needs assessment (e.g., politics, culture, language)
- The issues that had to be addressed for success
- Discussion questions for considering in-depth issues
- Appropriate references as well as some background information on the authors
- A few of the cases provide appendix material (e.g., data collection and management instruments)

This book is appropriate for practitioners, students, and scholars. Practitioners can use it to compare their how-to knowledge with the information contained in the cases and to consider whether and how to update their practices.

This book is a suitable text for graduate and undergraduate courses that teach needs assessment as the starting point for training, development, performance improvement, community development, and evaluation initiatives. It can be used as a companion to *A Practical Guide to Needs Assessment* (Sleezer, Russ-Eft, & Gupta, 2014). Also, it can serve as a resource for students assigned to conduct needs assessment projects, training projects, human resource development (HRD) projects, and evaluation projects in internship and directed study courses.

We hope that scholars use the cases in the book to compare the differences between needs assessment practices and instruction. Such comparison, coupled with thoughtful reflection and discourse, could move the field forward by identifying needed changes to both the practice and instruction of needs assessment.

References

Sleezer, C. M., Russ-Eft, D. F., & Gupta, K. (2014). *A practical guide to needs assessment* (3rd ed.). San Francisco, CA: Wiley & ASTD.

Acknowledgments

We want to thank retired professor Thomas Michael Power from the Université Laval, who alerted us to the limited number of current case studies that were appropriate for teaching needs assessments. We also thank the many practitioners who each provided the real-world cases for this book.

We are grateful to the practitioners and faculty members who helped us hone our practical how-to knowledge of needs assessment. Deane Gradous, our friend and editor, made this book easier to read. Helen Salmon, our editor at SAGE, offered many helpful suggestions, which improved our initial proposal. The external reviewers provided needed critiques to focus the text and the cases. Finally, we thank our families, especially Jack Eft and Jim Sleezer, whose support enabled us to be the best needs assessors and writers we could be.

SAGE and the editors would like to thank the following reviewers for their feedback:

Minjuan Wang, San Diego State University

Diane Gavin, St. Philip's College

Nikki DiGregorio, Georgia Southern University

Dawn L. Comeau, Emory University

Jill Stefaniak, Old Dominion University

Denise M. Cumberland, University of Louisville

Amy E. Patterson, Agnes Scott College

Gretta Wright, LaGrange College

Editors' Biographies

 **Darlene F. Russ-Eft**, PhD, is Professor Emeritus of adult and higher education, College of Education, Oregon State University (OSU). She received her BA from the College of Wooster in psychology and her MA and PhD from University of Michigan in cognitive psychology. She worked for international training companies as director of research before joining OSU, where she teaches doctoral and master's courses to senior leaders and practitioners. Her research focuses on issues related to leadership development and human resources development (HRD) program evaluation. Her most recent book is titled *Managing Social Science Research* (2017, Wiley). She is past president of the Academy of Human Resource Development (AHRD), past board member of the American Evaluation Association, and past editor of *Human Resource Development Quarterly*. In her previous role with international training companies and as a director for the International Board of Standards for Training, Performance, and Instruction (ibstpi), she has undertaken several studies examining global competencies related to HRD. She has received several awards for her research, including the Times Mirror Editor of the Year Award, the ASTD (now ATD) Research Article Award, and the AHRD Scholar Award. She was also inducted into the AHRD Hall of Fame.

(darlene.russeft@oregonstate.edu)

 **Catherine M. (Cathy) Sleezer**, PhD, helps individuals and organizations identify and address performance barriers and align training and development with goals. Grounded and guided by cutting-edge research and best practices, she has consulted successfully with a variety of organizations on needs assessment, training and development, executive coaching, strategic planning, organizational surveys, employee engagement, management development, new employee orientation, and team building. She received her PhD from the University of Minnesota and was a professor at Oklahoma State University before moving to the corporate world where she filled multiple roles for an international company. Cathy's work history also, includes serving as a faculty member at Penn State, where she directed the Institute for Research in Training and Development. More recently, she was the resident consultant for the University of Tulsa's Center for Executive and Professional Development. Cathy is a past director and president of the International Board of Standards for Training, Performance, and Instruction (ibstpi) and a past board member of the Academy of Human Resource Development (ASTD) and the ASTD (now ATD) Research Committee. Her co-authored books include *Human Resource Development Review: Research and Implications, A Practical Guide to Needs Assessment* (3rd edition), *Fieldbook of ibstpi Evaluator Competencies*, and *Managing Applied Social Research*.

(catherine.sleezer@gmail.com)

Contributing Authors' Biographies

James W. Altschuld is Professor Emeritus at The Ohio State University (OSU) and a charter member of its Emeritus Academy. For almost 30 years, he taught research methods and program evaluation courses for graduate students in the OSU College of Education and Human Ecology. In evaluation, he developed a sequence of four courses on models, the assessment of needs, and the design and implementation of evaluations for programs primarily in education, with a lesser emphasis for those in business, industry, and public health. He has in excess of more than 100 publications, including many books on needs assessment (over the past quarter of a century) and topics such as professionalizing the work of evaluators. He has received local and university awards for teaching, service to graduate students, and major assistance to a local school district. He was honored with a statewide award for evaluation from the Ohio Program Evaluator's Group, and at the national level, he was the recipient of the Alva and Gunnar Myrdal Award of the American Evaluation Association for major contributions to evaluation.

(altschuld.1@osu.edu)

Heather Champion is the Manager of Client Evaluation Services and Senior Evaluation Faculty for the Insights and Impact group at the Center for Creative Leadership. Heather has over 20 years of combined experience in research, evaluation, and leadership development with work across most industry sectors, including corporate and nonprofit. Since 2008, when Heather joined the Center for Creative Leadership (CCL), a top-ranked, global provider of leadership education and research, she has led numerous needs assessment, evaluation, and research studies, including work in North America, Asia, Europe, and Africa. She has experience with a wide range of evaluation methodologies, including success case methodology, the evaluation of action learning and action development, social network analysis, and leader analytics. In her role, she works with CCL staff, global clients, and external evaluators to design and conduct customized evaluations for CCL programs, products, and services. This work includes identifying organizational and leader needs, articulating program outcomes, selecting the most appropriate methods for evaluating initiatives for improvement and impact, and reporting the findings to key stakeholders. Heather has worked with clients from a broad range of sectors, including government, finance, manufacturing, and technology, but has extensive experience in the health sector and in early leadership development.

Heather earned a BA in psychology from North Carolina State University and an MS and PhD in developmental psychology from North Carolina State University. She completed a postdoctoral fellowship in adolescent health at Wake Forest University School of Medicine.

(championh@ccl.org)

Louise C. Chan is a consultant at FMP Consulting. She earned her MA in industrial-organizational psychology from Minnesota State University, Mankato. Ms. Chan attended the University of California, San Diego, where she graduated with a BS in psychology.

N. Anand Chandrasekar is a senior research faculty at the Center for Creative Leadership (CCL). In this role, Anand leads CCL's Asia-focused leadership development research and evaluation practice, partnering with CCL staff and clients to identify leadership needs and design, and to deliver leadership development solutions, articulate leadership solution outcomes, and evaluate the solutions for impact and improvement. A key area of his current research is on enhancing the ability of individuals and organizations to make learning from experience intentional, not incidental. Anand holds a BE degree in electrical and electronics engineering from the University of Madras and an MBus degree from Nanyang Technological University, Singapore.

(chandrasekara@ccl.org)

Yonjoo Cho, PhD (choyonj@indiana.edu), is an associate professor of instructional systems technology focusing on human resources development (HRD) at Indiana University. Her research interests include action learning in organizations, HRD, and women in leadership. She has published three books: *Trends and Issues in Action Learning Practice: Lessons From South Korea* (Cho & Bong, 2013) with Routledge, and *Current Perspectives on Asian Women in Leadership* (Cho, Ghosh, Sun, & McLean, 2017) and *Korean Women in Leadership* (Cho & McLean, 2018) with Palgrave Macmillan. She serves as an associate editor of the *Human Resource Development Review* and on the editorial board of the *Human Resource Development Quarterly, European Journal of Training and Development*, and *Action Learning: Research and Practice*. She has been a board member of the Academy of Human Resource Development and the Korea Action Learning Association. She received her PhD in instructional technology from the University of Texas at Austin.

(choyonj@indiana.edu)

Candice Clark is a PhD candidate in the College of Education at Oregon State University, where she is focusing on science and mathematics education in higher education settings. Candice received her master's degree in adult and higher education from Oregon State in 2018. Her undergraduate work in physics and mathematics began at Northeast Alabama Community College and was completed at The University of Alabama in Huntsville. For the latter half of her undergraduate education and for her graduate studies, Candice has been a Cooke Scholar. Cooke scholarships are highly prestigious academic scholarships awarded annually to a select few U.S. students; awards go toward supporting high-achieving students who face pronounced barriers to educational success. In her free time, Candice enjoys playing trombone and euphonium with volunteer groups in Oregon's Willamette River Valley.

(clarkca@oregonstate.edu)

Ginny Cockerill is the Assistant Director of Assessment at The University of Alabama in Huntsville. She received her MEd from Columbia International University in 2002 in Curriculum and Instruction. Ms. Cockerill has over 15 years of experience in higher education, focusing on assessment and data analysis. Her work has centered on guiding faculty, staff, and administrators in interpreting external and internal standards, developing and implementing plans and processes to ensure those standards are met, and reporting and analyzing those results.

(ginny.cockerill@uah.edu)

Denise M. Cumberland is an assistant professor in the Department of Educational Leadership, Evaluation, and Organizational Development at the University of Louisville. She teaches courses on organizational analysis, workplace ethics, organization change, and program evaluation. Her research interests include governance, leadership, and training within global organizations, franchising firms, and the nonprofit sector. She consults on topics such as change, conflict management, communication strategies, innovation, and teamwork. Dr. Cumberland received her PhD from the University of Louisville.

(denise.cumberland@louisville.edu)

Ariel M. Domlyn, MA, has experience conducting applied research domestically and internationally in the fields of medical anthropology, public health, and psychology. Ms. Domlyn specializes in developing and applying implementation science methods and health interventions at every level: individual, family, organization, community, state, and national. She has a master's degree in medical anthropology and is currently a doctoral candidate in clinical-community psychology at the University of South Carolina. There, she is a junior scholar with the SmartState Center for Healthcare Quality, an alumnus of the USC Graduate Civic Scholars Program, and a recipient of the Cecil Scott Trustee Fellowship.

(adomlyn@email.sc.edu)

Eric L. Einspruch, PhD, principal, ELE Consulting, LLC, in Lake Oswego, OR, has spent over 30 years leading, managing, and conducting research and evaluation studies to inform policy development and program improvement. Dr. Einspruch has conducted small-scale local evaluations, large multisite studies, large-scale epidemiological surveys of adolescent health behavior, and randomized controlled trials. He has extensive experience providing consultation and technical assistance. He is an award-winning author whose work has appeared in 18 peer-reviewed publications (15 journal articles, two books, and one book chapter), and he has held professional association leadership positions. Dr. Einspruch is an adjunct professor at Portland State University (PSU), where he teaches graduate, undergraduate, and certificate courses in program evaluation, research methods, data analysis, and emergency preparedness. In 2017, he received PSU's inaugural Adjunct Excellence Award for Research, which recognizes and honors the outstanding contributions of adjunct faculty and researchers. Dr. Einspruch may be contacted via www.eleconsulting.com.

(einspruch@eleconsulting.com)

Molly Engle is a retired professor of adult and higher education and an evaluation specialist at Oregon State University. She has spent the past 30 plus years evaluating community programs and the problems encountered with them. She has co-taught the Needs Assessment and Asset/Capacity Building professional development session at the American Evaluation Association with Dr. Altschuld for several years.

Jen Geary, PhD, is affiliated with the Trident Mediation, Counseling, Arts and Supports Foundation, which operates in Australia and Canada. She has written two books, two research theses, a chapter in an edited book, as well as numerous articles. She has published in a number of areas relevant to law, justice, and management. She holds a Bachelor of Social Work from Curtin University (1997); Bachelor of Laws from the University of New England (2012); a Master of Social Work from Monash University (2000); a Master of Social Policy from James Cook University (2001); a Master of Education in Distance Education from Athabasca University (2001); a Master of Education in Further Education and Training from University of Southern Queensland (2002); a Master of Arts in Psychology by Research from Deakin University (2015), and a PhD Social Science in Social Work and Social Policy from the University of South Australia (2008).

(tridentmediation@icloud.com)

P. Cristian Gugiu, PhD, was an assistant professor in the Quantitative Research, Evaluation and Measurement program in the Department of Educational Studies at The Ohio State University at the time this chapter was written. He received his training in psychometrics, statistics, and evaluation. He has 23 years of evaluation and research experience with a diverse portfolio with regard to content (education, medicine, psychology). Broadly speaking, he is interested in survey development and validation and the investigation of appropriate methods for handling ordinal data.

(crisgugiu@gmail.com)

Tara Kenworthy, MA, is a doctoral student at the University of South Carolina studying clinical-community psychology. Ms. Kenworthy has worked with nonprofit, governmental, and health care organizations to evaluate and improve the quality implementation of their initiatives. She is particularly interested in how implementation science can inform and improve integrated care initiatives.

(tlk@email.sc.edu)

Derek Koehl is a research associate at The University of Alabama in Huntsville. He received his MEd from The University of Texas at Brownsville in 1998 in educational technology. Mr. Koehl has over 13 years of experience as an instructional designer and educator and over 10 years of experience in business and organizational process optimization and consulting. His recent work focuses on the implications of language as an instructional technology and advancements in natural-language-processing algorithms and frameworks.

(dk0044@uah.edu)

Tim McGonigle, PhD, is a program manager at the Human Resources Research Organization (HumRRO). The HumRRO has developed methodologies that improve the accuracy and efficiency of the job analysis process and advance human resources practices that rely on job analysis data, such as employee selection, development, and career exploration programs. Dr. McGonigle has over 20 years of experience conducting job task analysis in support of a broad range of human resources program, including career development/exploration, workforce planning, assessment development and validation, and medical and physical ability standards. Numerous organizations have funded his research, including the Departments of Agriculture, Interior, Homeland Security, Transportation, Defense, and Veterans Affairs and the Office of Personnel Management, Centers for Disease Control, U.S. Air Force, and Army Research Institute. Dr. McGonigle earned a PhD in industrial-organizational psychology from Virginia Tech.

(TMcGonigle@HUMRRO.ORG)

Kelly A. McGreevey works with a health care consulting firm, assisting hospitals and health care organizations with developing a clinically integrated network. She is a skilled instructional designer with an eye for detail and a talent for creative problem solving. Ms. McGreevey holds a master's degree in human resource development from Northeastern Illinois University.

(kelly.mcgreevey@gmail.com)

Gary N. McLean, EdD, PhD hon., was president of McLean Global Consulting, Inc., a family business, and holds Canadian and U.S. citizenships. As an OD practitioner, he works extensively globally, especially in Asia. He is currently a Professor in the OD PhD program at Assumption University (Bangkok). He recently worked in the Graduate School of Management in the International Islamic University of Malaysia as "Renowned Scholar." He teaches regularly in the PhD program in human resources at National Institute for Development Administration and advises PhD students at Assumption University, both in Bangkok, Thailand. Previously, he was a senior professor at Texas A&M University. He is Professor Emeritus and co-founder of the HRD program at the University of Minnesota. He served as President of the Academy of Human Resource Development and the International Management Development Association. He served in editorial roles for several journals. His research interests are broad, focusing primarily on organization development and national and international HRD.

(gary.mclean@mcleanglobal.com)

Erich N. Pitcher, PhD, is Program Lead for Adult Education and Higher Education Leadership in the College of Education at Oregon State University. His most recent book is titled *Being and Becoming Professionally Other: Identities, Voices, and Experiences of U.S. Trans*Academic*, published by Peter Lang in 2018. He received his doctoral degree in higher, adult, and lifelong education from Michigan State University.

(enpitcher@gmail.com)

Ling Qian is an instructional designer at the University of Akron. She received a master's degree in instructional systems technology at Indiana University (IU). Before joining IU, she worked as faculty teaching educational technology at Hebei University in China for 8 years. Her research interests include multicultural perspectives of online instructional design and online pedagogy in active learning.

(lqian@uakron.edu)

Jonathan P. Scaccia, PhD, is a practicing community psychologist and an evaluation consultant with the Institute for Healthcare Improvement and the Finger Lakes Law and Social Policy Center. Dr. Scaccia was one of the initial developers of the $R = MC^2$ readiness model. His current research focuses on developing comprehensive methods to evaluate quantitative and qualitative differences in organizational readiness and enhancing strategies that can help to build readiness. These methods have been used in multiple projects and settings (community coalitions, schools, federally qualified health centers). Dr. Scaccia also works toward developing practical implementation science techniques usable by front-line practitioners.

(jonathan.p.scaccia@wandersmancenter.org)

Victoria Scott, PhD, is an assistant professor at the University of North Carolina at Charlotte. Dr. Scott focuses on interdisciplinary approaches to promote individual and collective wellness, systems-level capacity building, and organizational development. Dr. Scott works primarily with health care systems and community-based organizations. She is particularly interested in building organizational readiness in nonprofit and for-profit organizations, and the science and art of implementation science and quality improvement. Dr. Scott received the Society for Community Research and Action Early Career Award in 2015 in honor of her commitment to developing and promoting the field of community psychology. She also received the Don Klein Publication Award to Advance Community Psychology Practice for her co-edited book *Community Psychology: Foundations for Practice*, which aims to further the competencies of professionals who work in community settings.

(victoria.scott@uncc.edu)

Lauren A. Silverstein, PhD, chief impact officer, Jewish Federation of Greater MetroWest NJ. Prior to this position, she lived in Hartford, CT, where she was the founding director of Jr. Apprentice, a nonprofit program that introduces Hartford high school students to different careers and helps them develop job skills through hands-on apprenticeships with local employers. In addition to the nonprofit world, Lauren loves the classroom, and she taught at both the undergraduate and graduate levels in Education Leadership departments. Lauren received her PhD from the University of Pittsburgh, her master's degree in education from Harvard University, and her BA from Vassar College.

(LSilverstein@JFedGMW.org)

Melanie Suzanne Simpson is the Director of the Office of Institutional Research and Assessment at The University of Alabama in Huntsville. She has over 10 years of experience in higher education administration and student learning/ assessment and evaluation and over 15 years in public service. She received her EdD in professional studies with an emphasis in higher education administration from Delta State University in 2014. Dr. Simpson's most recent work has centered on developing models for measuring graduate student retention and graduation rates and ensuring that policies and procedures are met for institutional reporting, assessment, and accreditation.

(suzanne.simpson@uah.edu)

Dawisa Sritanyarat, PhD, is an assistant professor in the Graduate School of Human Resource Development in the National Institute for Development Administration, located in Bangkok, Thailand. Her areas of interest are not only human resource and organization development, but also higher education. With the interest in developing higher education study programs in Thailand systematically, she serves as an ASEAN University Network Quality Assurance (AUN-QA) assessor. Also, she is interested in outcome-based education and competency-based education. Her experiences in needs assessment are in the areas of project management, training and development, education quality assurance, and measurement and evaluation in organization.

(Dawisa.s@gmail.com)

Sequoia Star, MEd, with Sequoia Star Consulting and Oregon State University, holds a master's degree in adult education. She works as an independent consultant in the field of adult education and is courtesy faculty at Oregon State University. She has extensive background as a researcher conducting refereed research and evaluation in the public, private, and nonprofit sectors. Some of her more notable projects include project lead, lead researcher, evaluation, training, and curriculum developer on endeavors with OSU, Portland State University, University of Oregon, U.S. Department of Justice, The Robert Woods Johnson Foundation, The Ford Family Foundation, and Southwestern Oregon Community College. Ms. Star is a published author of journal articles and conference proceedings in the field of human resource development and has received numerous awards for academic excellence and social contribution, including the Oregon Governor Crime Victim's Service Award.

(sstar01@gmail.com)

Lindsay Strack, MPH, is the Manager of Research and Member Resources at WorldatWork, an organization delivering timely, practical, and relevant results on key total rewards issues. She earned her master's degree in public health from Northern Illinois University. Her experience includes conducting quantitative research in human resources, total rewards, public health, and health care.

(strack.lindsay@gmail.com)

Ratrapee Techawitthayachinda (Inging) is a PhD student of learning, literacies, and technologies at Arizona State University. She has a master's degree in instructional systems technology from Indiana University. Her research interests include computer-supported collaborative learning, group discourse and interactions, and cognitive and affective conflict in online learning.

(ratrapee@asu.edu)

Sandra L. Williams, PhD, is an associate professor and program coordinator of human resource development at Northeastern Illinois University. Her work focuses on core values and building trust in organizations. Dr. Williams created Ethics for Business Success and conducts research on mentoring, building trust in the workplace, and organizational change. She consults with organizations to create customized ethics training and trust-building seminars.

(s-williams24@neiu.edu)

Andrea Word is on the faculty in Curriculum and Instruction in the College of Education at The University of Alabama in Huntsville. She received her Ed.D. in Higher Education Administration from The University of Alabama in 2012. With backgrounds in both linguistics and higher education administration, Dr. Word's most recent research focuses on language within communication, with particular attention to teachers' design of instructional language. Her work prioritizes clarity of communication and its role in shared understanding within educational settings.

(worda@uah.edu)

Meina Zhu is a PhD candidate in instructional systems technology at Indiana University. She holds a master's degree in educational technology from Beijing Normal University in China. Her research interests include online instructional design, open education and massive open online courses, mobile learning, self-directed learning, and active learning.

(meinzhu@iu.edu)

Introduction

This chapter provides background information that makes the needs assessment cases in this book easier to understand and more useful. Here, you will find the following topics:

- Need: An important concept
- Overview of needs assessment
- Connections between needs assessment and program evaluation
- How to use the book
- Our favorite needs assessment resources

Need: An Important Concept

Needs assessment is a catchphrase with almost as many flavors as ice cream. This situation stems in part from the many definitions for the term *need*. Interestingly, *Merriam-Webster's* online dictionary (n.d.) defines *need* as "a lack of something requisite, desirable, or useful." Did you notice that the definition lacks information about what the *something* is, who might have the *something*, and how the *something* was determined?

To better understand the term *need*, consider the following examples:

- A teenager explains to her parents that she *will need* a new car.
- An individual addicted to meth *needs* drugs.
- The poor *need* food and clothing.
- The Finance Team *needs* a common procedure for auditing documents.
- This school *needs* a better science, technology, engineering, and mathematics (STEM) curriculum so its students are competitive.
- The community *needs* a neighborhood safety program.

Which example above focuses on an individual? A team? An organization? A community? Which example conveys a desire or a want? Something desirable? Something useful? A biopsychological state? A norm? A requirement? An obligation? A gap between the current condition and a goal? As the examples show, the term *need* can be interpreted in different ways.

Needs are seldom universally agreed upon, and their desirability, usefulness, and requirements can change quickly. For example, some community leaders may view a neighborhood program as desirable; others may view it as useless. Those views could change quickly if the community experiences a flood or obtains a grant. As Rossi, Lipsey, and Freeman (2004) pointed out in discussing social programs, "The resources, priorities, and relative influence of the various sponsors and stakeholders of social programs are dynamic and frequently change with shifts in political context and social trends" (p. 33). The same can be said of other types of decisions. A *need* reflects who the decision makers were, when they were asked, and how those who have a stake in addressing the *need* viewed the larger systemic, political, and cultural environment.

Each need must be precisely defined so that effective solutions or programs can be developed that address the decision makers' need. Needs assessment is an instrument for figuring out the important needs in a specific situation and how to address them.

Kettner, Moroney, and Martin (2017) stated that "Sometimes the need is obvious. . . . At other times the need is more subtle." Furthermore, they suggested four different perspectives on need: *normative need* (as defined by experts in the field), *perceived need* (as seen by those experiencing the need), *expressed need* (from those who seek out services), and *relative need* (needs and resources in one geographic area compared with needs and resources in another).

This section described how the term need contributes to the use of *needs assessment* as a catchphrase. The next section describes how the various applications of needs assessment as an instrument contribute to the confusion.

Overview of Needs Assessment

Assessing needs before implementing solutions is a foundation for such professions as training, education, human resource development, organization development, evaluation, health care, community development, and policy and program development (see Figure 1.1). Why? Needs assessments save time, resources, and frustrations—and, they increase the likelihood of success. Moreover, they distinguish true professionals from snake oil distributors who hawk their desired solutions regardless of the problem.

The use of *needs assessment* as a foundation for so many professions has led to various understandings of the term. Christensen (2016) offered advice for anyone who wants to find the definition of the terms needs assessment and training needs assessment: ". . . be prepared for an arduous search through the Internet and many texts and journal articles where authors have put their own spin, tweak, massage, and a coat of Rust-Oleum paint on the meanings. I say *the* because there is no single definitive explanation" (Para. 9). Watkins, West Meiers, and Visser (2012) stated that "the term needs assessment has taken on several definitions and has led to a number of related process models or approaches" (p. 15). They also identified some terms that are used as synonyms for needs

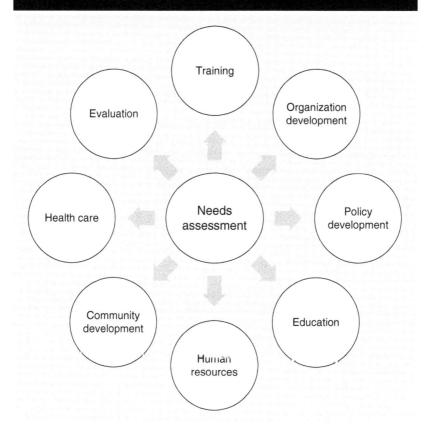

Figure 1.1 Some Professions That Rely on
          Needs Assessments

assessment: *gap analysis, performance analysis,* and *needs analysis.* Those are just a few flavors of needs assessment.

Consider the following example: Laura, the president of a mid-sized manufacturing firm, attended a party and overheard part of a conversation between a recently hired intern and the city's mayor. To Laura's surprise, the intern divulged that many of the firm's safety requirements were not met. Laura immediately determined that she would have a frank discussion with the intern.

Later, while driving home from the party, Laura again considered the intern's comment, and she realized that

- A gap between her firm's current safety practices and the city's mandated practices could have serious consequences for both her and the firm.

- The intern's comment to the mayor was Laura's first hint of a potential safety problem.

Laura then weighed three options for immediate action:

1. The risky option: Ignore the potential safety gap.

2. The expensive option: Mandate that all employees attend all the firm's safety training courses.

3. The smart option: Authorize a needs assessment to figure out if and where a safety gap exists, the behaviors and mechanisms that contribute to the gap, and potential future actions to close the gap.

Which of the three options would you advise Laura to take? We choose Option 3.

Most initiatives that involve human learning, training, performance improvement, or policy, community, or organization development begin with a needs assessment, which is "a diagnostic process that relies on data collection, collaboration, and negotiation to identify and understand gaps in learning and performance and to determine future actions" (Sleezer, Russ-Eft, & Gupta, 2014, p. 310). Watkins et al. (2012) pointed out that "the results of your needs assessment will then guide your subsequent decisions—including the design, implementation, and evaluation of projects and programs that will lead to achieving the desired results" (p. 6).

An *organization* is a group of people who work together to accomplish something. Examples include businesses, health care organizations, government agencies, foundations, nonprofit organizations, colleges and universities, communities, and military groups. Many large organizations have divisions that are responsible for specific areas of activity. These also can be called organizations. Examples include a federal or state government agency, a company's Human Resource Department, a community's Maintenance Operation, and a university's College of Education.

A *needs assessment* is influenced by the organization's politics, internal and external norms and cultures, specific language, unique interactions among people, financial and physical resources, and much more. A needs assessment is also influenced by the environment in which the organization exists. Do you think Laura should consider that her firm is in a city that recently experienced several toxic spills? We do!

An organization is composed of individuals and subgroups that interact to achieve organizational goals. The individuals and subgroups in Laura's firm who could play an important role in the needs assessment include

*   The members of the senior management team

*   The Safety Department that develops and monitors the firm's safety policies and practices

*   The Finance Department that must fund any future action to address the need

- The Operations Department that must adjust employees' schedules to implement the needs assessment solution(s) while, simultaneously, maintaining the firm's production schedule

- The Human Resource Department that hires and fires employees and monitors adherence to the firm's policies

- The Communication Manager who creates and disseminates messages about adherence to safety rules

The individuals and subgroups—which each have a stake in the needs assessment process and outcomes—are called *stakeholders*. The stakeholders' characteristics and interactions can affect the needs assessment process and its outcomes.

The *needs assessor,* or *analyst,* is the professional who conducts the needs assessment. The analyst could be an external consultant or an employee of the organization. Analysts, through their diagnostic skill levels and their information gathering preferences, influence the process and the results of a needs assessment (Sleezer, 1990).

Decision maker(s) are responsible for choosing to allocate resources to determine and/or address the needs. The decision makers affect the needs assessment process and results (e.g., their preferences for data sources, the type of data collected and more) (Sleezer, 1990).

Sleezer et al. (2014) stated that a needs assessment can diagnose the learning and performance issues of

- Individuals

- Teams

- Functional units (e.g., finance, operations)

- One or more organizations

- Interorganizational groups

- Communities

- Countries

- International efforts

Given its diagnostic role and ability to build consensus and buy-in, it is not surprising that needs assessment is the first step in the initiatives of so many professions. A needs assessment can specify the gaps (i.e., needs) that have the greatest priority in the current real-world environment and how each should be addressed. Usually, needs assessments identify more needs than there are resources available to address them. Therefore, the needs assessment process involves the analyst in interacting with people in social situations to understand and articulate the priority needs for a particular situation and to specify realistic solution strategies. The process involves

- Comparing the current and desired conditions

- Defining the problems or opportunities

- Figuring out the behaviors and mechanisms that contribute to the current conditions

- Determining what behaviors and mechanisms can be changed to produce the desired conditions

- Developing solution strategies

- Building support for action (Sleezer et al., 2014)

We have introduced "needs" as a concept, and then we discussed the various types of and contexts for needs assessments. This next section describes the connections between needs assessment and program evaluation.

Connections Between Needs Assessment and Program Evaluation

Some experts consider needs assessment to be the larger concept that subsumes program evaluation, while others see needs assessment as a segment within program evaluation. Certainly, if we consider professional organizations, the American Evaluation Association hosts a Topical Interest Group in needs assessment.

Regardless of one's perspective, we should acknowledge that the two processes are directly connected or linked. From the standpoint of training and the ADDIE model (Branson et al., 1975; Watson, 1981) that is used in Instructional Systems Design, for example, the two concepts are linked, as shown in Figure 1.2.

According to the model, assessment informs the design and development of a program or process. Then, following implementation, an evaluation can yield information as to whether more assessment and design and development should be undertaken.

Design thinking is a process that has gained recent popularity. It is an iterative innovation or problem-solving process. Linke (2017) stated that

At a high level, the steps involved in the design thinking process are simple: first, fully understand the problem; second, explore a wide range of possible solutions; third, iterate extensively through prototyping and testing; and finally, implement through the customary deployment mechanisms. (Para. 4)

Did you notice the similarities between design thinking and the ADDIE model? Both processes are similar, except for the lack of an evaluation step in the design thinking process.

Figure 1.2   Depiction of the ADDIE Model

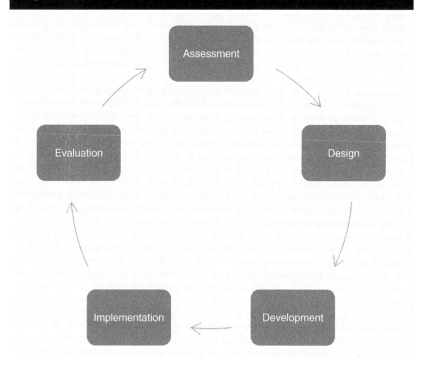

Both needs assessment and program evaluation use similar tools, techniques, and methods. These include the design of the effort, the methods for data collection, the approaches to ensuring reliability and validity, and the methods for analyzing the data. Also, whether using the ADDIE model or not, an evaluation determines whether the needs identified in the needs assessment have been addressed.

One important approach that can be used in both needs assessment and program evaluation involves the development of logic models. This approach was originally conceptualized by Wholey (1979) as a method to determine whether a program could be evaluated and which components would be appropriate to evaluate. According to Russ-Eft and Preskill (2009), the following questions can aid in developing a logic model:

- What are the assumptions underlying this program?

- What resources (human, financial, organizational) will be used to accomplish this program or process?

- What activities will be undertaken with the resources to produce the products and outcomes?

- What direct products (or outputs) will provide evidence that the program or process was actually implemented?

- What immediate outcomes do you expect from this program or process?

- What long-term outcomes do you expect? (p. 158)

A logic model can be used as part of a needs assessment, for example, to identify what might be added to ensure that the outputs and the outcomes can be achieved. As part of an evaluation effort, the logic model can help to focus that effort and determine the key questions to be answered. More details on logic models can be found in the following works: Jung and Schubert (1983); Kettner et al. (2017); McLaughlin and Jordan (1999, 2015); Rossi et al. (2004); and Strosberg and Wholey (1983).

How to Use the Book

The cases in this book offer insights about the practice of needs assessment in dynamic, real-world organizations and communities. The speed of change, the intense competition for organization and community resources, and the increased number of highly educated decision makers who are knowledgeable about social and performance processes in the workplace and in communities have affected expectations for professional-level needs assessments. In the past, students, program evaluators, and consultants, human resource professionals, and other professionals armed themselves with the jargon of needs assessment before meeting with decision makers (e.g., gap analysis, needs analysis versus needs assessment, performance improvement potential). They expected decision makers to learn the special language of needs assessment.

Today, decision makers expect those who conduct needs assessments to quickly understand the larger context for the needs assessment and to contribute their specialized knowledge—with bulls-eye accuracy—to organizational or community success. Few decision makers seek a one-size-fits-all needs assessment. Instead, they want a needs assessment that is custom-fit to their situation. Moreover, many decision makers expect those who lead needs assessment initiatives to know what they are doing—even when the analysts are conducting their first needs assessment project. Such expectations can challenge novices who may

- Have little experience in transferring needs assessment concepts that were learned in the classroom to the real-world, dynamic situations

- Lack confidence in conducting needs assessments in the presence of powerful decision makers who possess competing interests

This book invites both novice and seasoned analysts to look over the shoulders of practitioners, to examine needs assessment practice in action, to grasp the real-world issues that arise, and to understand a variety of needs assessment strategies and issues. Each case in this book examines the implementation of needs assessment in a specific situation. As such, it bridges needs assessment theories and actual practice.

The cases in the book are organized into five sections based on the five approaches to needs assessment described by Sleezer et al. (2014):

- A *knowledge and skills assessment* focuses on the knowledge and skill needs that may exist. Such needs are often addressed with training solutions.

- A *job and task analysis* gathers and organizes information about the scope, responsibilities, and tasks of particular job functions.

- A *competency-based needs assessment* determines the knowledge, skills, attitudes, values, motivations, and beliefs that people must have to be successful in a job.

- A *strategic needs assessment* focuses on the learning and performance gaps that exist within the context of an organization's business strategy.

- A *complex needs assessment* is used when a single approach alone is insufficient for assessing the needs.

Table 1.1 depicts the characteristics of the book's needs assessment cases. It groups the cases into the five approaches. Then, it presents the author(s), the case title, and the details as to the "who, what, and where" of each case. It should be noted that there is only one case that depicts a job-task analysis and only one case that uses a competency assessment. Some of the complex needs assessments do include these approaches, however.

In addition to the overview of the cases, Table 1.2 provides a listing of the cases and the chapter highlighting some issues that may be of interest. These have been classified into the following topics: (a) data collection, (b) data analysis, (c) presentation of results, and (d) overall process.

The last chapter in the book is a summary of lessons learned from all the case studies. Regardless of which case you read first, be sure to check out this chapter. It describes the insights and tricks of the trade that we gained from reviewing all the needs assessment cases. These insights can be used to improve future needs assessment practice and scholarship.

Table 1.1 Characteristics of Needs Assessment Cases

Author	Case Title	Where Needs Assessment Was Conducted	Who Conducted the Needs Assessment	Focus of Needs Assessment	How Data Were Collected	How Data Were Analyzed
Knowledge and Skill (6 Cases)						
Clark	Transitioning From Traditional to Digital: A Knowledge and Skills Needs Assessment for a Community Orchestra Context	Community orchestra within an urban area in the southeastern United States	A former member of the orchestra	Focused on determining the gap between knowledge and skills volunteers had and those they needed to complete a project involving the scanning and saving of music scores	Content mappings, surveys, and interviews	Likert scale responses from surveys of volunteers verified via follow-up interview; verified responses compared to minimum knowledge and skills required; content mappings revealed where knowledge and skills were underdeveloped
Cho, Zhu, Techawitthayachinda, & Qian	A Needs Assessment of Online Core Courses for Student Learning in Higher Education	A midwestern university	Faculty and graduate students of the university	How online courses are delivered for graduate students of an Instructional Technology (IT) Department for student learning	Interviews with seven instructors and 11 online graduate students who agreed to participate after a survey questionnaire	Used descriptive statistics for survey data and content analysis for interview data and a strengths, weaknesses, opportunities, and threats (SWOT) analysis to present

Author	Case Title	Where Needs Assessment Was Conducted	Who Conducted the Needs Assessment	Focus of Needs Assessment	How Data Were Collected	How Data Were Analyzed
					with 44 out of 96 online graduate students, a review of the literature on online education, and a document review of four peer institutions' IT programs	results (findings and recommendations) for the improvement of online core courses for student learning
Cumberland	A Needs Assessment for a Professional Association's Certificate Program	International professional association	Consultant experienced in franchising and in conducting needs assessments	Identified what would encourage a specific target population of long-standing credential holders to continue recertifying	Archival survey data, interviews conducted over the telephone	Archival data from the graduate satisfaction surveys were cross-tabulated; closed-ended data responses from long-standing credential holders were reviewed; Likert-style questions were analyzed with descriptive statistics; open-ended survey responses and interview transcripts analyzed using structural coding technique

(Continued)

Table 1.1 (Continued)

Author	Case Title	Where Needs Assessment Was Conducted	Who Conducted the Needs Assessment	Focus of Needs Assessment	How Data Were Collected	How Data Were Analyzed
Geary	A Public Legal Education and Information Strategy: Advancing Cybersecurity and Counterterrorism Processes	Over 50 locations in Australia, Canada, and the United States	Staff of the Trident, Mediation, Counseling, Arts and Supports Foundation	Collected and shared materials from Public Legal Education and Information (PLEI) to enable public to understand impacts of cybersecurity breaches and counterterrorism and to learn ways to protect themselves	Researcher was a participant-observer: collecting archival data, observing the public and their interactions, participating in public activities, and speaking with selected individuals. PLEI collected from various sources such as case law, legislation, international law, the general literature, and direct observations	Qualitative analysis and triangulation; development of corporate, theoretical, affiliations, program features, and location codes used to develop themes
Star	Paws-A-Tive Pals: Assessing the Needs of a Therapy Dog Organization	Grassroots organization in rural community on west coast of the United States	External consultant	Focused on developing clear definitions of work roles of governing body; transitioning newly elected officers and board; developing training for evaluators of new-member dog teams	Survey of officers and board members; personal interviews of selected officers and board members; literature review; review of extant documents (organizational guide, past newsletters, team evaluation forms, the membership list, the picture albums/scrapbooks, and the promotional flyer)	Quantitative data analyzed using descriptive statistics; qualitative data analyzed for thematic content; used constant-comparative method and content analysis to compare data to literature

Author	Case Title	Where Needs Assessment Was Conducted	Who Conducted the Needs Assessment	Focus of Needs Assessment	How Data Were Collected	How Data Were Analyzed
Star	Small Business Enrichment Training Needs Assessment	Small business organizations (about 200 organizations) in rural community on the west coast of United States	Small Business Enrichment Program (SBEP) engaged an external evaluator	Focused on determining entrepreneur's needs and desires for training	Explored available training programs; examined historical data; two surveys of small business organization clients and SBEP statewide directors and staff; interviews of 15 small business owners	Descriptive statistics reported for quantitative data; content analysis of qualitative data identifying themes
Job and Task (1 case)						
McGonigle	Enterprise-wide Job Task Analysis in a Large Organization	U.S. government agency that had dispersed sites	A consulting company	Constructed and validated over 600 role profiles that each included data for up to five career levels; provided career development information for roles filled by over 90% of organization's workforce	Background information on each role (e.g., position descriptions, vacancy announcements, and official titling and job grading standards), information from a Department of Labor database, feedback from subject matter experts (SMEs)	Content analyzed documents; created draft profiles for SME review and feedback

(Continued)

Table 1.1 (Continued)

Author	Case Title	Where Needs Assessment Was Conducted	Who Conducted the Needs Assessment	Focus of Needs Assessment	How Data Were Collected	How Data Were Analyzed
Competency (1 Case)						
Sritan-yarat	Assessing Needs for a PhD Study Program in Human Resource Development and Organization Development: A Case Study Focused on Quality Development in an Outcome-Based Education Approach	Human Resource and Organization Development PhD Program for the National Institute for Development Administration in Bangkok, Thailand	Steering team, comprised of the PhD program director, deputy dean for planning and development, and program coordinator	Focused on identifying expected learning outcomes for the human resource and organization development (HROD) program (doctoral degree) that were suitable for the labor market and related stakeholders, such as potential students, current students, alumni, and so on	Qualitative and quantitative data: a workshop among teaching staff, review by external experts, a workshop with alumni and employers, an open-ended survey of the program's visiting scholars, an online Likert survey of current students, alumni, and prospective students	HROD teaching staff workshop data were analyzed using content analysis, coding, and analyzing data; Likert survey analyzed using descriptive statistics

Author	Case Title	Where Needs Assessment Was Conducted	Who Conducted the Needs Assessment	Focus of Needs Assessment	How Data Were Collected	How Data Were Analyzed
Strategic (8 cases)						
Altschuld & Engle	Comprehensive Needs Assessment and Asset/Capacity Building: The Case of the Westington Schools	Middle-class suburban school district and community	External consultants in conjunction with internal district staff	Planning the future direction of the schools in the Westinghouse Schools, a rapidly growing community	Architectural study; demographic analysis; literature review; benchmarking; facilitated group meetings	Descriptive statistics; thematic analysis of group meetings
Chandrasekar & Champion	A Strategic Multiyear Needs Assessment: Leadership Development for a Global Firm	Leading textile manufacturing group in a South Asian country	Staff of a nonprofit organization focused on leadership education and research	Focused on identifying business challenges, culture of the company, leadership skills for success, and skill gaps of leaders	Combination of surveys, interviews, and focus groups	1st Year: Qualitative analysis of interviews and focus groups. 2nd Year: Survey data were organized into profiles on success, leadership, leadership gap, leadership attention index, and potential challenges. Qualitative data were analyzed into categories of challenges faced; profile of effective leader; sustaining the learning; indicators of impact. 3rd Year: Incidents around collaboration and change were reported.

(Continued)

Table 1.1 (Continued)

Author	Case Title	Where Needs Assessment Was Conducted	Who Conducted the Needs Assessment	Focus of Needs Assessment	How Data Were Collected	How Data Were Analyzed
Einsprusch	Needs Assessment in Rural Communities	Six communities on a large, remote U.S. island	External consultant	Identified most important behavioral health problem in each community to provide a focus for future work	Surveys (collected via interviews)	Quantitative survey data: descriptive statistics (i.e., frequency distributions); qualitative data were summarized
Gugiu	Assessing Needs of a Community College: A Mixed Methods Case Study	Community college in Latin America and the Caribbean	Two external consultants who were doctoral students	Focused on determining major factors (i.e., student needs), influenced by college's actions, facilities, policies, or resources, that affected student life	Surveys completed by 49 staff and 291 students; only 200 respondents provided responses to the open-ended inquiries	Thematically analyzed open-ended responses; eight categories identified: (a) safety and security, (b) student behavior and policy, (c) quality of life, (d) health and sanitation, (e) management, (f) factors that impact student learning, (g) staff job performance, and (h) resources. Likert-type items were analyzed using descriptive statistics and analysis of variance to compare student and staff responses.

Author	Case Title	Where Needs Assessment Was Conducted	Who Conducted the Needs Assessment	Focus of Needs Assessment	How Data Were Collected	How Data Were Analyzed
McLean	Needs Assessment for Employee Empowerment in a Large Multinational: A Case Study	Large multinational R&D	External consultant	Determining the needs and content for a workshop on employee empowerment	A literature review; a review of existing survey results, interviews, and focus groups	Reliability using Cronbach alphas; checked for multicollinearity; ran experimental factor analysis on half of data to determine if there were subfactors; ran confirmatory factor analysis on the second half; t-tests; chi-square analysis
Pitcher	Diverse Students' Needs Assessment Case Study	University in northwestern United States	Faculty member	Focused on determining how well students' needs were met by current programs and services of three cultural centers	Interviews conducted with center directors; archival data (enrollment trends); a survey of students for each center	Descriptive statistics for closed-ended questions; thematic analysis for open-ended questions; reports combined text, infographics, and data tables to convey findings; organized data around strengths and areas for growth
Silverstein	Spending Other People's Money Responsibly and Strategically: Using Needs Assessment in Philanthropy	New Jersey	The philanthropic organization	Focused on understanding community's needs in five impact areas	Survey instruments administered to all executive directors and lead staff of grantee organizations; face-to-face inquiry meetings held with all executive directors of grantee organizations	Data placemat created for each impact area. (A data placemat is a visual document [the size of a placemat] that displays themes from the collected data, typically in the form of charts and graphs.)

(Continued)

Table 1.1 (Continued)

Author	Case Title	Where Needs Assessment Was Conducted	Who Conducted the Needs Assessment	Focus of Needs Assessment	How Data Were Collected	How Data Were Analyzed
Strack	Case Study of a Total Rewards Association's Needs Assessment	Global professional association	Staff of the professional association	Focused on determining current challenges faced by association members and identifying what members needed and how they preferred to be served	Reviewed previous member satisfaction surveys; information gathering interviews with association staff; survey questionnaire to 125,000 individuals—all known current and previous members, customers, and friends of association	Descriptive statistics for surveys; content analysis for interviews
Complex (4 cases)						
Chan	Needs Assessment at FMP Consulting	U.S. federal government	FMP Consulting (consulting firm)	Conducted job analysis and competency modeling for a federal client to improve the selection process for numerous occupations within the organization	Identified key tasks from existing client documentations, drafted competencies and assessment items, conducted workshop with subject matter experts to review and validate drafted competencies and assessment items, job analysis survey	Descriptive statistics; used cut-off scores to eliminate tasks and competencies; linked tasks to competencies; developed assessment items; compiled information for each occupation into a master workbook

Author	Case Title	Where Needs Assessment Was Conducted	Who Conducted the Needs Assessment	Focus of Needs Assessment	How Data Were Collected	How Data Were Analyzed
Domlyn, Kenworthy, Scaccia, & Scott	Readiness for Integrating Behavioral Health and Primary Care: Application of the R = MC^2 Framework	One outpatient care organization within a metropolitan area in the southeastern United States	An evaluation team was led by two community psychology professors and assisted by three graduate students from two universities. No one on the team was affiliated with the organization undergoing the needs assessment	Assessed journey of integrating behavioral health and primary care by investigating changes in organizational readiness	(a) The Readiness for Integrated Care Questionnaire (RICQ), (b) readiness score reports, (c) follow-up phone calls, and (d) qualitative interviews	Average RICQ scores and changes in scores over time; interview transcriptions analyzed by two independent coders using grounded theory and reconciliation of differences in themes

(Continued)

Table 1.1 (Continued)

Author	Case Title	Where Needs Assessment Was Conducted	Who Conducted the Needs Assessment	Focus of Needs Assessment	How Data Were Collected	How Data Were Analyzed
Simpson, Cockerill, Word, & Koehl	Faculty and Student Perceptions of University Course Evaluations	Mid-sized, undergraduate, higher research activity institution located in the southern United States	Internal staff and faculty with staff and faculty from a neutral office for the focus groups	Focused on the course evaluation process to identify and address barriers to stakeholder engagement, to guide departmental and institutional support for instructional practice	Results from course evaluations for six semesters (Spring 2015 through Fall 2017) with both quantitative responses (Likert 4- and 5-point scales) and qualitative comments; focus groups with students and with faculty; an environmental scan of initiatives and procedures currently informing support of teaching across the institution; a review of the steps in the current evaluation process	Statistical analysis of the numeric ratings and a text analysis of the comments on student–instructor evaluations; review and analysis of focus group data

Author	Case Title	Where Needs Assessment Was Conducted	Who Conducted the Needs Assessment	Focus of Needs Assessment	How Data Were Collected	How Data Were Analyzed
Williams & McGreevey	Orchid Candy Company	Privately owned business in the United States	Human resource development (HRD) consultant advised two teams of graduate HRD students	Focused on issues of succession planning, strategic planning, leadership development, and employee engagement	Initial conference meeting, observational site visits, and review of archival data (such as quantitative data included financial numbers, and personnel numbers of turnover, hiring, workplace attendance, training attendance, production numbers); public data research; employee interviews; questionnaire survey of selected employees	Quantitative data analyzed using descriptive statistics; qualitative data analyzed by identifying themes, then coding and categorizing the themes; data cross-case analyzed for similarity and issue identification

Table 1.2 Chapters, Authors, and Selected Interesting Information

Data Collection		
Chapter	**Author Names**	**Interesting Information**
2	Clark	Focus group protocol and analysis
4	Cumberland	Interview questions
5	Geary	Public observations as unobtrusive data collection
7	Star—small business	Identification of primary, secondary, and tertiary stakeholders
8	McGonigle	Engaging of subject matter experts in data collection for a job-task analysis
9	Sritanyarat	Results in terms of expected learning outcomes
12	Einspruch	Open- and closed-ended survey questions
13	Gugiu	Mixed-method survey design
18	Chan	Use of subject matter experts in data collection for competency model development

Data Analysis		
Chapter	**Author Names**	**Interesting Information**
3	Cho, Zhu, Techawitthayachinda, & Qian	Strengths, Weaknesses, Opportunities, and Threats (SWOT) analysis
6	Star—dog therapy	Use of triangulation
21	Williams & McGreevey	SWOT analysis

Presentation of Results		
Chapter	**Author Names**	**Interesting Information**
16	Silverstein	Reporting formats, for example, data placemats
17	Strack	Table 17.1 Key Findings
20	Simpson, Cockerill, Word, & Koehl	Table 20.3 Areas for Improvement and Action Plans

Overall Process		
Chapter	Author Names	Interesting Information
10	Altschuld & Engle	Table 10.1 Beginning Key Activities, Table 10.2 Interim Undertakings, and Table 10.3 Concluding Events
11	Chandrasekar & Champion	Table 11.1 Depicting Process Over a 3-Year Period
14	McLean	Issues and challenges in the needs assessment
15	Pitcher	Influences on the work; issues that had to be addressed
19	Domlyn, Kenworthy, Scaccia, & Scott	Table 19.1 Definition of Components and Subcomponents Defining Readiness for Innovation

Our Favorite Needs Assessment Resources

Throughout this chapter, we referred to *A Practical Guide to Needs Assessment*, by Sleezer et al. (2014). However, we devoted little space in this book to explaining the many other needs assessment models, theories, and jargon. Below are some of our favorite resources:

- *The Needs Assessment Kit* (Altschuld, 2010)
- *Bridging the Gap Between Asset/Capacity Building and Needs Assessment: Concepts and Practical Applications* (Altschuld, 2014)
- *Training Needs Assessment: Methods, Tools and Techniques* (Barbazette, 2005)
- *Human Competence: Engineering Worthy Performance* (Gilbert, 1978, 2007)
- *Needs Assessment for Organizational Success* (Guerra-Lopez & Kaufman, 2013)
- *An Ounce of Analysis Is Worth a Pound of Objectives* (Harless, 1970)
- *Strategic Planning Plus* (Kaufman, 1992).
- *Analyzing Performance Problems* (Mager & Pipe, 1984)
- *Needs Assessment Basics* (2nd ed.) (McGoldrick & Tobey, 2016)
- *First Things Fast: A Handbook for Performance Analysis (Essential Knowledge Resource)* (Rossett, 2009)

- *Evaluation: A Systematic Approach* (7th ed.) (Rossi, Lipsey, & Freeman, 2004)

- *Improving Performance: How to Manage the White Space on the Organization Chart* (Rummler & Brache, 1995)

- *Evaluation in Organizations: An Approach to Enhancing Learning, Performance, and Change* (2nd ed.) (Russ-Eft & Preskill, 2009)

- *The Development and Validation of the Performance Analysis for Training Model* (Sleezer, 1990, 1991)

- *Needs Assessment: Perspectives From the Literature* (Sleezer, 1992)

- *Performance at Work: A Systematic Program for Analyzing Work Behavior* (Swanson, 1998)

- *Analysis for Improving Performance: Tools for Diagnosing Organizations & Documenting Workplace Expertise* (Swanson, 2007)

- *A Guide to Assessing Needs* (Watkins et al., 2012)

- *Figuring Things Out: A Trainer's Guide to Needs and Task Analysis* (Zemke & Kramlinger, 1982)

We recommend that you examine all or some of these resources, since each one provides some important insights.

REFERENCES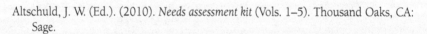

Altschuld, J. W. (Ed.). (2010). *Needs assessment kit* (Vols. 1–5). Thousand Oaks, CA: Sage.

Altschuld, J. W. (2014). *Bridging the gap between asset/capacity building and needs assessment: Concepts and practical applications*. Thousand Oaks, CA: Sage.

Assessment [Def. 1]. (n.d.). *Merriam Webster's Dictionary*. Retrieved from http://www.merriam-webster.com/dictionary/assessment.

Barbazette, J. (2005). *Training needs assessment: Methods, tools and techniques*. New York, NY: Wiley.

Branson, R. K., Rayner, G. T., Cox, J. L., Furman, J. P., King, F. J., & Hannum, W. H. (1975). *Interservice procedures for instructional systems development: Executive summary and model* (Vols. 1–5). TRADOC Pam 350-30, Ft. Monroe, VA: U.S. Army Training and Doctrine Command.

Christensen, B. (2016). Needs assessment vs. needs analysis: What's the diff? Retrieved from https://www.ispi.org/ISPI/Resources/PX/Articles/Editors__Pick/ Needs_Assessment_vs_Needs_Analysis__What_s_the_Diff_.aspx.

Gilbert, T. E. (1978). *Human competence: Engineering worthy performance.* New York, NY: McGraw-Hill.

Gilbert, T. E. (2007). *Human competence: Engineering worthy performance.* San Francisco, CA: Pfeiffer.

Guerra-Lopez, I., & Kaufman, R. (2013). *Needs assessment for organizational success.* Alexandria, VA: ASTD.

Harless, J. (1970). *An ounce of analysis (is worth a pound of objectives).* Newman, GA: Harless Performance Guild.

Jung, S. M., & Schubert, J. G. (1983). Evaluability assessment: A two-year retrospective. *Educational Evaluation and Policy Analysis, 5*(4), 435–444. https:// doi.org/10.3102/01623737005004435.

Kaufman, R. (1992). *Strategic planning plus.* Thousand Oaks, CA: Sage.

Kettner, P. M., Moroney, R. M., & Martin, L. L. (2017). *Designing and managing programs: An effectiveness based approach* (5th ed.). Thousand Oaks, CA: Sage.

Linke, R. (2017). *Design thinking, explained.* Retrieved from https://mitsloan.mit.edu/ ideas-made-to-matter/design-thinking-explained.

Mager, R. F., & Pipe, P. (1984). *Analyzing performance problems; or, you really oughta wanna* (2nd ed.). Belmont, CA: David S. Lake.

McLaughlin, J. A., & Jordan, G. B. (1999). Logic models: A tool for telling your program's performance story. *Evaluation and Program Planning, 22,* 65–72. doi: 10.1016/S0149-7189(98)00042-1

McGoldrick, B., & Tobey, D. (2016). *Needs assessment basics* (2nd ed.). Alexandria, VA: ATD Press.

McLaughlin, J. A., & Jordan, G. B. (2015). *Using logic models: Handbook of practical program evaluation.* New York, NY: Wiley.

Need. (n.d.). *Merriam-Webster's Dictionary.* Retrieved from https://www.merriam-webster.com/dictionary/need.

Rossett, A. (2009). *First things fast: A handbook for performance analysis (Essential knowledge resource)* (2nd ed.). San Francisco, CA: Jossey-Bass.

Rossi, P. H., Lipsey, M. W., & Freeman, H. E. (2004). *Evaluation: A systematic approach* (7th ed.). Thousand Oaks, CA: Sage.

Rummler, G. A., & Brache, A. P. (1995). *Improving performance: How to manage the white space in the organization chart.* San Francisco, CA: Jossey-Bass.

Russ-Eft, D., & Preskill, H. (2009). *Evaluation in organizations: A systematic approach to enhancing learning, performance, and change* (2nd ed.). New York, NY: Basic Books.

Sleezer, C. M. (1990). *The development and validation of a performance analysis for training model* [Dissertation]. University of Minnesota, St. Paul, MN.

Sleezer, C. M. (1991). Developing and validating the performance analysis for training model. *Human Resource Development Quarterly, 2*(4), 355–372.

Sleezer, C. M. (1992). Needs assessment: Perspectives from the literature. *Performance Improvement Quarterly, 2*(5), 34–46.

Sleezer, C. M., Russ-Eft, D. F., & Gupta, K. (2014). *A practical guide to needs assessment* (3rd ed.). San Francisco, CA: Wiley & ASTD.

Strosberg, M. A., & Wholey, J. S. (1983). Evaluability assessment: From theory to practice in the Department of Health and Human Services. *Public Administration Review, 43*(1), 66–71.

Swanson, R. A. (1986). *Performance at work: A systematic program for analyzing work behavior.* San Francisco, CA: Wiley.

Swanson, R. A. (2007). *Analysis for improving performance: Tools for diagnosing organizations and documenting workplace expertise* (2nd ed.). San Francisco, CA: Berrett-Koehler.

Watkins, R., West Meiers, M., & Visser, Y. L. (2012). *A guide to assessing needs.* Washington, DC: The World Bank.

Watson, R. (1981, October). *Instructional system development.* Paper presented to the International Congress for Individualized Instruction. EDRS publication ED 209 239.

Wholey, J. (1979). *Evaluation: Promise and performance.* Washington, DC: Urban Institute.

Wholey, J. (1994). *Handbook of practical program evaluation.* San Francisco, CA: Jossey-Bass.

Zemke, R., & Kramlinger, T. (1982). *Figuring things out: A trainer's guide to needs and task analysis.* Boston, MA: Addison-Wesley.

Knowledge and Skills Assessments

"Its purpose is to identify the knowledge and skills required."

(Sleezer, Russ-Eft, & Gupta, 2014, p. 31)

Transitioning From Traditional to Digital

A Knowledge and Skills Needs Assessment for a Community Orchestra Context

Candice R. Clark

Abstract

This case study describes a mixed methods knowledge and skills needs assessment conducted for a community orchestra in a large urban city in the southeastern United States. The orchestra transitioned their music library from a paper system with physical storage to an electronic system with cloud-based

Where Was the Needs Assessment Conducted	Who Conducted the Needs Assessment	Focus of Needs Assessment	How Data Were Collected	How Data Were Analyzed
Community orchestra within an urban area in the southeastern United States	A former member of the orchestra	Focused on determining the gap between knowledge and skills volunteers had and those they needed to complete a project involving the scanning and saving of music scores	Content mappings, surveys, and interviews	Likert scale responses from surveys of volunteers verified via follow-up interview; verified responses compared to minimum knowledge and skills required; content mappings revealed where knowledge and skills were underdeveloped

storage. The transition relied on volunteers from the orchestra taking home music scores, scanning them, and saving them to an application. A needs assessment was conducted to identify the gap between the knowledge and skills volunteers had and those they needed to complete the project. The goal of the assessment was to use the findings to develop training materials for both current and future volunteers.

Background

The orchestra maintained a storage building containing approximately 550 scores of sheet music. When scores were accessed for practice or performances, the librarian located them, withdrew them from storage, and transported them to the venue. Due to inhibitive factors, such as the librarian's physical limitations, transportation difficulties caused by traffic, and costly damage to scores during location changes, the orchestra needed an alternative method for score storage and retrieval. To overcome these challenges, the executive board opted to migrate sheet music storage to Dropbox, an online platform.

Profile of the Organization

The orchestra was a community orchestra located in a large urban city in the southeastern United States. The group's mission was to share both classical and contemporary orchestral music with the greater metropolitan area. It did this by providing free concerts to communities in surrounding areas.

The orchestra was founded in 1999 to bring together legal professionals who shared a love of instrumental music. At the time of the assessment, the orchestra consisted of some 35 volunteer musicians from a variety of professions, as well as students and retirees. Its members' skill levels ranged from intermediate to professional. The median age of the group's members was 75. Their lingua franca was English.

As a 501(c)(3) organization, the orchestra depended on donations from patrons in the community and grants for the arts to provide community-accessible concerts. The funding they received went toward purchasing music scores, making copies, paying legal fees, paying music and equipment storage fees, and miscellaneous other expenditures.

Governance Structure

The orchestra's 35-member group was comprised of a principal director and 12 sections of instrumentalists, for example, the violin section. Each section was led by a section principal who was selected by and from within their section.

The principal director, president, librarian, and concertmistress formed the orchestra committee (i.e., committee). These individuals were elected by the orchestra as a whole. The committee was responsible for managing the practical matters the orchestra faced, for example, scheduling performances.

The principal director, the president, and a group of five lawyers made up the executive board. The board was responsible for addressing legally oriented matters, for example, the legality of accepting donations, and system issues. The board's lawyers were past members of the orchestra or family members of past or present orchestra members.

The technical advisor position was filled through appointment by the committee. The technical advisor was responsible for consulting with the orchestra on technical issues, for example, website changes. The technical advisor acted as a by-invitation, ad hoc, nonvoting member of the committee and the board. The role was held by a past member of the orchestra.

Figure 2.1 depicts a simplified view of the orchestra's structure.

Figure 2.1   A Simplified View of the Orchestra's Structure

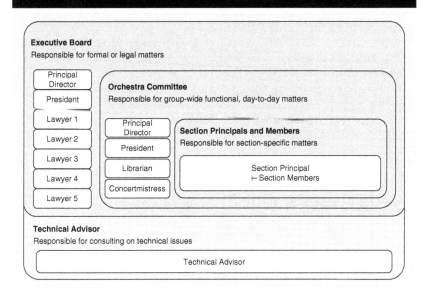

Executive Board
Responsible for formal or legal matters

Principal Director
President
Lawyer 1
Lawyer 2
Lawyer 3
Lawyer 4
Lawyer 5

Orchestra Committee
Responsible for group-wide functional, day-to-day matters

Principal Director
President
Librarian
Concertmistress

Section Principals and Members
Responsible for section-specific matters

Section Principal
⊢ Section Members

Technical Advisor
Responsible for consulting on technical issues

Technical Advisor

Preassessment Information

During a regular board meeting, members chose to move to an electronic storage system to solve the issues with storing, accessing, and transporting scores. After consulting with the technical advisor, the board determined that the most cost-effective solution was Dropbox, an online file-hosting platform that offered cloud-based electronic storage. However, to make the solution cost-effective, orchestra members would need to volunteer to scan the paper library's documents and save electronic copies to the Dropbox application on their local computers. Several board members questioned whether volunteers had the appropriate skills to perform the tasks necessary for completing the project.

The technical advisor suggested that the orchestra conduct a needs assessment with its volunteers. By assessing what volunteers already knew about these processes and comparing it with what they needed to know, training materials could be developed.

Boundaries of the Needs Assessment

As a community-based, nonprofit organization, the orchestra had limited funds to conduct a needs assessment, so it was essential to locate a needs assessor willing to donate the required time and labor. A further restriction stemmed from the culture of the organization. Whenever possible, the orchestra called on past and present members to complete projects. Accordingly, it needed to find an assessor connected to the organization who was willing and able to donate the required services.

The orchestra found only one person affiliated with them who met these criteria: me. I had experience with needs assessment and had been trained in the collection and analysis of both qualitative and quantitative data. After holding a preliminary meeting with the board, I agreed to conduct a knowledge and skills needs assessment (Sleezer, Russ-Eft, & Gupta, 2014). The goal of the assessment was to determine the difference between the knowledge and skills volunteers already had related to the document scanning and saving processes and using Dropbox, and the ones they would need.

Needs Assessment Process

The orchestra's ultimate goal was to ensure that volunteers had the training they needed to scan music scores and save those scores to Dropbox. The assessment would provide information for creating appropriate training materials.

Model for the Needs Assessment

The development of this needs assessment rested on a couple of primary assumptions. The first was that the assessment was an integral first step in instructional design for the group's training needs. Second, the instructional goals of the group were an appropriate base for making decisions during the development of the needs assessment plan. Given these assumptions and the goal of the needs assessment, I drew on the Rothwell and Kazanas (1992) seven-step model to guide the assessment's design and implementation.

While I utilized the Rothwell and Kazanas (1992) model for needs assessment management, the remainder of this manuscript is written in terms of a separate five-phase assessment process. As this five-phase process aligns with the phases the key players experienced, communicating about the assessment in terms of those phases facilitated making the project accessible to more people.

Phases of the Needs Assessment

The five main phases of the assessment process were (a) preassessment planning, (b) assessment design, (c) assessment administration, (d) data analysis, and (e) communicating and disseminating results. See Figure 2.2 for which key individuals and groups participated in each phase of the assessment process.

Phase I: Preassessment Planning

During the preassessment planning phase, I held an in-person focus group with the board, committee, and technical advisor. Participants were chosen based on their positions within the organization or their connection to the project. The committee represented the orchestra. The lawyers ensured the legality of decisions. The technical advisor offered input on the scanning and saving processes.

The focus group was held over Skype, and it used a semi-structured protocol (see Appendix A). Qualitative analysis of the focus group's discussion resulted in themes around four issues to be addressed before proceeding with the needs assessment. By the conclusion of the focus group one or more action items had been developed to address each issue. (For example, one issue was how to solicit volunteers. An action item associated with resolving this issue was for the president to announce that a survey would be posted on the group's intranet.) In the days following the focus group, the documents, artifacts, and

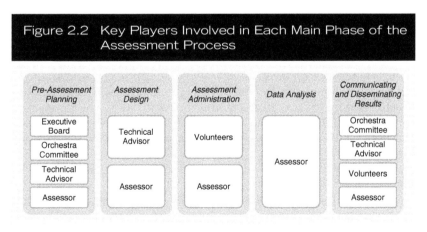

Figure 2.2 Key Players Involved in Each Main Phase of the Assessment Process

Pre-Assessment Planning	Assessment Design	Assessment Administration	Data Analysis	Communicating and Disseminating Results
Executive Board	Technical Advisor	Volunteers		Orchestra Committee
Orchestra Committee				Technical Advisor
Technical Advisor			Assessor	
	Assessor	Assessor		Volunteers
Assessor				Assessor

reports that resulted from each action item were returned to me. See Appendix B for a complete listing of issues, themes, decisions, action items, and data returned.

Soliciting Volunteers. During the focus group, two issues around finding volunteers were settled: who would be selected, and how they would be selected. All understood that volunteers would self-select from within the orchestra. However, it was unclear if all the volunteers would have access to the necessary resources, such as the internet and a scanner. The group decided that I would develop a screening survey to be sent out prior to final participant selection. This survey collected information on whether potential volunteers had the resources needed to participate. (See Appendix C for the Resources Survey.) Potential volunteers who responded to the survey and indicated they had the necessary resources took part in the needs assessment.

When choosing how to solicit volunteers, the group decided the technical advisor would place the resources survey on the group intranet. In turn, the president would announce during practice that anyone who wished to help with the project should respond to that survey. Finally, I agreed to monitor survey responses and communicate final outcomes to the group.

In the 2 weeks after the resources survey was posted, 14 potential volunteers had responded. Results indicated that three participants did not have appropriate resources to scan and save documents, two were not permitted to download Dropbox, and one expressed lack of access to a scanner. Of the 11 remaining participants, four indicated that they already used Dropbox, and seven others were willing to download it. Overall, 11 volunteers (22% of the total orchestra population) were capable of acting as volunteer scanners. These 11 participants took part in the needs assessment.

Phase II: Assessment Design

The purpose of this assessment was to find the gap between the knowledge and skills volunteers had and those they needed to be competent scanners. To find this gap, two questions needed to be answered. First, what knowledge and skills did volunteers already have? Second, what knowledge and skills did volunteers need to have? In the assessment design phase, the technical advisor worked with me to develop content mappings, survey instruments, and interview protocols to help answer these questions.

The assessment design had three parts. First, to help me understand what volunteers needed to know, the technical advisor created two content mappings: one for scanning and saving, and one for Dropbox. Each content mapping contained explicit lists of the knowledge and skills necessary for the scanning and saving processes.

Second, I used the content mappings to design two data collection instruments: a survey and a postsurvey interview protocol. The survey gauged volunteers' knowledge, skills, and comfort levels with the scanning and saving processes as well as with Dropbox. The interview protocol allowed volunteers to ask questions about the process and/or their responsibilities, and it gave me a chance to validate volunteers' survey responses. Volunteers' completion of the survey and follow-up interview afforded me a robust picture of each volunteer's level of familiarity with scanning and saving and with Dropbox.

Third, the assessment compared the data in the content mappings (what volunteers needed to know) with data from the data collection instruments (what volunteers already knew). That comparison highlighted the gap between what volunteers knew and what they needed to know.

The basic flow of the design phase is shown in Figure 2.3.

Phase III: Assessment Administration

In this phase, the 11 volunteers identified during the preassessment planning phase worked with me to provide information about their individual levels of knowledge and skills. Data were collected from three primary sources: content mappings, surveys, and interviews. The content mappings were discussed in the assessment design section and will not be discussed further here.

Figure 2.3 Flow of the Assessment Design Phase Including Key Questions and What Was Developed to Answer Each Question

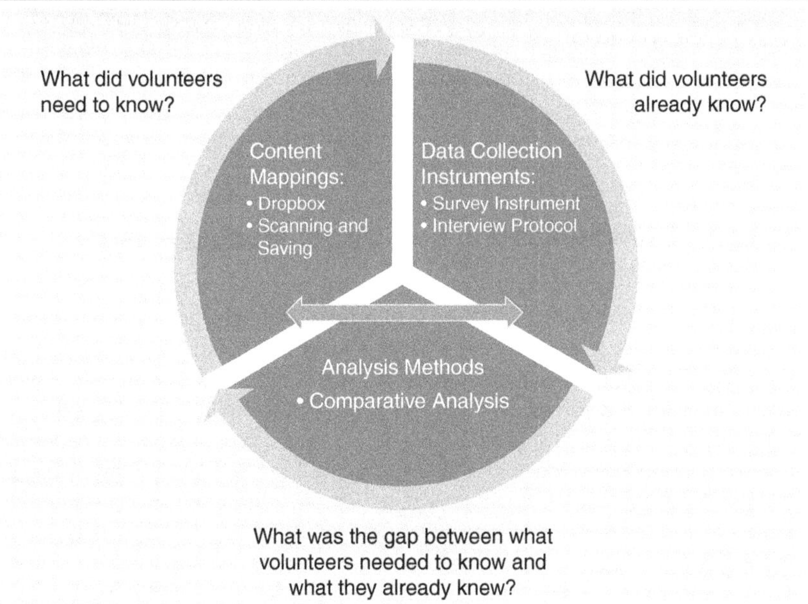

What did volunteers need to know?

What did volunteers already know?

Content Mappings:
• Dropbox
• Scanning and Saving

Data Collection Instruments:
• Survey Instrument
• Interview Protocol

Analysis Methods
• Comparative Analysis

What was the gap between what volunteers needed to know and what they already knew?

Surveys. At the end of the 2-week period in which volunteers responded to the Resources Survey, I emailed each volunteer the Knowledge and Skills Survey (Appendix D). The survey used Likert scale items to assess volunteers' knowledge, skills, and comfort levels with the scanning and saving processes and with Dropbox. During the survey, volunteers set up one-on-one follow-up phone interviews with me.

Postsurvey Interviews. Before the interviews, I reviewed volunteers' survey responses. Then, I contacted each volunteer at their preferred time for a 1-hour interview. During the interview, I worked with the volunteer on two fronts. First, I asked questions about the volunteer's survey responses. Next, I briefly explained the library transition plan and allowed the volunteer to ask questions about the transition process and their responsibilities toward the project. The interviews were not structured; exact procedures evolved organically throughout each interview.

Phase IV: Data Analysis

Data from the survey and postsurvey interviews were analyzed both qualitatively and quantitatively. The Likert scale responses from each volunteer's Knowledge and Skills Survey were verified via qualitative information from the follow-up interview. I used comparative analysis methods to contrast verified responses with what the technical advisor had determined to be the minimum knowledge and skills required of volunteers. Comparing the information from the content mappings with volunteers' responses revealed where volunteers' knowledge and skills about the scanning and saving processes or Dropbox were underdeveloped. Differences in what volunteers already knew and what they would need to know were coded on a scale of 1 to 4 for each category on the survey, where one indicated "knowledge/skill/comfort level far below necessary level" and four indicated "knowledge/skill/comfort level meets or exceeds necessary level."

Phase V: Communicating and Disseminating Results

A summary of the findings for the assessment is presented in Figure 2.4. The figure contains information on each volunteer's knowledge, skills, and comfort levels with the scanning and saving processes and with Dropbox. It also has information on what machine types and operating systems volunteers were using. The codes of how well a volunteer's levels of knowledge and skills met the minimum levels of knowledge and skills necessary are represented in a code-to-color correspondence. Codes of 1 are represented by dark gray, 2 by medium gray, 3 by light gray, and 4 by white, where dark gray indicates knowledge/skill/comfort level far below necessary level, and white indicates knowledge/skill/comfort level meets or exceeds necessary level. Also shown is whether a volunteer is using a PC or a Mac (P or M) with a Windows, Apple, or Linux (W, i, L) operating system. Note all names are pseudonyms that preserve gender identity.

	Scanner					Dropbox		System	
	Experience	Confidence	Page merging	Merger support	Changing settings	Download support	Comfort	Machine	OS
Jennifer								P	W
John								M	L
Aaron								M	i
Cora								P	W
Christina								P	W
Harry								M	i
Donald								M	i
Richard								M	i
Mary								P	W
Eunice								P	W
Elizabeth								M	i

As the needs of the board, the committee, and the technical advisor varied based on how they would use results, reports of findings were tailored to each group.

Communicating With the Board. The board had to ensure that dissemination of the findings did not violate confidentiality laws for the organization. Three days after the findings were compiled, I met with the board via Skype to present the results. An executive summary of the findings was presented. Additionally, the board requested all reports, documents, etc., based on the findings be emailed to them for review before being disseminated to others.

Communicating With the Committee. The president sat on both the board and the committee. He was asked to take the executive summary of the findings to the next committee meeting and discuss the assessment's results.

Communicating With the Advisor. The report for the technical advisor contained an in-depth account of the needs assessment's findings. Along with the executive summary, the report included volunteers' survey responses aggregated by survey item along with verbal descriptions and quotations about specific areas where people believed they needed the most support. The information in the report and with the content mappings were to have formed the basis for the technical advisor to develop training materials. These materials were to have included high- and low-level training and download support materials for the scanning and saving processes, high- and low-level training and download support materials for using Dropbox, and a handbook for future technical advisors.

Influences

The orchestra's roots as a community-based volunteer organization resulted in it having a supportive culture for completing this needs assessment. Orchestra members understood that they were participating in something that would provide them the training they needed to support their group. Further, I had previously been a member of the organization for many years. Due to this relationship and my understanding of their culture, orchestra members were inclined to trust me and open up about their needs.

One major boundary was how closely the needs assessment was tied to that group, in that place, at that time. The age range of the population of volunteers, the culture of the organization, and many other factors could affect the generalizability of the assessment's results.

Issues and Challenges

As a nonprofit organization, the orchestra had a limited budget for planning and conducting the assessment and developing training. To overcome this problem, the orchestra called on current and former members. While those who volunteered were integral to the project's success, many voiced reticence to participate in a technically oriented undertaking, citing a lack of technical knowledge. To assuage participants' concerns, I clarified that the needs assessment would enable the development of training materials that would meet volunteers' specific training needs. Further, holding a phone conversation with each volunteer after he or she completed the online questionnaire helped ensure that volunteers had understood questions' intent and had been able to reflect their knowledge accurately on the survey.

The results of the needs assessment may be applicable only to the population sampled at this specific place in this particular time due to factors such as volunteer technical knowledge, language, and skill levels. Care had to be taken to communicate results with the technical advisor in a way that supported the development of training materials to meet the needs of a range of learners, rather than training to match directly the nuances of individual learners' needs.

DISCUSSION QUESTIONS

1. What are the advantages and disadvantages of using a focus group during the preassessment planning phase rather than individual interviews, given the structure of this group?

2. As time passes, will the training documents developed from the 11 volunteers' responses become outdated such that the needs assessment will need to be repeated? Why, or why not?

3. What other approaches to needs assessment, if any, might have been used in this case?

4. Consider how the group's characteristics (culture of the group, age range of group members, status as a nonprofit, structure of governance, size of group, etc.) influenced how the results of the needs assessment were communicated. How would changes in one of the group's characteristics have affected the dissemination of results?

5. How did these instruments used in this assessment (see Appendices A through D) communicate knowledge of the transition project, understanding of the orchestra culture, and respect for those who participated in the needs assessment?

REFERENCES

Rothwell, W. J., & Kazanas, H.C. (1992). *Mastering the instructional design process: A systematic approach.* San Francisco, CA: Jossey-Bass.

Sleezer, C. M., Russ-Eft, D. F., & Gupta, K. (2014). *A practical guide to needs assessment* (3rd ed.). San Francisco, CA: Wiley & ASTD.

Appendix A

Semi-structured Protocol for Focus Group

Introductory Discussion (5 minutes)	The director will open the Skype meeting by introducing the topic and why we are all there. We should all note the times in our current locations, which will span from coast to coast in the United States and extend to Italy.
Background (10 minutes)	**I give background on the problem.** • What the issue is • What the cause of the issue is • What the major complications arising from the issue are • What we see as a possible long-term solution to the problem (Time is allowed at the end for questions from the group.)
Today's Discussion Agenda (5 minutes)	**I give an overview of today's topics.** (Time is allowed at the end for questions from the group.)
Topic 1 (10 minutes)	**Determine expectations for volunteers in terms of work and skills.** • I lead this discussion but open the floor to group members.
Topic 2 (10 minutes)	**Determine a method for soliciting volunteers.** • I lead this discussion but open the floor to group members.
Topic 4 (5 minutes)	**Legal concerns.** • Are there any potential legal issues arising from this solution to the issue? • I lead this discussion but open the floor to group members.
Topic 3 (10 minutes)	**Settle on a method for determining volunteers' skill levels.** • I lead this discussion but open the floor to group members.
Recap (5 minutes)	I recap what we determined during the meeting, along with giving reminders of any data collection tasks assigned during the meeting.
Final Thoughts (5 minutes)	I check to see if anyone has any further questions.
Planning Further Communication (5 minutes)	The group makes decisions about to whom official further communication should be addressed throughout the remainder of the project.

Appendix B

Focus Group Data: Issues, Themes, Decisions, Action Items, and Data Returned

ISSUE 1: Volunteer Workload

Theme(s): The librarian and president expressed concern about the workload placed on volunteers. Uncertainties arose over the time needed from each volunteer, and the skills the volunteers would need to have.

Decision(s): Volunteers from the orchestra will take home some number (to be determined) of scores each week, scan them, and return them.

Action Item(s): The librarian will tally the number of scores currently in the orchestra's library.

Data Returned: The librarian estimated the number of scores needing to be cataloged electronically as some 550. This number would be used for projections of how long the paper-to-digital conversion process should take in terms of weeks, given the number of volunteers.

Note: Of particular concern to the librarian was how to keep track of which volunteers had which scores and which scores had been returned.

ISSUE 2: Soliciting Volunteers

Theme(s): Suggestions on how to solicit volunteers included a sign-up sheet, an announcement during rehearsal, and a link on the orchestra's intranet. The technical advisor pointed out that this is a technology based volunteer position; thus, it was reasonable to ask people to respond to the request electronically.

Decision(s): Volunteers' responses to the survey will be collected on the internet. Volunteers will be told about the survey at practice.

Action Item(s): The president will announce to the group that the survey will be posted. The technical advisor will place the survey on the intranet.

Data Returned: The president announced during practice that the orchestra was looking for volunteers. The technical advisor posted the survey that I had created on the orchestra's intranet (see "Resources Survey," Appendix C).

ISSUE 3: Legal Concerns

Theme(s): The lawyers foresaw no major legal concerns. However, the director suggested the final plan be presented to the board. The librarian suggested checking with music publishers to verify there would be no conflict.

Decision(s): Lawyers will be presented with the final plan. Publishers will be contacted.

Action Item(s): The director will present the plan to the lawyers at the upcoming board meeting. The librarian will call several major publishers.

Data Returned: Neither the lawyers nor the publishing company found any legal issues with the approach.

ISSUE 4: Volunteers' Resources and Skills

Theme(s): The president and librarian both mentioned the need to make sure potential volunteers had the resources necessary to volunteer (computer, internet, scanner, etc.).

Decision(s): A survey will be sent out prior to the needs assessment to determine if volunteers have the necessary resources.

Action Item(s): I will create a resources survey. Additionally, I will monitor response rates to the survey and report back to the focus group.

Data Returned: I created the Resources Survey to collect data on if potential volunteers had the resources necessary to volunteer. Within 2 weeks of the survey being posted, 14 potential volunteers had responded. Results indicated three participants did not have appropriate resources to scan documents, two indicated they did not have permission to download Dropbox on the computer connected to their scanner, and one indicated they did not have access to a scanner. Of the 11 remaining volunteers, four participants indicated they already had Dropbox, and the seven others were willing to download it. Overall, 11 volunteers (22% of the total orchestra population) were found capable of acting as volunteer scanners.

Appendix C
Resources Survey

[Orchestra] Members:

[The president] recently announced that the [orchestra] is transitioning from the current paper library managed by [the librarian] to an electronic, cloud-based storage and management system. The board has decided to use Dropbox as the cloud-based storage location. To convert the paper library over to an electronic library stored in Dropbox, the orchestra has asked for volunteers. From here, we (those of you who volunteer and I) will go through three phases.

Phase I: We will determine if you have the necessary resources (computer, scanner, programs, internet) to volunteer with this project. This is done through this survey.

Phase II: After you complete this survey, I will contact those of you that indicate you have the needed resources directly via email. I will ask you to respond to a few questions about how comfortable you are with the scanning and saving processes. (Do not worry if you are not familiar with these; see Phase III.) At the end of the survey, I will have you schedule a short phone call with me to discuss details.

Phase III: Using what you tell me [the technical advisor] will create training tutorials both for scanning and saving and for Dropbox. These documents can be used as training materials for those of you with little experience, as guidebooks for those of you who are more experienced, and as reference documents as you continue to add scores to the library in the years to come.

Thank you all for participating in this exciting adventure!

Candice

Your first name:

[   ]

Your last name:

[   ]

What type of computer and operating system will you be using? List as many computers as you may use (consider at work, at home, etc.).

	What Is the Computer Type?			What Is the Operating System?				What Is the Computer Style?		
	PC	Macintosh/ Apple	Other/I do not know	Windows	iOS	Linux	Other/I do not know	Laptop	Desktop	Other/I do not know
Computer 1	O	O	O	O	O	O	O	O	O	O
Computer 2	O	O	O	O	O	O	O	O	O	O
Computer 3	O	O	O	O	O	O	O	O	O	O

Do you have internet access on the computer connected to your scanner?

O Yes

O No

O Other (please specify) _____

Where do you have access to a scanner? (Please select all that apply.)

O At home

O At work

O Other (please explain) _____

O I do not have access to a scanner.

Is Dropbox currently installed on the computer you would use for scanning documents?

O Yes

O No

O I do not know.

Display this question if yes is not selected for the previous question.

Would you be willing to install Dropbox (a free program)?

O Yes

O Maybe

O No

O I do not know.

Please enter the email address you would like me to use to contact you regarding the next steps.
[   ]

Appendix D
Knowledge and Skills Survey

Thank you for volunteering to help with scanning the [orchestra's] scores into the new library!

Please answer these questions about how comfortable you are with scanning and saving documents. At the end of the survey, we will set up a time to talk on the phone to discuss details of the project and answer any questions you may have. This survey should take less than 5 minutes to complete.

Do you have experience with the scanner you will likely use?

◯ Yes

◯ No

Display this question if yes is selected for the previous question.

How much experience do you have with the scanner?

	None	Very little	Some	Very much	Extensive
My experience level	◯	◯	◯	◯	◯

Display this question if no is selected for the previous question.

How much confidence do you have in your ability to scan (or learn to scan) a document?

	None	Very little	Some	Very much	Extensive
My confidence level	◯	◯	◯	◯	◯

Do you know how to scan multiple pages to one document?

◯ Yes

◯ No

◯ Not sure

Does your scanner scan multiple pages to one document?

◯ Yes

◯ No

◯ Not sure

If your scanner will not allow for scanning multiple pages into one document, would you be willing to download free PDF merging software?

○ Yes

○ Would consider

○ No

Do you know how to

	Not sure	No	Yes
Save a document as a PDF (or scan directly to PDF)?	○	○	○
Change the DPI (resolution) of a scan?	○	○	○
Choose a save location?	○	○	○

Have you ever used Dropbox before?

○ Yes

○ No/I do not know.

Display this question if yes is selected for the previous question.

How comfortable are you working with Dropbox?

○ Not

○ A little

○ Somewhat

○ Very

○ Extremely

What is your *first choice* of date and time to talk?

Date	○ Wed 22 Mar	○ Fri 24 Mar	○ Sat 25 Mar	○ Sun 26 Mar	○ Mon 27 Mar	○ Tue 28 Mar	○ Wed 1 Apr	○ Fri 3 Apr	○ Sat 4 Apr	○ Sun 5 Apr	○ Mon 6 Apr	○ Tue 7 Apr
Time (EST)	○ 7 AM	○ 8 AM	○ 9 AM	○ 10 AM	○ 11 AM	○ 12 AM	○ 1 PM	○ 2 PM	○ 3 PM	○ 4 PM	○ 5 PM	○ 6 PM

What is your *second choice* of date and time to talk?

Date	○ Wed 22 Mar	○ Fri 24 Mar	○ Sat 25 Mar	○ Sun 26 Mar	○ Mon 27 Mar	○ Tue 28 Mar	○ Wed 1 Apr	○ Fri 3 Apr	○ Sat 4 Apr	○ Sun 5 Apr	○ Mon 6 Apr	○ Tue 7 Apr
Time (EST)	○ 7 AM	○ 8 AM	○ 9 AM	○ 10 AM	○ 11 AM	○ 12 AM	○ 1 PM	○ 2 PM	○ 3 PM	○ 4 PM	○ 5 PM	○ 6 PM

Please indicate the best number to reach you.
[   ]

Would you prefer me to email you or text you to confirm the time for our call?

○ Email

○ Text

My number is
Feel free to save it in your phone or write it down now.
Thank you for taking the time to do this for [the orchestra]. I look forward to talking to you soon!
Candice

A Needs Assessment of Online Core Courses for Student Learning in Higher Education

Yonjoo Cho, Meina Zhu, Ratrapee Techawitthayachinda, and Ling Qian

Abstract

This case describes a needs assessment of online core courses in an Instructional Technology (IT) Department at a U.S. midwestern university. The purpose of the needs assessment project was (a) to identify the gap between the current state and the desired state, and (b) to provide recommendations for the overall quality of student learning. To that end, we collected data from a survey of 96 online graduate students, 11 follow-up student interviews, and seven instructor interviews. We also collected secondary data including the literature on online education to see the current state of the research area and four peer institutions' online degree programs in instructional technology to compare and contrast. We used a strengths, weaknesses, opportunities, and threats (SWOT) analysis to analyze the data and present findings and recommendations to improve online core courses for student learning. Below is an overview of the case.

Where the Needs Assessment Was Conducted	Who Conducted the Needs Assessment	Focus of Needs Assessment	How Data Were Collected	How Data Were Analyzed
A midwestern university	Faculty and graduate students of the university	How online courses are delivered for graduate students of an Instructional Technology (IT) Department for student learning	Interviews with seven instructors and 11 online graduate students who agreed to participate after a survey, a survey questionnaire with 44 out of 96 online graduate students, a review of the literature on online education, and a document review of four peer institutions' IT programs	Used descriptive statistics for survey data and content analysis for interview data and a strengths, weaknesses, opportunities, and threats analysis to present results (findings and recommendations) for the improvement of online core courses for student learning

Background

Needs assessment is defined as "a process for figuring out how to close a learning or performance gap" (Sleezer, Russ-Eft, & Gupta, 2014, p. 17) by comparing the current condition to the desired condition. Recognizing that a need for a review of the IT program at a midwestern state university in the United States had never been undertaken, a project team was formed and approached the department chair for approval to conduct the needs assessment. That team consisted of four members including a doctoral student and two master's students, as well as a faculty member who played a facilitator role in guiding the project process.

As the IT program is considered one of the earliest programs in the United States and the world, it attracts many students who have diverse backgrounds, coming from 21 different countries, although many online students are U.S. residents (Cho, Boling, & Kwon, 2017). The department has offered online master's degree programs since 2000 and the first online EdD degree at the university in 2011. Due to the increased student demand for online IT degrees, the number of graduates from the online master's degree program has surpassed that of the residential master's degree program since 2013. Before graduation, students in all online degree programs (i.e., certificate, master's, and EdD) should take five core courses including Foundations of IT, Instructional Design, Instructional Development, Evaluation, and Needs Assessment.

Preassessment Information

Although the IT Department's offering of both residential and online degree programs remains popular, to make it more attractive to students and for their learning, there is a need to assess the degree programs' current strengths and make recommendations for improvement. While there is ample anecdotal evidence that the five online core courses are meeting some of the student needs, there is no empirical evidence on the extent to which those core courses are meeting the student needs from a student learning perspective. In the role of the project team, we defined student learning as the integration of learning objectives (goals), content (subject matter), and learning environments (instructional design, technology, and tools).

In this context, we chose five online core courses to identify the gap between the current state and the desired state and to provide recommendations for the overall quality of student learning. The project participants included online students and instructors. To collect data, we conducted a literature review, interviews, a survey, and document review to benchmark four peer institutions' IT degree programs. The frame factors restraining the scope of this needs assessment project included (a) a limited timeline to complete the project within a semester; (b) faculty availability due to their busy schedule; and (c) possible bias generated from the project team of residential students who may have limited understanding of online students' needs and challenges.

Needs Assessment Process

We worked through four steps for the needs assessment process including initiation, data collection, data analysis (SWOT analysis), and results (findings and recommendations; see Figure 3.1).

To get started, we met with the department chair as our client to determine the scope of the project and to identify frame factors constraining the scope of the project. The chair provided a list of faculty members who have taught or are teaching online core courses and agreed to help us conduct a survey with students through the department office. After developing a one-page proposal and receiving a permission letter from the chair, we began collecting data.

Figure 3.1 Needs Assessment Process

Initiation	Data Collection	Data Analysis	Result
• Initial meeting with client • Identify frame factors • One-page proposal • Permission letter	• Literature review • Document review • Interviews • Survey	• Statistical analysis of the survey data • Content analysis of the interview data • SWOT analysis	• Positive and negative findings • Recommendations • Final report • Presentation

Data Collection

To collect data, we conducted a literature review, a survey, interviews, and a document review. Each data collection process is described below.

Literature Review. We reviewed the literature on online education to understand the current state of the research area (e.g., Kozan & Richardson, 2014; Lawson & Lawson, 2013; McGee, Windes, & Torres, 2017; Zhang, Lin, Zhan, & Ren, 2016). Understanding key concepts identified in the literature on online education served as a useful lens to assess the needs of online students. To that end, we reviewed five bodies of literature that represent common themes in online education including: online education (general), instructor presence and feedback, group collaboration, student engagement, and use of technology.

Online students seek interactions with instructors through *just-in-time* feedback, instructor presence, and positive student engagement (Garrison, Anderson, & Archer, 1999; Wicks, Craft, Mason, Gritter, & Bolding, 2015). Instructors attempt to use different ways (e.g., project-based learning) to engage students in class participation in online courses (Cho & Brown, 2013; Darabi, Arrastia, Nelson, Cornille, & Liang, 2011; Ertmer, Sadaf, & Ertmer, 2011; Pazzaglia, Clements, Lavigne, & Stafford, 2016). Through group collaboration, students learn from their peers, engage in learning, and improve their performance (Huggins & Stamatel, 2015). Research (King, 2014; Kirby & Hulan, 2016) has shown that technology (e.g., learning management systems [LMS]) plays a critical role in online education.

Survey. We developed an online survey using *Qualtrics* and performed a pilot test with six graduate students in the department. Based on their feedback, we revised the survey. The final survey included two questions on demographics, five 5-point Likert scale questions on student learning of each online core course, two multiple-choice questions about online teaching tools, and an open-ended question on suggestions.

Figure 3.2 shows one of the Likert scale questions. As can be seen in the sample, the survey asked each student about a specific course that the person

Figure 3.2 A Sample Survey Question

Q4. For *R511: Instructional Technology Foundations*, please rate your agreement/disagreement with the statements that describe your perception on this course.
Caution: Agree is on the left side, and Disagree on the right side

	Strongly agree	Agree	Neutral	Disagree	Strongly disagree	Not applicable
Learning objectives are clear.	O	O	O	O	O	O
Navigation of the online course is clear.	O	O	O	O	O	O
Course materials include different media formats to facillitate students' learning.	O	O	O	O	O	O
Assessment methods are appropriate to measure what I have learned.	O	O	O	O	O	O
Grading policies are clearly presented.	O	O	O	O	O	O
The course encourages students to interact with each other.	O	O	O	O	O	O
The course is relevant to my work.	O	O	O	O	O	O
The instructor delivers learning content clearly.	O	O	O	O	O	O
The instructor provides students with constructive feedback on assignments.	O	O	O	O	O	O
The instructor provides feedback promptly.	O	O	O	O	O	O
I would recommend this course to other students.	O	O	O	O	O	O

was taking. Most students were enrolled in one of the three online degree programs (certificate, master's, or EdD).

We sent an email with a link to the online survey to 96 online students who enrolled in at least one core course through the department office. We sent them a reminder twice, 1 week and 2 weeks later, to increase the response rate. Of 96 online students who had taken at least one of the five core courses, 44 students (45.8% response rate) responded to the survey, and 11 students who had taken the survey volunteered for interviews. Of 44 respondents, 30 were female, 13 were male, and one did not answer.

Interviews. We developed three versions of the interview protocol, one each for online students, instructors, and administrators (the department chair and associate dean of Graduate Studies) who were also the department's faculty. Interview questions for students included students' experience in and perceptions of online courses. Example questions are the following: What do you think are the (dis)advantages of online courses? Can you please give us an example of online classes that you enjoyed? What would you suggest to improve online classes in instructional systems technology (IST)? Interview questions for instructors asked about their online teaching experiences and suggestions. Interview questions for administrators included their perceptions of online core courses.

We conducted interviews with 11 online students via Zoom because they were scattered throughout the United States. We interviewed seven instructors including two administrators who have been involved in developing online degree programs. Two other instructors were not available due to schedule conflicts. Interviews took a total of 389 minutes (6.48 hours) and approximately 20 to 25 minutes each. To ensure validity, we used member checks by asking interview participants to fact-check their transcripts. Five faculty members (71%) and nine students (82%) corrected their transcripts, while the other faculty and students made no changes.

Document Review. To benchmark our peer institutions' IT degree programs, we reviewed the websites of four peer institutions' programs including Florida State University, University of Georgia, Penn State University, and Purdue University. We found that their admission requirements were almost the same, except our IT degree program's higher graduation requirement (36 credits) compared to peer institutions' 30 or 35 credits. Reviewing our peer institutions' online degree programs helped us better understand the current state of our IT degree programs. We also reviewed the U.S. Department of Education's (2017) National Educational Technology Plan to understand the role of technology in education.

Data Analysis

We analyzed the survey data using descriptive statistics embedded in *Qualtrics,* and the responses were combined across the online courses to which students were responding. Content analysis was used to analyze the interview data. After transcribing the interview data verbatim, we chose an instructor transcript as a sample, independently read it, and identified codes (the smallest unit of information), categories (the next level of information), and themes. Through the iterative process of individual and collective analysis of the rest of the transcripts, we delivered the final 35 coding categories (e.g., reputation, instructor's timely feedback, support, and resources).

SWOT Analysis

The SWOT analysis (Leigh, 2010) includes internal strengths and weaknesses that are relatively easy to manipulate within a short timeframe, whereas external opportunities and threats are difficult to control and take time to make things happen. We used a SWOT analysis as the final step of data analysis to generate strengths, weaknesses, opportunities, and threats of the online core courses for student learning.

In this section, we present the results of the SWOT analysis (Figure 3.3). The online core courses had internal strengths (e.g., high reputation) and weaknesses (e.g., instructors' low teaching presence), and external opportunities (e.g., increased demands for instructional designers) and threats (e.g., increased competition with other degree programs). It should be noted that some of these findings relate specifically to student learning, while others relate to the factors affecting students, the quality of the instruction, or the draw of the course.

Strengths

The online students articulated many strengths of the online core courses including reputation, quality, flexibility, accessibility, project-based learning,

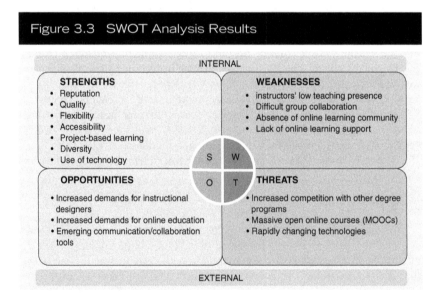

Figure 3.3   SWOT Analysis Results

diversity, and use of technology. The strong reputation came from the IT Department's long history as leading the field (Cho et al., 2017). For instance, students who took the Foundations of IT indicated that it encouraged them to interact with each other when working on group projects, while students who took the Instructional Design indicated that learning objectives were clear, and different media formats (e.g., videos) were effectively used to facilitate student learning.

Most online students, who had full-time jobs and family commitments, wanted to receive further education while working, so taking courses at any time and any place was crucial. Online students had positive attitudes toward project-based learning embedded in online core courses in which they conducted "authentic and meaningful projects." Students also appreciated learning things from different perspectives.

Weaknesses

We also found weaknesses including instructors' low teaching presence and timely feedback, challenging group collaborations, and a lack of online learning community and online learning support for technology. Some students encountered difficulties in receiving instructors' timely feedback. Due to the department's use of project-based learning, online students had to complete real group projects in core courses. Online team collaboration was a challenge due to team members' different places and time zones. A lack of physical presence in online classes also impacted students' feeling of belonging. Due to the absence of an orientation in the beginning, some online students were unsure about the registration and enrollment procedures. Students stated that some technology tools used in class were not current and adequate for group collaboration. As the university has recently adopted Canvas as the university's LMS and Zoom for communication in place of Oncourse and Adobe Connect, some students were frustrated in adjusting to new learning environments.

Opportunities

We found from the document and literature review that online courses provide opportunities: increased demands for instructional designers, global demands for online education, and emerging communication and collaboration technologies. Given a recent trend report on higher education (Berrett, 2016) in which the rise of instructional design was listed among the 10 key shifts in higher education, the graduates of the IT Department can easily find a job as an instructional designer locally and nationwide in diverse organizations. As universities are increasing online degree programs (Allen & Seaman, 2013), a growing number of working professionals desire to receive further education to stay current and get promoted while working, which will help the IT Department increase online courses. Increase of emerging communication tools also provides instructors with opportunities to use different teaching methods so that online students can effectively learn and communicate in class and teamwork.

Threats

Also from the document and literature review, we identified threats to the online core courses: increased competition with other degree programs, massive open online courses (MOOCs), and rapidly changing technologies. The IT Department in this case requires a relatively high GPA and credit requirements. Prospective students might choose other programs due to their flexibility in enrollment and graduation requirements. MOOCs providers (e.g., Coursera, edX) offer online courses on diverse subjects, whereas some top universities in the world offer free courses (Bonk et al., 2018). Students are expected to keep up with rapidly changing technologies to stay current; therefore, instructors are required to teach with those technologies.

Findings and Recommendations

Based on the data analysis (SWOT analysis), we present the following positive and negative findings (Table 3.1).

Based on the positive and negative findings, we provided recommendations to the department chair that ranged from easy to difficult as follows:

1. Optimize student experience during onboarding. To that end, provide an online orientation and detailed instructions for students in the beginning.

Table 3.1 Positive and Negative Findings

Positives	Negatives
• Online students access courses anytime and anywhere. • Online courses are designed by experts in IT who are supportive. • Faculty's teaching of both online and residential courses is beneficial because recorded residential courses increase teacher presence. • Learning objectives and guidelines for assignments are well-designed. • Students receive different perspectives from other students from all over the world as well as instructors from different areas of interest.	• New students do not feel that they receive adequate support from instructors. • Teamwork is difficult due to different time zones and work schedules. • Students do not receive immediate feedback from some instructors. • Canvas discussion forums and course structures are not sufficiently user-friendly. • Some course materials include outdated technologies; course content is K–12 education-focused.

2. Encourage student involvement in the online learning community. Online students can play an active role in taking responsibility for their learning and actively seeking information and resources to be part of the online learning community.

3. Leverage what is going well (e.g., research findings, flexibility, diverse backgrounds, and shared resources) and build on it.

4. Build an online teaching community. To that end, create standards for instructors to set the same expectations and have regular meetings for online teaching such as "critical friends groups," as in Cho and Brown (2013, p. 751), in which teachers share project ideas and give each other feedback to tackle challenges in project-based learning in class.

5. Update course delivery tools and ask the campus technology unit to improve some of the Canvas functions (e.g., the discussion forum for quality discussion).

Upon the project team's presentation of findings and recommendations, the department chair provided an overall positive feedback. Among the five recommendations, student onboarding as a low-hanging fruit and the involvement of online students in the learning community have shown certain progress because there was consensus in the department to consider orientation and the involvement of online students for the learning community as the first steps needing specifications. Both residential and online students have recently been invited to the university campus in mid-August before getting started to have a 1-day orientation to get to know the IT Department, degree program requirements, curriculum, and most importantly, people (i.e., students, faculty members, and staff). These efforts are being evaluated as critical to build a sense of a learning community in the department.

Influences

In the beginning of this needs assessment project, the department chair gave us preliminary advice that we should not approach needs assessment from a negative perspective, meaning that we should not have the preconception that there must be problems to fix in the department. To follow up on his advice, we had to be sensitive in wording and questioning in the data collection process and tone down some areas for improvement that we identified when presenting to the chair who thought there would be few issues in online core courses. Therefore, we learned a lesson that for a needs assessment to be more impactful, the buy-in of the top management, the department chair in this case, is extremely important to make recommendations effective in the organization.

Issues and Challenges

....

We focused the scope of the project on student learning and did not involve the needs of the instructors and their professional development. From the survey, for instance, we gathered only the current students' perceptions to identify their needs. Given that survey response rate levels in organizational research range from 35.7% to 52.7% (Baruch & Holtom, 2008), the 45.8% response rate we received showed a decent number of survey respondents, but it was not large enough to claim that we gathered most students' learning needs. Due to the limited number of respondents, the study findings should be interpreted with caution. With more survey responses, we might have a much better understanding of the online student needs for the online core courses. In addition, due to the faculty members' busy schedules, we could not interview all instructors in the department. Interviews with all instructors might help us capture the instructors' perspectives in full.

We attempted to triangulate data collection using multiple methods from multiple sources. Data collection methods included a survey and interviews as well as a literature and document review. To acquire firsthand data, observation would help us examine the online teaching and learning process, though it is challenging to do so online. Lastly, as three graduate students who participated in this needs assessment project were residential students, their understanding of the online students' needs and challenges might have been a limitation in capturing a full picture of student learning and satisfaction.

DISCUSSION QUESTIONS

1. The project team approached the client (the department chair in this case) and recommended the use of a needs assessment. Typically, the client is the one requesting a needs assessment. What issues or problems might arise from this reversal in the person or group requesting the project? What advantages might appear?

2. How do needs assessment and evaluation differ? The department chair in this case asked us this question after our final presentation. To him, a needs assessment can be considered formative evaluation in instructional design. Students can discuss similarities and differences between formative evaluation and needs assessment to have a better understanding of the latter.

3. How can a client who has a strong positive outlook on the current IT department's online degree programs be approached? Persuasion can be a challenge if clients do not have the same level of criticality about performance problems in the organization (online student learning in this case).

REFERENCES

Allen, I. E., & Seaman, J. (2013). *Changing course: Ten years of tracking online education in the United States* [Report]. Retrieved from https://www.immagic .com/eLibrary/ARCHIVES/GENERAL/OLC_US/O130110A.pdf.

Baruch, Y., & Holtom, B. C. (2008). Survey response rate levels and trends in organizational research. *Human Relations, 61*(8), 1139–1160. doi: 10.1177/0018726708094863

Berrett, D. (2016, February 29). Instructional design: Demand grows for a new breed of academic. *The Chronicle of Higher Education.* Retrieved from http:// chronicle.com/article/Instructional-Design/235425?cid=cp32.

Bonk, C. J., Zhu, M., Kim, M., Xu, S., Sabir, N., & Sari, A. (2018). Pushing toward a more personalized MOOC: Exploring instructor selected activities, resources, and technologies for MOOC design and implementation. *The International Review of Research on Open and Distributed Learning, 19*(4), 92–115.

Cho, Y., Boling, E., & Kwon, K. (2017). Improving human learning and performance at Indiana University [Special issue]. *Performance Improvement, 56*(3), 34–44. doi:10.1002/pfi.21695

Cho, Y., & Brown, C. (2013). Project-based learning in education: Integrating business needs and student learning. *European Journal of Training and Development, 37*(8), 744–765. doi:10.1108/EJTD-01-2013-0006

Darabi, A., Arrastia, M. C., Nelson, D. W., Cornille, T., & Liang, X. (2011). Cognitive presence in asynchronous online learning: A comparison of four discussion strategies. *Journal of Computer Assisted Learning, 27*(3), 216–227. doi:10.1111/j.1365-2729.2010.00392.x

Ertmer, P. A., Sadaf, A., & Ertmer, D. J. (2011). Student-content interactions in online courses: The role of question prompts in facilitating higher-level engagement with course content. *Journal of Computing in Higher Education, 23*(2/3), 157–186. doi:10.1007/s12528-011-9047-6

Garrison, D. R., Anderson, T., & Archer, W. (1999). Critical inquiry in a text-based environment: Computer conferencing in higher education. *The Internet and Higher Education, 2*(2), 87–105. doi:10.1016/S1096-7516(00)00016-6

Huggins, C. M., & Stamatel, J. P. (2015). An exploratory study comparing the effectiveness of lecturing versus team-based learning. *Teaching Sociology, 43*(3), 227–235. doi:10.1177/0092055X15581929

King, S. B. (2014). Graduate student perceptions of the use of online course tools to support engagement. *International Journal for the Scholarship of Teaching and Learning, 8*(1), Article 5. Retrieved from https://doi.org/10.20429/ ijsotl.2014.080105.

Kirby, E. G., & Hulan, N. (2016). Student perceptions of self and community within an online environment: The use of VoiceThread to foster community. *Journal of Teaching and Learning With Technology, 5*(1), 87–99. doi:10.14434/jotlt.v5n1.19411

Kozan, K., & Richardson, J. C. (2014). Interrelationships between and among social, teaching, and cognitive presence. *The Internet and Higher Education, 21*, 68–73. doi:10.1016/j.iheduc.2013.10.007

Lawson, M. A., & Lawson, H. A. (2013). New conceptual frameworks for student engagement research, policy, and practice. *Review of Educational Research, 83*(3), 432–479. doi:10.3102/0034654313480891

Leigh, D. (2010). SWOT analysis. In R. Watkins & D. Leigh (Eds.), *Handbook of improving performance in the workplace: Selecting and implementing performance interventions* (Vol. 2, pp. 115–140). Silver Spring, MD: ISPI.

McGee, P., Windes, D., & Torres, M. (2017). Experienced online instructors: Beliefs and preferred supports regarding online teaching. *Journal of Computing in Higher Education, 29*(2), 331–352. doi:10.1007/s12528-017-9140-6

Pazzaglia, A. M., Clements, M., Lavigne, H. J., & Stafford, E. T. (2016). *An analysis of student engagement patterns and online course outcomes in Wisconsin* (REL 2016-147). Retrieved from https://ies.ed.gov/ncee/edlabs/regions/midwest/pdf/REL_2016147.pdf.

Sleezer, C. M., Russ-Eft, D., & Gupta, K. (2014). *A practical guide to needs assessment* (3rd ed.). San Francisco, CA: Wiley & ASTD.

U.S. Department of Education. (2017, January). *National educational technology plan.* Retrieved from https://tech.ed.gov/files/2017/01/NETP17.pdf.

Wicks, D. A., Craft, B. B., Mason, G. N., Gritter, K., & Bolding, K. (2015). An investigation into the community of inquiry of blended classrooms by a faculty learning community. *The Internet and Higher Education, 25*, 53–62. doi:10.1016/j.iheduc.2014.12.001

Zhang, H., Lin, L., Zhan, Y., & Ren, Y. (2016). The impact of teaching presence on online engagement behaviors. *Journal of Educational Computing Research, 54*(7), 887–900. doi:10.1177/0735633116648171

CHAPTER

4

A Needs Assessment for a Professional Association's Certificate Program

Denise M. Cumberland

Abstract

This case describes a knowledge and skills needs assessment for an international professional association's educational certificate program. The needs assessment was conducted to identify what would encourage a specific target population, long-standing credential holders, to continue recertifying. A two-step data collection process involved analyzing archival data from annual surveys over a 2-year period, followed by interviews with 12 long-standing credential holders. The outcome of this needs assessment led to innovative and customized educational programming efforts, as well as efforts to provide distinction to those who recertify and devise platforms for this group to socialize and connect in person and online. Below is an overview of the case.

Where the Needs Assessment Was Conducted	Who Conducted the Needs Assessment	Focus of Needs Assessment	How Data Were Collected	How Data Were Analyzed
International professional association	Consultant experienced in franchising and in conducting needs assessments	To identify what would encourage a specific target population of long-standing credential holders to continue recertifying	Archival survey data, interviews conducted over the telephone	Archival data from the graduate satisfaction surveys were cross-tabulated; closed-ended data responses from long-standing credential holders were reviewed; Likert-style questions were analyzed with descriptive statistics; open-ended survey responses and interview transcripts were analyzed using structural coding technique

Background

As organizations seek to elevate the skills of their employees, as well as garner stature for their industry, many associations have stepped up and created certificate programs to provide professional development educational curriculum for their membership (Barrows & Walsh, 2002; Black & Everard, 1992; Huang & Weiler, 2010; Samuels, 2000). For professional certification programs to be optimally effective, however, they must be designed and delivered in a manner that meets the needs of the individuals who pursue these opportunities (Cumberland, Petrosko, & Jones, 2018).

Founded in 1960, the International Franchise Association (IFA) is an organization that represents franchisors and franchisees. With 15,800 members, the IFA is the largest association that supports the franchising sector (IFA, 2017 Annual Report). The IFA defines franchising as a business relationship where "the franchisor provides to another party (the franchisee) the right to operate a business that sells products and/or services produced or developed by the franchisor, under the franchisor's business format and management system and identified by the franchisor's trademark" (Rudnick & Wieczorek, 2016, p. 4). On the one hand, franchisors must recognize franchisees as business owners who desire autonomy, and on the other hand, the franchisor must exert rigid controls over specific processes. This hybrid business format can create tension in the relationship.

As stated in the association's guiding principles, the IFA works to educate franchisors and franchisees on beneficial methods and business practices to improve franchising. Members include franchise organizations, individual franchisees, as well as consultants and companies that support the franchise sector in legal, marketing, and the business development arena. The IFA's Educational Foundation initiated programs in the early 1990s to educate and train franchisors and franchisees on methods and business practices that would improve the industry (www.franchise.org/cfe.asp). In 1996, the Institute of Certified Franchise Executives (ICFE) was launched. A program manager was hired, and an official Board of Governors established to oversee program standards, approve curriculum, and provide the Certified Franchise Executive (CFE) designation when participants completed the program.

Profile of the Organization

The ICFE mission is to "enhance the professionalism of franchising by certifying the highest standards of quality training and education" (www.franchise.org/cfe). The ICFE provides educational programs and a course of study and assessment that leads to the designation as a CFE. The designation of CFE indicates that a participant of the program has obtained through experience, education, and testing, an advanced set of skills distinctly applicable to the field of franchising.

Participants in the certificate program may work in or be closely associated to the franchising industry. Individuals must apply, meet eligibility requirements, and pay an application fee. Once accepted, candidates need to earn 3,500 credits to complete the program. Credits are secured based on experience, participation at IFA-sponsored events, and educational programming from approved workshops, webinars, and online classes. Credits and costs associated with the educational components vary. Candidates must also take and pass an online exam to qualify for the certificate. Participants who complete the program are awarded the CFE designation at the IFA annual convention. There are currently over 1,300 graduates of the program. Much of the growth in the program has occurred over the last 5 years, with graduating classes averaging over 125 students between 2010 and 2017 (R. DuPont, personal communication, April 16, 2018). To maintain certification, individuals must earn a total of 1,200 credits every 3 years following the year they earned certification.

Preassessment Information

As the incoming IFA Education Foundation president was meeting with franchise executives, she was hearing from long-standing certificate holders that they could no longer find relevant educational courses. The Education Foundation president reached out to me based on my experience working in franchising, my role as an educator, and my experience in conducting needs assessments, to determine what these seasoned executives identified as their primary learning gaps, as well as other factors that would encourage them to recertify. We set up a conference call to discuss current knowledge, identify stakeholders, and align on the focus for the needs assessment. We agreed on five basic questions to guide the research:

- What do we know about these long-standing credential holders?

- What subject areas do these long-standing credential holders perceive as learning opportunities?

- What educational formats/platforms would be appealing to this group?

- What other motivators would attract this group to continue to recertify?

- Are there any other unmet needs this group has with respect to education?

Next, a letter of agreement was developed outlining expectations of steps, what support would be needed from the client (president, Franchise Education Foundation), and the timeline.

Needs Assessment Process

In this instance, I relied on a knowledge and skills training needs assessment for a specific population of certification holders, thought to be underserved with the current educational course offerings. Knowledge and skills needs assessments are applicable when existing training and development curriculum needs require updating to meet organizational changes (Sleezer, Russ-Eft, & Gupta, 2014). When the ultimate goal of a knowledge and skills needs assessment is to customize learning programs to capture the interest of a specific group (Barbazette, 2006), the focus is typically on the following:

- Gaining insight into the group's opinions with respect to learning needs

- Examining what motivates this group of learners

- Identifying preferences for types of educational contexts

- Understanding any characteristics of the group that would influence programming development (e.g., physical, social, cultural factors)

I relied on needs assessment models promoted by Altschuld and Kuman (2010), and Sleezer et al. (2014). Both of these needs assessment models focus on making data-driven and responsive recommendations. Both also advocate the use of a systematic approach that suggests three phases to a needs assessment when addressing a complex issue such as addressing the training and nontraining needs of a specific target population (Sleezer et al., 2014). The three phases of this knowledge and skills assessment include the preassessment, assessment, and postassessment.

The initial preassessment phase in our case began with research and discovery focused on the current number of educational courses available to long-standing credential holders, which in this case turned out to be zero. This led next to the formation of a needs assessment committee (NAC). The NAC was comprised of the client (the new president of the Education Foundation), the prior Education Foundation president, the director of the CFE Program, and me to develop an agreed-upon work plan to conduct the needs assessment. The assessment phase, where the identified gaps were studied, involved examination of archival data and telephone interviews with a pool of 12 CFEs who had been credentialed for over 10 years. Finally, in the postassessment phase, the findings were used to produce recommendations.

Altchuld and Kuman's (2010) traditional needs assessment approach invites multiple stakeholders' views and considers the political environment. Altschuld and Kuman defined stakeholders at three different levels, including individuals receiving the service, the providers, or the organization as a whole. For this assessment, Level 1 stakeholders were the participants in the program who had held the credential for over 10 years. Level 2 stakeholders varied, but primarily consisted of the ICFE Board, which has oversight of the program, and the IFA's Educational Foundation, which could be impacted from a reputational standpoint. Finally, Level 3 stakeholders were members of the IFA.

Data-Gathering Approach

With respect to a knowledge and skills needs assessment for a specific target group, appropriate methods to collect information may include interviews, observations, existing records, focus groups, and surveys. Using at least two methods bolsters the validity and reliability of the data (Sleezer et al., 2014). Both interviews and observations allow you to explain why this information is sought, and this can help alleviate any suspicions that may arise. Second, specific groups can be hard to reach in a mass approach, or resources can be wasted by collecting data from individuals who are not considered pertinent to the assessment.

To understand the perceptions and needs of long-standing credential holders, the assessment phase was conducted using two data collection methods. The first relied on archival survey data from Graduate Satisfaction Surveys conducted over a 2-year period. The second phase of data collection relied on telephone interviews with long-standing CFEs. The client also expressed interest in a possible follow-up survey to all long-standing credential holders, once initial data from the interviews were analyzed. Outlined below is the protocol used to collect the data via archival records and interviews.

Archival Survey Data. Using database information to obtain a current and future picture of the organization or issue is a recommended protocol in needs assessment models (Altschuld, 2010; Sleezer et al., 2014). Graduate Satisfaction Surveys were readily available and easily accessible. This is important because the review of database information is a very timely and cost-efficient method for understanding the situation at hand. In addition to providing graduate demographics, it also yielded information concerning their overall satisfaction with the program. Furthermore, respondents' recommendations for optimizing the program were available in response to an open-ended question. I analyzed archival data information (described below) to help inform the next phase of data collection: *interviewing.*

Interviews. The second phase of data collection consisted of in-depth, semi-structured interviews with seasoned credential holders. The interviews were used to elicit perceptions about unmet needs, satisfaction with current programming, and gather ideas for types of learning modalities that would appeal to this group. Telephone interviews were conducted with 12 graduates who had held the credential for over 10 years. The interviewees were chosen by the client and the program director. The interviewees ranged in age, gender, and title. Furthermore, these individuals came from various-sized organizations to ensure that large, medium, and small franchise systems were represented. Most interview sessions lasted approximately 45 minutes. The interview questions were developed by the author for the purpose of this research (see Appendix A for the interview questions).

Data Analyses

The archival data from the Graduate Satisfaction Surveys were first cross-tabulated in the survey software program to report only on long-standing certificate holders. Next, the closed-ended data responses were reviewed for logic and consistency to determine if any pattern of responses suggested any respondents did not understand the questions. Next, the answers to all Likert-style questions were analyzed by the software program, which reported percentages for each response (e.g., strongly agree, agree, neither agree nor disagree, disagree, strongly disagree), as well measures of central tendency. The open-ended survey responses and interview transcripts were analyzed using Saldaña's (2009) *structural coding* technique. Well suited for both of these types of datasets, structural coding uses a question-based code. The research questions served as the initial label or indexing device. After reading and rereading the data, participant statements were classified under the appropriate label. Next, each series of statements within the segments was read, and more descriptive codes were assigned. This straightforward coding process allows for frequency counts to be used to assess common opinions, attitudes, or perceptions. Finally, statements quoting particularly illustrative expressions were noted. These would be used as quotations in the final report to capture the full sense of respondents' beliefs and understandings.

Results of the Needs Assessment

What Did We Learn?

A cross tabulation of surveys from 2 years of data located 52 respondents who had held their credential for over 10 years. Respondent data revealed the following demographic profiles:

- Most held high-ranking positions (e.g., CEO/president or other C-Suite positions).

- They had been in their current position for a long time, with over one-third holding their position for over 15 years.

- Education levels tended to be high, with almost one-third of the participants holding a master's degree.

- Over three-fourths of them were over the age of 50.

With respect to overall satisfaction with the program, this group indicated strong scores with close to 90% very satisfied/satisfied. After reviewing responses to the survey's open-ended question, "How can the program be improved?" the following needs emerged:

- Greater variety of course topics

- Improvements in the overall recertification process

- Formal recognition of noteworthy members (e.g., retirees or long-term CFEs)

The 12 interviews with seasoned credential holders allowed for deeper exploration of views with respect to the program, as well as ways to optimize the program to meet their needs. All respondents indicated that having their CFE had proven to be valuable early in their career. The majority felt that the relevancy of the course topics had diminished as they had progressed in their profession. This was reflected in the comment: "When you climb into the executive rank you need special technical knowledge and the current programming for this group is weak." This sentiment was further illustrated as 10 of the participants indicated that they were supportive of the program, but their own participation was based on habit.

When asked why they pursued professional development, a large number of the respondents indicated their motivation was to gain knowledge and remain up-to-date in a continually changing business environment. Several respondents also mentioned that the CFE designation provided them credibility. A follow-up question asked how they currently obtain the knowledge or information that they are seeking if not through educational programming. Eight interviewees indicated they solve this issue by reaching out to their peer network for information on the topic. The next most popular method for securing information included reading books and checking the Internet.

What New Educational Content Is Needed?

Seven interviewees wanted to learn more about franchise development based on different life stages of the organization. Seven participants also indicated that leadership development for the C-suite was a topic of interest. A focus on finance emerged from a third of the interviewees as a needed educational component. Specifically, this included a desire for more education around structuring international deals, private equity ownership, and financial education at different franchisor stages. Marketing also resonated as a need with a third of the interviewees, with each specifically mentioning social media. With respect to education about the human resources function, engaging long-term franchisees, as well as working with different generations, surfaced as desirable content.

What Learning Formats Are Desired?

A third of the respondents stated that they prefer learning from well-known experts and that the facilitator makes a huge difference in their interest and attendance. A third also indicated they favored learning from brainstorming through panels or peer groups. Specific probes about varying educational formats provided the following data.

Online Courses

These offered the least appeal to the respondents, and the majority of those interviewed indicated they were not "fans" or had not taken any online courses in a long time. Several commented on these formats being *"bulky"* or *"cumbersome."*

Several suggested that online courses were more appropriate for when you want to get "basic information across." When probed on what makes for a good online experience, the comments centered on having a good learning-management system and offering interactive assessments throughout to keep the learners' attention.

Webinars

Most respondents were either positive or at least neutral about the value of webinars as learning opportunities. Several mentioned that they rarely participate due to time issues. Others, who more actively engage in webinars, suggested the following tips for making webinars effective:

- Using well-known and highly respected speakers
- Ensuring the topics target specific attendees
- Providing a strong technology interface
- Limiting the time to 20 minutes or no longer than an hour
- Having interactive elements to be able to engage with the speaker
- Providing some follow-up with the attendees other than a survey

Conference Workshops

A vast majority of respondents indicated that they valued the networking opportunity provided by conference workshops. A probe asked what determined their attendance. Similar to webinars, the respondents indicated that relying on well-known experts was critical and that the session must be focused on the needs of a specific audience. When asked about what methods of facilitation helped them learn, the respondents listed roundtables, case studies, and panels.

Learning Teams/Clubs

Nine of the 12 respondents thought learning teams or clubs were appealing, and several indicated they either participated in CEO groups in their cities, or they used these in their own organizations. Suggestions for how to execute included

- Clear guidelines (i.e., meeting monthly, participants only allowed to miss one session, having a goal, limiting size to no more than 8–12 participants, having a facilitator, using a good matching program to establish the mentor–mentee pairs, embracing the case study approach, and working on a specific issue).
- Participants are from the same business discipline.
- Participants are at the same level (peers).

- Applications are required.
- Using technology such as Google Chat.

Coaching/Mentoring

All respondents favored the idea of coaching or mentoring. Several mentioned that they currently mentor others. Many respondents suggested there be a shadow component and credits awarded to both the mentor and mentee. All respondents indicated the need for clear guidelines to be established in a mentoring relationship. There were different views on the optimal length of mentor programs, as some respondents liked 6 months, while others thought a year to 3 years was appropriate.

What Motivators Would Facilitate Continual Recertification?

Most respondents indicated that they liked having the CFE designation and enjoyed learning something new. The majority of those interviewed suggested some additional acknowledgement for those with over 10 years would increase the value of staying certified. The most noted idea was for some form of title enhancement such as *CFE Fellow* or *Distinguished CFE*. One respondent mentioned that Toastmasters has various "levels" and could be a model. Another commented, "It isn't why I do it, but I would love being recognized as a 'fellow'— this is where our programming is under-developed." One-quarter of respondents mentioned being listed as part of a speaker's bureau on the IFA website would be motivation to remain involved. Other ideas offered by the interviewees to create additional reasons for recertifying included

- Some type of "pin"
- Eligibility to author an article for the IFA's journal, *Franchising World*
- Recognition at the IFA convention with an exclusive networking event

What Other Ideas Surfaced for Meeting Educational Needs?

The most noted idea was to create a method to connect the long-standing credential holders so that they could network with each other (e.g., LinkedIn groups). A handful of other ideas surfaced, such as offering language classes, developing a series of programs just for senior executives, and having small groups who serve as resources. One interviewee summed up by saying, "Don't make certification painful for those of us who have been doing it for a long time. Give us cool stuff that we can sign up for."

Influences

Based on findings from this needs assessment, these long-standing credential holders are higher in role stature and have worked longer in the franchising industry. The needs assessment showed that more relevant courses in the educational curriculum were needed to attract and maintain involvement of this group of stakeholders. The client, the NAC, and I agreed that our recommendation would include new customized programming be developed for long-standing CFEs. Furthermore, we decided to recommend that these long-standing credential holders be recognized with new title enhancements, special events, and select social media networking opportunities. The next step was to present the findings to the ICFE Board of Governors, a stakeholder group that would ultimately decide what action to take.

It was important to frame the needs assessment as an opportunity to augment current programming. The purpose was not to suggest that current courses were inadequate, as those courses serve individuals in earlier career stages. Rather, our goal was to identify what type of new customized programming would appeal to this group of long-standing credential holders. The board embraced the recommendations, but due to time constraints, it wanted to begin with one pilot workshop that would be held at the annual IFA convention. After a well-attended and highly rated full-day program dedicated only to long-standing CFEs at the convention, more programming is under development. Additionally, the board opted to create a task force to examine how to execute title enhancements and to determine what types of special networking events to create for this group.

Issues and Challenges

The first challenge with a knowledge and skills needs assessment, such as this one, is gaining access to the designated target group. In this case, attempting to reach senior leaders for 35–45 minute interviews was not something the needs assessor could assume would be easy to accomplish. To avoid the problem of access, I requested the client secure the interviews by providing a list of dates and times when I could conduct the telephone interviews. By providing a spreadsheet of dates and times, the client filled out the name of the person to be interviewed, and I contacted each person on that date and time. This eliminated potential access issues.

The desire to engage in a follow-up survey, to identify how widely held the opinions expressed from the interviews were, proved to be the second challenge. There was not adequate time to field a survey, analyze the data, and provide a report to the Board of Governors prior to the IFA convention. It is possible that the limitation of having primarily interview data resulted in board members wanting to take a slower approach to executing the recommendations.

DISCUSSION QUESTIONS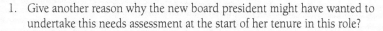

1. Give another reason why the new board president might have wanted to undertake this needs assessment at the start of her tenure in this role?

2. Looking at Appendix A, what other interview questions or probes would you have asked?

3. Assuming time had been available, develop survey questions for long-standing credential holders based on the qualitative data findings.

4. What other recommendations would you suggest based on the findings?

5. What are some success factors that the ICFE could use to assess the impact of the changes made based on the needs assessment?

REFERENCES

Altschuld, J., & Kumar, D. (2010). A generic needs assessment model and steps. *Needs assessment: An overview*. Thousand Oaks, CA: Sage.

Barbazette, J. (2006). *Training needs assessment: Methods, tools, and techniques*. San Francisco, CA: Pfeiffer.

Barrows, C. W., & Walsh, J. (2002). "Bridging the gap" between hospitality management programmes and the private club industry. *International Journal of Contemporary Hospitality Management, 14*(3), 120–127. https://doi .org/10.1108/09596110210424411

Black, H. S., & Everard, K. E. (1992). The Academy of Administrative Management: Path to the professional management certification. *Management World, 20*(1), 6–7.

Cumberland, D. M., Petrosko, J., & Jones, G. (2018). Motivations for pursuing professional certification. *Performance Improvement Quarterly, 31*(1), 57–82. https://doi.org/10.1002/piq.21256

Huang, S., & Weiler, B. (2010). A review and evaluation of China's quality assurance system for tour guiding. *Journal of Sustainable Tourism, 18*(7), 845–860. http://dx.doi.org/10.1080/09669582.2010.484492

International Franchise Association. (n.d.). Certified Franchise Executive Program. Retrieved from https://www.franchise.org/cfe-home.

International Franchise Association. (2017). *Annual report: We are franchising*. Retrieved from http://ifa-annual-report.s3-website-us-west-2.amazonaws .com/2017-annual-report/.

Rudnick, L., & Wieczorek, D. (2015). What is franchising. In *ICFE study guide for franchise executives* (pp. 1–17). Washington, DC: IFA Educational Foundation.

Saldaña, J. (2009). An introduction to codes and coding. *The coding manual for qualitative researchers*. Thousand Oaks, CA: Sage.

Samuels, J. B. (2000). Certification: A continually perplexing issue facing hospitality, tourism, and related professions. *Journal of Hospitality & Tourism Education, 12*(1), 47–51.

Sleezer, C. M., Russ-Eft, D., & Gupta, K. (2014). *A practical guide to needs assessment* (3rd ed.). San Francisco, CA: Wiley & ASTD.

Appendix A

How would you describe the Certified Franchise Executive programming options available to you over the last several years?

As you think about your work, what topics or issues do you continually seek more information on?

How are you currently securing this information?

If you could design a way to learn more about [insert topic they mentioned], what would this educational format look like?

Thinking about the following types of learning formats, let me know why it would or would not appeal.

- Webinars
- Workshops
- Online courses
- Learning teams/clubs
- Coaching

Why is professional development important to you?

What would motivate you to pursue ongoing professional development programs from the International Franchise Association?

Do you have any other ideas for how the International Franchise Association can meet your educational needs?

CHAPTER

5

A Public Legal Education and Information Strategy

Advancing Cybersecurity and Counterterrorism Processes

Jen Geary

Abstract

These combined needs assessments present generalities about assessing cybersecurity and counterterrorism in over 50 unique locations. A nonprofit organization presents informal, public needs assessments that address the public's knowledge and skill needs related to cybersecurity and counterterrorism. These assessments were conducted with the public in selected locations in Australia, Canada, and the United States. Public Legal Education and Information (PLEI) was an approach used to assess needs, engage with the public, and advance the public's capacity to shape regulatory and policy decisions linked to cybersecurity and cyberterrorism. Below is an overview of the case.

Where the Needs Assessment Was Conducted	Who Conducted the Needs Assessment	Focus of Needs Assessment	How Data Were Collected	How Data Were Analyzed
Over 50 locations in Australia, Canada, and the United States	Staff of the Trident Mediation, Counseling, Arts and Supports Foundation	Collected and shared materials from Public Legal Education and Information (PLEI) to enable public to understand impacts of cybersecurity breaches and counterterrorism and to learn ways to protect themselves	Researcher was a participant-observer: collecting archival data, observing the public and their interactions, participating in public activities, and speaking with selected individuals. PLEI collected from various sources such as case law, legislation, international law, the general literature, and direct observations	Qualitative analysis and triangulation; development of corporate, theoretical, affiliations, program features, and location codes used to develop themes

Background

Cybertechnology consists of computers, communicative and network elements, data, and media (Baase, 2003). The human risks associated with technology and cyberterrorism present a global challenge for states (Tehrani, 2017). There is not a universal definition of terrorism (Brunst, 2010). Debates about what is and what is not terrorism can be traced back at least to the 1920s. Furthermore, Tehrani mentioned that at a fundamental level, the Internet comprises joined computer networks to transmit typescript, graphic, and sound. Cybersecurity involves procedures and practices to safeguard technology, including mainframes, nets, hardware, and data from unlawful contact or targeting to exploit others (Department of Homeland Security, n.d.; Editor, 2017).

Stories of cybersecurity and cyberterrorism disruptions and attacks permeate the news. Examples include accounts of extremist groups using computer technology to recruit members, transfer funds, intimidate vulnerable people, and more. Terrorist incidents could be of relatively low occurrence, but the public may experience high fear and vulnerability because of them (Anderson, 2017; Kirmayer, Lemelson, & Barad, 2007).

There are gaps in scientific knowledge and the social scientists' understanding of technology, cybersecurity, and counterterrorism (Nacos, 2002). Similar to other studies, research linked to cybersecurity and counterterrorism is subject to data breaches. Many laws require practitioners, researchers, administrators, retailers, and others to adopt reasonable precautions to limit or prevent privacy and security risks.

Often data storage is on multiple devices that are located in diverse geographical areas (Bandler, 2017). Valuable data could be destroyed through human agency and in natural disasters such as fires. Also, anonymous parties both domestically and internationally may be able to steal, set a ransom, mine, and otherwise exploit data (Claypoole & Payton, 2017). There is merit in developing contingency plans should there be data loss or cybersecurity breaches (Social Impact Assessment Unit, 1996).

In 2017, Tehrani noted that unlawful cyberactivity events have become better planned and recurrent. There has been a seeming increase in the number of countries that experience terrorist incidents, although deaths that are attributable to terrorist activities declined in 2016 and 2017 (Institute for Economics and Peace, 2017).

Profile of the Organization

The Trident Mediation, Counseling, Arts and Supports Foundation was established as a Canadian nonprofit organization in 2017. The Trident Mediation, Counseling, and Support Foundation was founded as a provincial organization in 1998. Thus, the Trident Mediation, Counseling, Arts and Supports Foundation is a national organization, and the Trident Mediation

Counseling and Support Foundation exists at the provincial level. They are sister organizations. The Foundations' staff consists of two full-time directors and networks of professionals who are in Australia, Canada, and the United States. The Foundation and networks work to improve the lives of individuals, couples, families, and organizations across the Canadian provinces, as well as across nations and in international jurisdictions. The Foundation meets its mission through direct service delivery, publications, and innovations. It provides outreach and diverse services to the public as part of its social responsibility agenda. An essential part of the Foundation's strategy is to develop collaborations between the private and public sectors. The *public* includes the individuals in a specific location, and it also refers to the relationship between the government and the public involving power, rights, aptitudes, and like aspects. The Foundation is inspired by an ethic to serve and protect. For the Foundation, an underlying value is the development of holistic practices partly through, for example, needs assessments and research.

The Foundation used Public Legal Education and Information (PLEI) to engage with the public and advance the public's capacity to shape regulatory and policy decisions linked to cybersecurity and cyberterrorism. PLEI can be used to develop the psychological, legal, policy, and social purposes related to cybersecurity and counterterrorism. PLEI includes assessing the needs of

- The public at large

- The relationships between the public and government

- Government behaviors (as exemplified in laws, cultural practices, official behaviors and decisions, etc.)

Preassessment Information

A director of the Foundation conducted all of these needs assessments often in conjunction with Foundation networks. Locations were selected based on publications and recommendations from governments about the incidents of cybersecurity breaches, and cyberterrorism, and their importance. Boundaries for the work included

- Members of the public who communicated such matters as issues about cybersecurity or cyberterrorism and their consequences

- The communicated matters had components from the social sciences, including education, law, psychology, social policy, social work, management, and business studies, etc. (Russ-Eft, Sleezer, Sampson, & Leviton, 2017).

Needs Assessment Processes

This case illustrates informal needs assessments as described by Sleezer, Russ-Eft, and Gupta (2014). Further, the case used a knowledge and skills assessment process to help the public at large deal with the relationships between the public and government and with government behaviors (as exemplified in laws, cultural practices, official behaviors, and decisions, etc.). PLEI as implemented in these needs assessments relied on collecting archival data, observing the public and their interactions, participating in public activities, and speaking with selected individuals. When PLEI was implemented, information was collected from various sources such as case law, legislation, international law, the general literature, and direct observations. The literature supports the use of data from multiple sources and approaches (e.g., Goldstein, 1986; Russ-Eft & Preskill, 2009; Sleezer et al., 2014).

PLEI is not designed to provide legal advice, and the Foundation does not offer this service; rather, the public is encouraged to consult with a lawyer who is familiar with immediate and local issues. The provision of legal support, such as information and research, is often not the same as giving legal advice as to the relevance of law to the public situation. The public needs that are identified when implementing PLEI can be used to create strategic solutions (e.g., legal education that could be applied across the disciplines and information).

The Foundation also incorporated a social planning approach to needs assessments that combined extensive and intensive requisites. The public often has extensive needs to access education and administrative proceedings and to be safe (Social Impact Assessment Unit, 1996). Communities of interest also have intensive requisites to access PLEI regardless of such factors as age, gender, ethnicity, infirmity, or social or economic status. The Foundation noted debates, endeavored to be inclusive, strived to open communication channels, and facilitated relationship building between the private and public sectors. These activities were directed toward developing a shared identity and purpose to learn what the public wants and to begin to address it needs; this is consistent with ideas offered in many publications (e.g., Cook, & Dampier, 1998; Russ-Eft & Preskill, 2009; Selman, Selman, Social Impact Assessment Unit, 1996; Spencer, 1998). The Foundation also incorporated an approach from Patton (2002), and it viewed the public in different locations and participated

> in whatever is going on, without taking notes; and using documents or reports prepared for other purposes (e.g. clinical case notes) to generate research data in situations where no additional human subject protection permission is required because the data are routinely collected, and findings will be reported only in the aggregate. (p. 191)

The Foundation recognized the challenges that could have happened had experiments or questionnaires been administered at public places (Patton, 2002).

These challenges included losses of originality, spontaneity, and freedoms of speech and expression. Russ-Eft and Preskill (2009) mentioned unobtrusive means for undertaking evaluations and indicated that such methods do not interrupt everyday activities. Had the Foundation been aloof during its observations and taken comprehensive notes, this would have been conspicuous. The Foundation showed interest in public activities and encouraged the public to enter into dialogue with each other. This helped to ease tensions and to create an environment that was conducive to information sharing. Observational research can be resource intensive in terms of hours and financial costs (Russ-Eft et al., 2017). The Foundation and others in the public interest were and continue to be willing to invest in these needs assessments.

Data Collection and Analysis Methods

The Foundation set out to develop anticipatory inquiry and future thinking (Patton, 2002; Wadsworth, 1991) on the needs for PLEI on cybersecurity and counterterrorism. The Foundation apprised, empathized, and empowered (Wadsworth, 1991) the public through PLEI. Means for carrying out these needs assessments included content analysis, developmental, formative, summative, outcome, impact, individual, collective, organizational, systemic, observational, and combined processes (Castro, 1991; Russ-Eft & Preskill, 2009; Schuemer, 1991).

The Local Government and Shires Associations of New South Wales (2000) and the Social Impact Assessment Unit (1996) indicated that social planning involves issues that lie at the threshold of social recognition. The Foundation held assumptions that were based on its experiences, discussions with the public, and reflections on the literature review (Russ-Eft et al., 2017).

Data Collection

At each location in Australia, Canada, and the United States, the Foundation collected, published information, and engaged as a participant-observer at public venues. These venues included public markets, libraries, and cafés—representing over 50 unique locations. These efforts required about 35,000 hours of voluntary services and were conducted at selected communities in the three countries. Needs were identified that could reflect political, administrative, and cognitive aspects of cybersecurity or cyberterrorism.

The Foundation, when it conducted these needs assessments, relied on interdisciplinary practice. This approach is consistent with Selman et al.'s (1998) advice on the role of interdisciplinary practice. More specifically, the Foundation relied on interdisciplinary collaboration and maintained an active presence in diverse communities of interest that ranged from local, to national, to international levels. The Foundation met with the public mainly on a face-to-face basis.

Data Analysis

Wolcott (1988, p. 192) wrote: "The strength of fieldwork lies in its [triangulation] obtaining information in many ways rather than solely one." The broad term *triangulation* seems to have a shared application in qualitative research. However, its meaning may be interpreted differently by various researchers (e.g., Bogdan & Biklen, 1998). Triangulation could denote studies where one or more data sources are applied (Bogdan & Biklen, 1998; Naumes & Naumes, 1999; Neuman, 1997). This researcher in this study was not confined to one dataset alone. This helped her to limit bias in this study.

In addition, this researcher applied codes to manage and limit complex data. Codes were linked to phenomena that arose in the needs assessments and the literature. There are varying kinds of codes. These incorporate theoretical, affiliations, program features, and location codes (Bradley, Curry, & Devers, 2007). As this researcher developed the codes she reflected upon, for example, the objects behind public activities, what outcomes she was able to achieve in facilitating the public understanding of PLEI on cybersecurity and counterterrorism. As this researcher coded data, she organized the materials and noted important elements that formed common themes or dissimilarities.

The codes led to themes, which in turn gave rise to statements, phrases, or groupings, and these were the subject of analysis (Ryan & Bernard, 2003). Central themes arose from the interpretive analysis (Patton, 2002). These reflected particular public issues. When text is analyzed, certain themes and part themes can emerge. This helps to create hierarchies of themes and half-themes (Ryan & Bernard, 2003). Examples of themes include public awareness of technological risks, hazard reduction, and the advancement of human rights, such as dignity and privacy, social and political liberties, safety and well-being. Bates (2000) recognized that technology impacts upon teaching, awareness, and learning management. Themes were compared against the entire set of data sources to locate interrelationships or otherwise between phenomena.

Results

Based on the literature and its observations the Foundation reflected, acted, and planned for sustainable change as described by Social Impact Assessment Unit (1996) and Wadsworth (1984). The public has experienced either directly or indirectly cybersecurity breaches or cyberterrorism. Public concerns included food terrorism, which has been identified by many (e.g., Kinsey, Stinson, Degeneffe, Ghosh, & Busta, 2006, 2009).

The economic and social benefits of inclusive Farmers' Markets have been recognized (BC Association of Farmers' Markets, 2014; Bloomberg Opinion Editorial Board, 2018; University of Guelph, 2014). New arrivals to Australia, Canada, and the United States could fall victim to cybersecurity breaches. They may enter the job market and industry through Farmers' Markets (Bloomberg

Opinion Editorial Board, 2018; University of Guelph, 2014). New arrivals benefited from PLEI on cybersecurity and counterterrorism. They were given tools to assist them to address the multiple impacts of cybersecurity breaches, including fear, financial, and other commercial exploitation.

The Foundation found that there is worth in having accessible services where the public congregates and of meeting them on their own terms to develop shared goals through empathetic engagements. There is merit in having diverse entry points to PLEI services in a range of locations including through the Internet and in-person. The public could continue to have access to PLEI about, for example, protecting their use of social media, computers, the Internet, and networks. The public benefits from having opportunities to receive timely assistance through the Internet, telephone, or face-to-face. Advantages of phone- and Internet-based help are that individuals and groups can access legal and health services possibly without self-identifying to other people that they need for such support. This can help to limit stigma that could be attached to seeking out and accessing formal assistance (Goffman, 1963).

There is a clear role to develop initiatives that incorporate various public views. This consists of a range of professionals, legal and allied educators, policy developers, psychologists, researchers, and others. PLEI would ideally continue to be available through publications and an organizational website. This information may include writings and images on cybersecurity, counterterrorism, social media, computers, the Internet, and networks. For example, the digital divide can result in individuals with low incomes relying on unsecured computer networks that are subject to exploitation, financial crimes, etc. In spite of the fears generated by such stories, some individuals are unaware or confused about whether they are vulnerable to cyberterrorism attacks and how to protect themselves using cybersecurity. Additional information would incorporate updates on policy and international developments regarding computers, the Internet, networks, and social media. The Foundation and others could offer pragmatic policy guidance to develop the safe and successful implementation of these technologies, including infrastructure build-out considerations.

The public saw the benefit of PLEI materials that were comprehensive and written in plain English (Social Impact Assessment Unit, 1996). Information currency that is disseminated as open source could help the public to make informed decisions about how security measures should be monitored, and violence lessened (Selman et al., 1989; Social Impact Assessment Unit, 1996).

PLEI in and of itself is likely to be insufficient to address safety issues. There is a role for other support services such as bargaining, counseling, mediation, technological, and psychological to augment PLEI innovations. Means to develop collaboration between the public and private sectors include education, training, coordination, communication, and networking (Russ-Eft & Preskill, 2009; Selman et al., 1989; Spencer, 1998). The private sector including professional, scholarly, trade, and community of interest organizations could potentially provide knowledge and other resources in such areas as needs assessments (Social Impact Assessment Unit, 1996).

The Internet, markets, libraries, and cafés can be ideal public spaces for PLEI purposes. The public is likely to benefit from having tools to assist it to respond to natural and human disasters. The public called for a diverse set of service options covered by the public or private insurance sectors (Spencer, 1998). The Foundation continues to develop comprehensive and varied services, and regularly offers the public PLEI. This is ideally before the public's challenges reach damaging proportions. Timing was also important, and the public saw the benefits of convenient scheduling to meet its work, leisure, home, or life obligations and a need for short wait. The public envisioned that short-term and ongoing PLEI could be delivered through print, audio, telephone, the Internet, or face-to-face (Selman et al., 1989). In sum, the Foundation offers, for example, some legal and qualitative support services to assist the public to meet life demands and stresses. It was viewed that PLEI should not be solely a means to address surface problems, but also focus on the core causes of public educational, legal, and psychological stresses, not just the symptoms.

There is a role for learning from various locations what they have applied to advance PLEI and to increase the public safety. As an example, in 2016, the Foundation visited San Diego and learned about preventative education to enhance the public safety when natural disasters, such as earthquakes, occur. In San Diego, the government informed the public about such matters as where they should be situated and how to equip and build their homes to lessen the dangers that are often associated with earthquakes. The Foundation applied a similar educational model to increase PLEI on cybersecurity and counterterrorism. For example, the Foundation advised the public of such rudimentary matters as not allowing its Web browsers to remember financial details and having software in place to limit third party's illicit interception.

Issues and Challenges

The Local Government and Shires Associations of New South Wales (2000) suggested that a needs assessment begins with participation and influences community building. Politics, culture, and interaction among people in social situations often have impacts on initiatives (Social Impact Assessment Unit, 1996; Spencer, 1998). The Foundation is accustomed to and values interdisciplinary teamwork with a range of stakeholders from the public including technological developers, international, federal, and government officials.

The Foundation faces the challenges of providing timely assistance face-to-face, through the telephone, or over the Internet to the public. It delivers "one-stop shopping" with such services as counselling, mediation, and support to begin to address a diversity of factors that range from mental health to social issues. It also offers supportive services such as conflict management; employee and family assistance; gambling reduction or prevention; qualitative research; therapies: individual, couple, and family; Public Legal Education and Information; and tutoring.

Influences

Organizations are often required to notify stakeholders when data breaches have occurred (Bandler, 2017). These organizations may be concerned that if they admit to being the victims of computer crimes, then they could lose shareholder and public confidence, and credibility. The concerns include anxieties about how stolen or lost personal or financial information might be misused. Computer and related crimes seem to signal psychosocial adaptions to changing and extreme environments in which violence occurs. There has been an advent of computers and other technologies in human conflict. There is value in developing a preventative model, and raising public awareness of computers, the Internet, networks, and social media.

Public well-being may be developed through meaningful legal information, referral, research, reform, and support services (Social Impact Assessment Unit, 1996). Given the issues arising from gathering data from organizations, these needs assessments focused on the public and gathered data in public spaces. These public spaces were located in Australia, Canada, and the United States. Influences were somewhat different in the three locations.

Western Australia is not immune from security breaches. In 2016, the auditor-general suggested that Western Australia had poor cybersecurity. In 2018, the Australasian Oil & Gas Exhibition & Conference (2018) stated, "Australia's multi-billion-dollar export earning oil and gas industry is under increased threat from terrorists and pirates according to a leading maritime security specialist." Cybersecurity threats also have implications for Queensland, and this has a gas production value of over 1 billion dollars. There is a maritime security threat. Oregon's, Washington's, and Vancouver Island's coast have been described as the graveyard of the Pacific (Patail, 2014; Wilma, 2006). There are natural hazards for vessels, and these are heightened with cybersecurity threats.

A key aspect of Canadian society is the importance of human rights and public education. In Canada, laws and programs that are inconsistent with the *Canadian Charter of Rights and Freedoms* can be struck down. In 2015, the Supreme Court of Canada struck down the *Cyber-safety Act* (2013), as it was thought to have been inconsistent with the *Canadian Charter of Rights and Freedoms* and generally a failure. But, perhaps its pioneering drafters recognized that activities such as cyberbullying have harmful consequences (Boon, 2015). There are also negative outcomes when human rights are suspended or disregarded.

In July 2018, this researcher traveled from Central to Southern and Coastal Oregon. She had opportunities to speak with and to develop a rudimentary understanding of the impact of the digital divide and to work with front line services for state and federal government employees. The government workers were small in number and the discussions about programs were isolated. However, this dialogue is reflective of this researcher's experiences with employees in Canada.

There are shortcomings with the delimiting of human administration and advent of technology. For example, staffing for first responder systems, such as fire lookouts, shipping, and lighthouses, has been slashed. Modern technology contributed to the scaling down of lighthouses, with the modern division of labor (Oregon State Parks, 2018). Communications and navigational networks such as Global Positioning Systems are subject to tampering, and they can fail (Madden, 2018; Saul, 2013). This writer understands that when bushfires are noted, state employees may need to rely on cell phones, and they could be out of range and experience the digital divide (McFadden, 2017; Vick, 2017). This may contribute to injuries and loss of lives. This underresourcing is reflective of her experiences with employees in Canada. The have-nots in search of connectivity could use unsecured and unsafe Wi-Fi, and other technology, and be susceptible to data breaches. The haves may be compelled to pay wrongdoers a ransom to have their data restored. Furthermore, wrongdoers could commit other unlawful online activities including credit card or similar fraud (Bandler, 2017). Legal developments to limit such unlawful activities as cyberattacks often lag behind technological innovations.

DISCUSSION QUESTIONS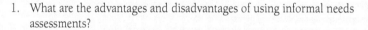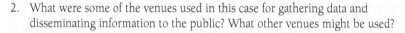

1. What are the advantages and disadvantages of using informal needs assessments?

2. What were some of the venues used in this case for gathering data and disseminating information to the public? What other venues might be used?

3. This work used unobtrusive measures. How might unobtrusive measures be used in other needs assessment efforts?

4. The three countries in which data were collected were English-speaking countries, Australia, Canada, and the United States. How might the cultures of these countries have affected the results?

5. In what ways, if any, might data collection undertaken in other countries need to be modified?

REFERENCES

Anderson, J. (2017). The psychology of why 94 deaths from terrorism are scarier than 301,797 deaths from guns. *QUARTZ*. Retrieved from https://qz.com/898207/the-psychology-of-why-americans-are-more-scared-of-terrorism-than-guns-though-guns-are-3210-times-likelier-to-kill-them/.

Australasian Oil & Gas Exhibition & Conference. (2018). Australian LNG and oil shipments under terrorist threat. Retrieved from https://aogexpo.com.au/lng/australian-lng-oil-shipments-terrorist-threat/.

Baase, S. (2003). *A gift of fire: Social, legal and ethical issues for computers and the Internet* (2nd ed.). New Jersey, NJ: Pearson.

Bandler, J. (2017). *Cybersecurity for the home and office: The lawyer's guide to taking charge of your own information security.* Washington, DC: American Bar Association.

Bates, A. W. (2000). *Managing technological change.* San Francisco, CA: Jossey-Bass.

BC Association of Farmers' Markets. (2014). *Economic and social benefits study.* Retrieved from http://www.bcfarmersmarket.org/resources/subpage/economic-and-social-benefits-study.

Bloomberg Opinion Editorial Board. (2018, June 1). *U.S. farms can't compete without foreign workers.* Retrieved from https://www.bloomberg.com/opinion/articles/2018-06-01/u-s-farms-need-more-immigrant-workers.

Bogdan, R. C., & Biklen, S. K. (1998). *Qualitative research in education: An introduction to theory and methods.* Boston, MA: Allyn and Bacon.

Boon, J. (2015). *The "colossal failure" of Nova Scotia's Cyber-Safety Act.* Retrieved from https://www.thecoast.ca/halifax/the-colossal-failure-of-nova-scotias-cyber-safety-act/Content? oid=5099688.

Bradley, E. H., Curry, L. A., & Devers, K. J. (2007). Qualitative data analysis for health services research: Developing taxonomy, themes and theory. *Health Services Research, 42*(4), 1758–1772. Retrieved from http://www.ncbi.nlm.nih.gov/pmc/articles/PMC1955280/.

Brunst, P. W. (2010). Terrorism and the Internet: New threats posed by cyberterrorism and terrorist use of the Internet. In M. Wade & A. Maljevic (Eds.), *A war on terror?* (pp. 51–78). New York, NY: Springer. Retrieved from https://www.google.com.au/url? sa=t&rct=j&q=&esrc=s&source=web&cd=1&ved=0ahUKEwiH2NiPp5jYAhVLmpQKHb6qBn4QFggpMAA&url=http%3A%2F%2Fwww.springer.com%2Fcda%2Fcontent%2Fdocument%2Fcda_downloaddocument%2F9780387892900-c1.pdf%3FSGWID%3D0-0-45-855750-p173866338&usg=AOvVaw1y9a5Z1TWD68BL4Abgi7RU.

Canadian Charter of Rights and Freedoms, Part I of the Constitution Act (1982), being Schedule B to the Canada Act 1982 (UK), 1982, c 11.

Castro, A. S. (1991). System evaluation: Some reflections on current tertiary practices in Australia and Hong Kong. In R. Schuemer (Ed.), *Evaluation concepts and practice in selected distance education institutions* (pp. 69–80). Hagen, Germany: FernUniversität.

Claypoole, T., & Payton, T. (2017). *Protecting your internet identity. Are you naked online?* Lanham, MD: Rowman and Littlefield.

Cyber-safety Act (2013). c. 2.

Department of Homeland Security. (n.d.). *Cybersecurity overview.* Retrieved from https://www.dhs.gov/cybersecurity-overview.

Editor. (2017). Definition of cyber security. *Economic Times.* Retrieved from https://economictimes.indiatimes.com/definition/Cyber-security.

Goffman, E. (1963). *Stigma: Notes on the management of spoiled identity.* Englewood Cliffs, NJ: Prentice-Hall.

Goldstein, I. L. (1986). *Training in organizations: Needs assessment, development, and evaluation* (2nd ed.). Monterey, CA: Brooks/Cole.

Institute for Economics and Peace. (2017). *Global Terrorism Index: Measuring and understanding the impact of terrorism.* Retrieved from https://lnt.ma/wp-content/uploads/2017/11/global-terrorism-index-2017.pdf.

Kinsey, J. D., Stinson, T. F., Degeneffe, D. J., Ghosh, K., & Busta, F. F. (2006, September). Consumer response to a new food safety issue: Food terrorism. Paper presented at IUFOST XIII Congress of Food Science and Technology: Food Is Life. Nates, France. Retrieved from http://www.foodlawment.hu/downloads/consumers_response_to_new_food_safety_issue_food_terroris.pdf.

Kinsey, J. D., Stinson, T. F., Degeneffe, D. J., Ghosh, K., & Busta, F. F. (2009). Consumer response to a new food safety issue: Food terrorism. In *Global issues in food science and technology* (pp. 145–161). San Diego, CA: Elsevier Science. https://doi.org/10.1016/B978-0-12-374124-0.00010-7.

Kirmayer, L. J., Lemelson, R., & Barad, M. (2007). Preface. In L. J. Kirmayer, R. Lemelson, and M. Barad (Eds.), *Understanding trauma. Integrating biological, clinical and cultural perspectives.* New York, NY: Cambridge University Press, xxiii–xxvii.

Local Government Association and Shires Associations of New South Wales. (2000). *Ground rules: Social planning for local government.* New South Wales, Australia: Local Government Association and Shires Associations of New South Wales.

Madden, R. (2018). *ECDIS: What happens when the GPS signal goes away?* Retrieved from https://www.maritime-executive.com/blog/ecdis-what-happens-when-the-gps-signal-goes-away#gs.Hhp=0M8.

McFadden, R. (2017, August). Digital divide deepens for low income, disabled, indigenous, and ageing Australians. *Probono.* Retrieved from https://probonoaustralia.com.au/news/2017/08/digital-divide-deepens-low-income-disabled-indigenous-ageing-australians/.

Nacos, B. L. (2002). *Mass-mediated terrorism: The central role of the media in terrorism and counterterrorism.* Lanham, MD: Rowman and Littlefield.

Naumes, W., & Naumes, M. J. (1999). *The art and craft of case writing.* Thousand Oaks, CA: Sage.

Neuman, W. L. (1997). *Social research methods: Qualitative and quantitative approaches*. Boston, MA: Allyn and Bacon.

Oregon State Parks. (2018). *Oregon Coast lighthouses*. Salem, OR: Oregon State Parks. Retrieved from https://oregonstateparks.org/index.cfm? do=main .loadFile&load=_siteFiles/publications/2018_Lighthouses_Brochure.pdf.

Patail, M. (2014). *The shipwrecks of the Northwest*. Retrieved from https://www .pdxmonthly.com/articles/2014/3/6/the-shipwrecks-of-the-northwest- march-2014.

Patton, M. Q. (2002). *Qualitative research and evaluation methods*. Thousand Oaks, CA: Sage.

Russ-Eft, D. F., Sleezer, C. M., Sampson, G., & Leviton, L. (2017). *Managing applied social research: Tools, strategies, and insights*. San Francisco, CA: Jossey-Bass.

Russ-Eft, D., & Preskill, H. (2009). *Evaluation in organizations: A systematic approach to learning, performance, and change* (2nd ed.). New York, NY: Basic Books.

Ryan, G. W., & Bernard, H. R. (2003). Techniques to identify themes. *Field Methods, 15*(1), 85–109. Retrieved from http://nersp.nerdc.ufl.edu/~ufruss/documents/ ryan%20and%20bernard%20themes.%20FM%2015(1).pdf.

Saul, J. (2013). *Governments confront rising threats to ships from signal jamming*. Retrieved from https://www.reuters.com/article/shipping-navigation-gps- idUSL5N0E926V20130530.

Schuemer, R. (Ed.). (1991). Introduction and preface. *Evaluation concepts and practice in selected distance education institutions* (pp.1–37). Hagen, Germany: FernUniversität.

Selman, G., Selman, M., Cooke, M., & Dampier, P. (1989). *The foundations of adult education in Canada* (2nd ed.). Toronto, Canada: Thomson Educational.

Sleezer, C. M., Russ-Eft, D. F., & Gupta, K. (2014). *A practical guide to needs assessment* (3rd ed.). San Francisco, CA: Wiley & ASTD.

Social Impact Assessment Unit. (1996). *Social issues in development assessment: A resource book for social planners in Queensland*. Brisbane, Australia: Department of Families, Youth and Community Care.

Spencer, B. (1998). *The purposes of adult education: A guide for students*. Toronto, Canada: Thomson Educational.

Tehrani, P. M. (2017). *Cyberterrorism: The legal and enforcement issues*. London, England: World Scientific.

University of Guelph. (2014, December 1). *Program helps immigrants sell taste of homeland*. Retrieved from https://news.uoguelph.ca/2014/12/program-helps- immigrants-sell-taste-of-homeland/.

Vick, K. (2017). The digital divide: A quarter of the nation is without broadband. *Time*. Retrieved from http://time.com/4718032/the-digital-divide/.

Wadsworth, Y. (1984). *Do it yourself social research*. Melbourne, Australia: Victorian Council of Social Service and Melbourne Family Care Organisation.

Wadsworth, Y. (1991). *Everyday evaluation on the run*. Melbourne, Australia: Action Research Issues Association.

Wilma, D. (2006). *Graveyard of the Pacific: Shipwrecks on the Washington Coast*. Retrieved from https://www.historylink.org/File/7936.

Wolcott, H. F. (1988). Ethnographic research in education. In M. Jaegar (Ed.), *Complementary methods for research in education* (pp. 188–206). Washington, DC: American Educational Research Association.

Paws-A-Tive Pals

Assessing the Needs of a Therapy Dog Organization

Sequoia Star

Abstract

A small but growing dog therapy organization, Paws-A-Tive Pals, incorporated to provide therapeutic canine visits to confined residents of assisted-living facilities. Since the organization's inception, job descriptions and training for the governing body had not taken place. Additionally, training for evaluators of new-member dog teams was an expressed need. Through this needs assessment, the organization was provided critical insight into ways to enhance governance and maintain creditability within their volunteer service community. Below is an overview of the case.

Where the Needs Assessment Was Conducted	Who Conducted the Needs Assessment	Focus of Needs Assessment	How Data Were Collected	How Data Were Analyzed
Grassroots organization in rural community on west coast of United States	External consultant	Focused on developing clear definitions of work roles of governing body; transitioning newly elected officers and board; developing training for evaluators of new-member dog teams	Survey of officers and board members; personal interviews of selected officers and board members; literature review; review of extant documents (organizational guide, past newsletters, team evaluation forms, the membership list, the picture albums/scrapbooks, and the promotional flyer)	Quantitative data analyzed using descriptive statistics; qualitative data analyzed for thematic content; used constant-comparative method and content analysis to compare data to literature

Background

Paws-A-Tive Pals Incorporated (PP) was a quickly growing grassroots organization that experienced rapid evolution in the constitution of its governing body. The need for guidance regarding the formalization of leadership roles and training for incoming officers and board members became clear to the organization's founders quite early on. These needs were recognized when founding members, having served their terms, left their positions. Concerns became evident when it was realized that new leadership had neither the benefit of organizational history nor the management knowledge of the founding members. Prior to this needs assessment, no job descriptions or formalized training were in place for the organization.

There were also concerns about the evaluation of new-member teams (dog–human teams). No formal training or documented guidelines existed to identify or clarify the conducting of new-member dog-team evaluations. These needs were recognized as vital in ensuring that dogs were evaluated accurately for social suitability in fulfillment of the role of participating dog-therapy team members. It was with these goals in mind that the organization's founding members commissioned the needs assessment.

Profile of the Organization

PP is recognized as a federally authorized 501 (c) 3 nonprofit membership corporation. The mission of the organization is to enhance the psychological and physical well-being of residents of assisted-living facilities and hospitals through the provision of therapeutic visits with certified therapy dogs. In addition to therapeutic visits, the organization provides read-to-dog programs for local schools, dog safety courses for children, and American Kennel Club (AKC) canine good citizen testing. PP is located in a rural community on the west coast of the United States. The current membership of the organization is approximately 50 visiting dog-team members and nonvisiting supporting members. The organization is entirely volunteer, with no remunerated positions.

As a result of significant growth, PP provides hundreds of service visits per year. Due to the volunteer structure, the corporation's annual budget is small. The organization is supported through small grants and several ongoing and annual fundraising endeavors. To increase awareness of the therapeutic effects of the canine–human bond, PP members participate in numerous community events.

PP conducts monthly membership and board meetings. The governance of the corporation is carried out by three officers and a board of three directors. The requirements for membership include: (a) the belief in, and agreement with, the goals of the organization; (b) participation in the activities of the organization; and (c) payment of nominal annual dues.

Preassessment Information

Historically, it has been difficult to recruit members to run for the organization's officer and board positions. Reportedly, members had expressed a lack of understanding as to the expectations of the governing roles. One of the stated desires of conducting the needs assessment was that future members might be more inclined to volunteer for leadership roles. It was expressly believed that if clear, specific job descriptions were in place and potential candidates had some certainty that there would be ongoing training, volunteerism for leadership roles would increase.

Seamless Training Protocols for Organizational Transitions

The assessment was necessitated by rapid growth that made clear that a lack of historical institutional knowledge existed within leadership. As only oral expectations for the officers and board existed, there was confusion by new board members as to their job descriptions and duties. Tensions grew around the internal fears of not having adequate information to conduct business according to state and federal regulations. The assessment sought to support incoming leadership, enhance the governance of PP through ascertaining the degree of existing "gaps between current and desired job performance" (Tobey, 2005), and identify training and nontraining solutions. It should be noted, however, that not all members were on board with the work necessary to concretize the roles of leadership and implement ongoing training.

Dog-Member Teams: Testing Qualifications

Through ongoing discussions, leadership surmised that training the dog-team evaluators would help ensure that only truly qualified dogs would be approved. They further theorized that more skilled owners and dogs would enhance the organization's viability within the service-provision community. And most importantly, having trained and skilled owners and dogs would help to ensure care-facility resident safety and concurrently reduce the organization's liability.

Needs Assessment Process

The assessment was conducted over the course of 3 months by an external consultant with participation from the primary level (Altschuld & Witkin, 2000) of organization leadership. These primary level individuals were the recipients of the outcomes of the assessment and to whom the assessment was directed.

The primary purpose of the assessment was twofold: (a) to make certain that the work roles of the governing body were clearly defined and realized, and (b) to transition newly elected officers and board as seamlessly as possible. The secondary purpose, the evaluator training assessment, was to make certain that each dog evaluated by PP was capable of performing to the field's best practices and the standards of the organization. Additionally, this portion of the needs assessment explored potential gaps between optimals and actuals (Rossett, 1987) with regard to the performance of team evaluators.

The gathering of data was accomplished through survey, personal interviews, literature, and extant documents. Open-ended questions were included in the interviews, while close-ended yes/no questions were the format for the survey. The interview questions sought to learn (a) what the officer's and board's prior experience was in organizational governance; (b) how they saw their roles evolving; (c) what they viewed as training needs; and (d) what, as training team evaluators, they felt would be especially helpful in that role. Extant documents provided organizational background, while literature offered comparison for gathered data.

Assessment Approach and Methods

Since the primary goal of the assessment was to help identify whether there was a necessity to formalize knowledge and skill needs of the governing body, the approach for the project was a knowledge and skills assessment (Sleezer, Russ-Eft, & Gupta, 2014). This approach was deemed applicable because of recognized and self-identified knowledge gaps of incoming officers, the demands of their roles, and the rapid growth of the organization.

Data Collection

As noted, data collection was triangulated. The decision to use multiple methods for data sources was made based on the desire to facilitate the validation of data from multiple approaches (Russ-Eft & Preskill, 2009). The included methods are discussed below.

Survey. Surveys were an important data source for determining actual training needs with regard to the officer's and board's roles. This method was also used to identify training needs of evaluation teams. Each survey consisted of closed-ended yes/no questions and served as knowledge tests (Russ-Eft & Preskill, 2009). Instrument validity was determined through review of theoretical literature and consultation with peer experts in the field of organizational training who approved the survey's content.

The surveys were administered to officers and board members at the same time the interviews were conducted. Survey questions were kept to questions requiring a yes/no response. The use of quantitative data sources is encouraged by Tobey (2005) when the desire is to extract hard data measures that are consistent and reliable.

Interview. Seven semi-structured interviews (Russ-Eft & Preskill, 2009) of officers and board members were conducted. The data gathered from these interviews provided clarifications of job descriptions and inquiry into perceived training needs. This method of data collection was chosen for the following reasons: flexibility for interviews to evolve as necessary, the ability to enlist support for the assessment, and the appropriateness of the tool for subject matter analysis (Rossett, 1987). The interviews included both quantitative and qualitative questions.

Ample time, at least 1 hour, was afforded each interviewee to discuss ideas and concerns regarding the clarification of tasks and roles. The board members were also queried to help clarify job description and duties for teams that conducted the dog-team evaluation. The supporting reference and rationale for using this data source was Goldstein and Ford (2002). In this volume the authors stated that interviews "provide maximum opportunity for the client to represent himself [/herself] spontaneously on his [/her] own terms" (p. 55).

Literature. Nonprofit trade literature (Cumfer & Sohl, 2005; Goldstein & Ford, 2002; Grimm, 2018) was compared to collected data. Relevant sections of these documents and volumes were reviewed, coded, and then compared with the coded data collected during the project. This comparison was done to ensure stated, desired outcomes met with nonprofit standards.

Extant Data. Extant data provided existing information regarding gaps between "optimal performance or knowledge and actual performance or knowledge" (Rossett, 1987, p. 52). Extant data also made it possible "to determine the relationship between [officer and board member] effort and organizational goals" (p. 52).

The extant documents data sources included the PP organizational guide, past newsletters, team evaluation forms, the membership list, the picture albums/scrapbooks, and the promotional flyer. These documents provided a wealth of organizational background information.

Data Analysis

Descriptive statistics were used to express the surveys' quantitative data. In terms of qualitative data, both the constant comparative method of comparing literature to the collected data and content analysis (Russ-Eft & Preskill, 2009) of deriving categories from the collected datasets were employed. Specifically, qualitative data were analyzed for thematic content using coding and categorization.

Findings

Survey results supported the need for conducting the assessment. Respondents noted that they were not formally trained in their job duties when they became either an officer or board member. Six of the seven believed that their position's written description was not detailed enough and did not assist them in knowing the expectations of their positions. Six felt that training for their particular position would be helpful. All seven said they would be willing to participate in such training.

The data collected via interview provided even richer detail of the needs of the officers, board, and new team evaluators. When asked where they had learned about their current PP job duties, respondents identified informal channels as the sole process of learning. One-hundred percent stated that they had no explicit training at the time they took office. While all had cursory knowledge of their job descriptions and duties, only a small percentage could provide a comprehensive overview of the responsibilities of their position. Six noted that they experienced the roles of the board and officers changing/evolving with the growth of the corporation.

During interviews, great confusion was expressed around new team evaluator duties and processes. When queried about the training needs for new team evaluators, all seven respondents (evaluators were comprised of board members and officers) felt they would benefit from specific training.

When asked about nontraining issues regarding new dog-team evaluations, and what clarification they would like in place for conducting evaluations, 100% of respondents had ideas for improvement. The following were two of the more notable ideas for improving dog evaluations: leave dog-evaluation duties to those officers and board members who were certified with the AKC Canine Good Citizen test; and clarify how strict in their evaluations the evaluators must be.

Literature in the form of nonprofit guidance for the state (Cumfer & Sohl, 2005), as well as nonprofit organizational volumes and articles, provided best practice process options for creating codified training materials. The handbook provided gap analysis data based on PP's existing organizational governance and training procedures against those of best practices. These documents were also useful for comparison and contrast during the organizational scan phase. Once specific training needs were identified through the other data sources, these documents became invaluable in describing the implementation to address these needs.

Extant data were found valuable both as a preliminary data source and for the overall assessment. Existing data reinforced both initial concerns: lack of job descriptions and training for officers/board members, and the lack of documented processes and training for new dog team evaluations.

The *PP Flyer* (the organization's newsletter) provided data for the organizational scan phase. Findings from the *Flyer* provided detailed insight into the existing oversight of the organization. These data helped flesh out the organizational culture, which was found to be casual but orderly.

Inspection of the *PP Guide*, which was the organization's one existing document of organizational guidance, revealed one-to-three-sentence job descriptions for the officers and no job description for board members. Review of the organization's by-laws, within the document, showed confusion regarding the roles of the board. This was noted through the use of the terms *board of directors* and *officers* interchangeably in some sections of the document and then differentiated in others.

For dog-team evaluators, the evaluation form was the singular existing guidance resource. The document listed the evaluation tests with short descriptions of each test. Beyond this form, the organization had no existing documents that communicated the nuances of conducting evaluations for dog-team evaluators.

The members' contact information list detailed the expansion of the corporation over the past several years. It was a data source that provided a historical reference point and illuminated how quickly membership had grown.

Most instructive was the lack of existing data for procedures and training. This deficit supported the identified needs for additional procedural resources and training for the officers, board, and evaluation teams.

Lastly, during the organizational scan, it was frequently conveyed that clearly defined procedures regarding transference of information and the conducting of evaluations were lacking. The majority of interviewees believed that the job description for new team evaluators was not comprehensive. Six stated that the processes for conducting evaluations and then transferring information were not clearly defined. Respondents also believed they would benefit from new team evaluator training. Again, all seven said they would be willing to participate in training if it were offered.

Findings expressed a need for ongoing in-service officer/board training for newly elected members. These trainings would also serve as refreshers for existing members. In terms of ongoing training, yearly officer/board training retreats would be useful. If specific training needs were outside the knowledge base of standing officer/board members, subject matter experts could be enlisted to provide specialized training.

Findings of training and nontraining needs for new team evaluators would encourage an extensive examination of current processes and procedures. The PP's governing body could define the goals for new team evaluations, that is, whether these evaluations were to be merely cursory checks, or an exhaustive examination of canine applicants. Clear and comprehensive procedural descriptions could then be developed. Specifically, role-play scenario trainings would offer trainees the opportunity to eye-witness hands-on demonstrations of mock evaluations. Lastly, as much confusion existed about the actual conducting of evaluations and subsequent channeling of information, information management and dissemination processes were areas in need of examination and reform.

Lastly, the creation of written comprehensive job descriptions for board members and new team evaluators was highly encouraged. Being specifically requested by respondents, it would be helpful if descriptions included definitions for each position with itemized task lists.

Results

Based on findings from combined data sources, several conclusions for PP's training and nontraining needs could be identified:

- Comprehensive and concretized job descriptions for the board and officers were nonexistent. Initial and ongoing training in duties for this group was also absent. The governing body of the organization was elected and then left to an unwritten, fragmented knowledge-base for conducting the daily activities of the organization.

- Additionally, the new dog-team evaluators experienced a lack of understanding in the expectations of evaluation duties. Many evaluators had never evaluated a dog and its handler. This lack of training ultimately posed a safety risk for the organization's clients (e.g., children and facility clientele) and financial liability for the organization.

As leadership development is vital to the success of organizations (Grimm, 2018), identifying and formalizing the competencies necessary for managing the corporation has been a defining moment for this organization. While there are certain universal training needs in core competencies of nonprofit management (e.g., financial management, fundraising, organizational planning), to be comprehensive, it is vital to assess the individualized needs of discrete agencies, no matter their size. And although there is immense "power in learning through storytelling, case study, discussion questions, and organic conversation" (Grimm, 2018, n.p.), this assessment confirmed that undertaking exploration of formal learning needs can be vital to small organization success.

Since the organization's leadership had no previous experience with a needs assessment process, short orientation presentations and ongoing debriefings were conducted during board meetings. Being readily available in these ways increased transparency while ameliorating any hesitancy or concerns. These sessions explained the assessment structure, process, and the support desired of participants. At each subsequent meeting, the assessor was available to answer questions regarding the process. The assessor remained accessible to stakeholders by both phone and email.

In terms of supporting the grassroot political and knowledge structure, final deliverables were both more and less formal. While a final written report was made, a final presentation to the membership, including a PowerPoint slideshow, made understanding outcomes more accessible.

Influences

Organizational leadership showed a strong investment in the community's recognition of their efforts. They desired to be viewed as a legitimate provider of a valuable service. Therefore, the process of assessment and the ensuing recommendations for the governing body were predominantly viewed as positive toward the accomplishment of this goal.

Influences to alter the structural functioning of an organization can impart political impacts (Russ-Eft & Preskill, 2009), and this assessment proved this point. However, by virtue of the nonprofit being a small grassroot program, any challenging impacts of political ramification were primarily localized to within the organization.

The organization's close-knit nature was a political influence impacting the decisions of the methods employed by the assessor. Based on a casual organizational structure, direct one-to-one personalized communication was most fitting (Goldstein & Ford, 2002). Therefore, interviews were conducted as a primary data source.

Issues and Challenges

It was not understood by the entirety of leadership that a needs assessment would be necessary or valuable. The stakeholders who initially bought in were hopeful that the outcome would justify the undertaking. They wished to legitimize their concerns of lack of formalized organizational structure and training. There was very little explicit resistance to the assessment process. The resistance that did exist was mainly the result of the perceived additional work necessary to accomplish the assessment. Those who initially questioned the process ultimately expressed gratitude for its outcome.

Full buy-in by organization stakeholders was a limited challenge. While some of the governing body recognized that rapid growth and other factors warranted an assessment, others did not. A lack of knowledge of the needs assessment process also inhibited buy-in. Another issue was officer and board availability for interviews.

Lastly, remaining flexible to scheduling needs of the participants was important. This was valuable, as there were a number of last-minute interview cancellations and rescheduling.

DISCUSSION QUESTIONS

1. The data collection included interviews, surveys, and a review of extant data. What are the advantages and disadvantages of undertaking all these data collection efforts?

2. The assessor had certain issues, challenges, and limitations while conducting the assessment. What other options might be implemented for resolution of the stated concerns?

3. This assessment was conducted within a small organization, making it easier to engage processes for key stakeholders' needs to be respected and considered. This supportive approach had a huge impact on participant buy-in to the assessment process. What varying assessment actions might need to be implemented to affect the same outcome for a larger organization?

REFERENCES

Altschuld, J. W., & Witkin, B. R. (2000). *From needs assessment to action: Transforming needs into solution strategies.* Thousand Oaks, CA: Sage.

Cumfer, C., & Sohl, K. (2005). *Oregon nonprofit handbook.* Portland, OR: Technical Assistance for Community Services.

Goldstein, I. L., & Ford, J. K. (2002). *Training in organizations.* Belmont, CA: Wadsworth.

Grimm, G. (2018). Nonprofit leadership development: The importance of leadership in nonprofit organizations. Retrieved from https://thirdsectorcompany.com/importance-leadership-nonprofit-organizations/.

Rossett, A. (1987). *Training needs assessment.* Englewood Cliffs, NJ: Educational Technology.

Russ-Eft, D., & Preskill, H. (2009). *Evaluation in organizations: A systematic approach to enhancing learning, performance, and change* (2nd ed.). New York, NY: Basic Books.

Sleezer, C. M., Russ-Eft, D., & Gupta, K. (2014). *A practical guide to needs assessment* (3rd ed.). San Francisco, CA: Wiley & ASTD.

Tobey, D. (2005). *Needs assessment basics.* Alexandria, VA: American Society for Training and Development.

CHAPTER

7

Small Business Enrichment Training Needs Assessment

Sequoia Star

Abstract

Entrepreneurial training for small business organizations can be crucial to the continued economic development of a region by enhancing the competence of small business principals (Lans, Hulsink, Baert, & Mulder, 2008). This assessment explored the current training programs of a rural region's small business community (200 small organizations), identified current training gaps, and examined implications of future training needs. Below is an overview of the case.

Where the Needs Assessment Was Conducted	Who Conducted the Needs Assessment	Focus of Needs Assessment	How Data Were Collected	How Data Were Analyzed
Small business organizations (about 200 organizations) in a rural community on the west coast of United States	Small Business Enrichment Program (SBEP) engaged an external evaluator	Focused on determining entrepreneurs' needs and desires for training	Explored available training programs; examined historical data; two surveys of small business organization clients and SBEP statewide directors and staff; interviews of 15 small business owners	Descriptive statistics reported for quantitative data; content analysis of qualitative data identifying themes

Background

The Small Business Enrichment Program (SBEP) is a statewide nonprofit organization providing entrepreneurs with necessary supports to convert innovative ideas, products, and services into successful businesses. The list of assistance provided by the SBEP includes general business advising, financial planning support, marketing assistance, bookkeeping assistance, employee management, accessing capital, and mentoring/training. Services are provided by qualified mentors and instructors for an annual average of 200 clients.

The sponsor of the training needs assessment was the SBEP, which is housed within a community college in a rural region of a western state. Historically, SBEP training offerings were provided based on perceived, rather than formally researched needs. A need for more strategic approaches to planning and providing business training was recognized by the director. Previous research has shown that successful entrepreneurial training is action oriented, supportive of experiential learning, problem solving, project based, creative, and involving peer evaluation (Jones & English, 2004). Focusing on the above attributes, the principal purpose of this assessment was to establish, through analysis of extant and newly garnered data, the training needs of the region's small business organizations (SBOs). Second, nontraining business needs were also identified.

Staffing

An external consultant evaluator was engaged to conduct the assessment. The evaluator holds a master's degree in the field of adult education and subscribes to principles of The Standards for Educational Evaluation, and The American Evaluation Association (2013). The consultant worked closely with the program director and other primary stakeholders to engage and query a representative sample of those impacted by the assessment's solutions.

Significance, Impact, and Value

This assessment was significant in that it analyzed business training needs for a population of approximately 200 SBOs. Given that 50% of small business start-ups fail in the first 5 years and 66% by 10 years (United States Small Business Administration, 2015), training and support are crucial for enhancing the success rate of SBOs (Katz, 2007). Therefore, the assessment's primary intent was to provide rich data for the provision of SBO training interventions.

Return on Investment

According to data published by the U.S. Small Business Administration Office of Advocacy (2014), SBO births have the largest impact on gross state product, state personal income, and total state employment of any other factor. They concluded that state efforts to promote small business formation and success are more fruitful for generating economic growth than virtually any other policy option.

This has been especially true for the SBEP's region, given its economic base is overly concentrated in small business. The locale is more dependent on very small business than either the state in general or the country as a whole (U.S. Census Bureau, 2015). Ninety percent of the SBOs have 20 or fewer employees (Northwest State Employment Department, 2016). Correspondingly, examination of SBEP's entrepreneurial training programs is paramount to facilitating the birth and retention of regional SBOs (Katz, 2007). During this region's lagging economic recovery, it would not be overstated to say that economic recovery and stability were dependent upon quality SBO training opportunities.

Profile of the Organization

Programs such as the SBEP are part of a statewide network of business centers. These programs are generally housed within community colleges. The SBEP's goals included providing education and services for business success. The program offered the following information about their service provision:

> SBEP offers training for businesses, from getting started to planning an exit strategy. Training is provided that will enable you to improve skills and learn new technologies. Our resources include business planning software, market research, financial analysis, and referrals. (SBEP program website)

Regional Context

The state and the region are identified as rural and frontier (U.S. demographic data, 2016), respectively. Historically, the largest employers have been the natural resource and mining industries. While these industries have remained key employers, as resources have dwindled, additional industries have developed.

Stakeholders

The audience and stakeholders for the assessment were varied. They included the SBEP director, the community college dean of instruction, the SBEP state director and upper management personnel, SBEP client SBOs and training attendees throughout the region, directors and other staff of the statewide network, SBEP instructors, and community business leaders.

Primary Stakeholders

Primary stakeholders were the administrators who manage the SBEP and the statewide network. Primary stakeholders were further defined as any person who had the authority to approve modifications to, and/or allocate funding for, current and future SBEP training practices.

Secondary Stakeholders

Current SBEP training participants and clients were classified as secondary stakeholders. Also considered secondary were statewide program directors and staff. Additional other secondary stakeholders were those regional business instructors and college personnel who may have had common SBO clients.

Tertiary Stakeholders

Future potential training participants/consumers would be considered tertiary stakeholders. This demographic would be highly interested in knowing if and how SBEP training can fulfill business-related training gaps and enhance small business success rates. Additionally, training instructors may have strong interest in the assessment data, as they may be useful for fashioning and delivering future training interventions.

Assessment Description and Data Gathering

The assessment's approach was the Knowledge and Skills Assessment (Sleezer, Russ-Eft, & Gupta, 2014). This approach was deemed appropriate due to the fulfilling of "critical success factors" (p. 92) for a knowledge- and skills-based assessment. These factors included (a) buy-in from stakeholders, (b) necessary financial resources, and (c) the availability and ability of personnel to conduct the assessment. The choice for this approach was based on the fact that SBEP's trainings were to be evaluated and updated using the assessment findings.

Ongoing meetings between the consultant and primary stakeholders were held during all phases of the assessment as opportunities to refine process, examine issues, and report project status. For ease of implementation and interim reporting, the assessment was divided into four phases: Phase I, assessment planning; Phase II, data gathering; Phase III, data analysis; and Phase IV, report preparation/delivery. Below are discussions of the structure of each of the assessment's phases.

Phase I: Assessment Planning

Phase I involved several preparatory meetings with primary stakeholders and the development and pilot testing of data-gathering tools. During these initial meetings, the scope and direction of the assessment were defined. Planning matrices were created by the consultant, which included the purpose, processes, outcomes, and projected due dates for each step of the assessment. Obtaining agreement and buy-in for the plan was relatively straightforward and relied on the sharing of empirical data with primary stakeholders. Once empirical data were presented, as a basis for processes, decision makers were readily willing to engage with the assessment.

The decision to keep stakeholders well informed, throughout the life of the assessment, began during the planning phase. As a result, schedules for interim reporting of project progress were also created. Meeting with stakeholders regularly and respectfully addressing their desire for information and concerns went far in the retention of the initial buy-in for the project. Phase I also included the designation of test subjects, identification of data tools and strategies, survey development, and the discovery of extant data sources.

Participant Subjects

The implemented participant sampling method was nonprobability purposive (Vehovar, Toepoel, & Steinmetz, 2016). The rationale for employing this strategy was that response data were being sought from narrowly defined, specified populations (i.e., SBOs within the region and program directors from SBEP programs). Participants were identified through SBEP databases. The client subjects were prior consumers of the SBEP services and/or trainings and SBEP statewide staff.

Survey Instruments

During Phase I of the assessment, two survey instruments were developed. The first was created for dissemination to SBEP clients to determine general attitudes regarding SBO training, descriptions of past training experiences, interest in future trainings, and training methods of choice (i.e., in person, Web-based synchronous, asynchronous, or combination of the three). The questions for this survey were researched and formatted after initial planning meetings with the SBEP regional director.

Once agreement was reached, the survey was put into the pilot-test format. At this juncture, a project introduction email was sent to pilot-test subjects. At the end of the pilot-test survey were another 12 questions specific to the qualities of the survey itself. These questions were asked to identify changes that would enhance survey validity. Based on feedback of testers, reevaluation and restructuring of the survey instrument ensued.

The second survey was created to collect training information from other statewide SBEP personnel including trainers and directors. This survey was also pilot tested and administered during Phase II of the assessment.

Phase II: Data Gathering

To better understand needed training requirements, data sources were triangulated. Mixed method data collection (Creswell, 2015), both quantitative and qualitative, was employed. To gain an understanding of SBEP training needs, data collection tools were strategically developed with input from stakeholders. Below is a discussion of the data-gathering tools and procedures.

Historical Data. The program's historical training data were obtained from program files and electronic databases. Original raw data were acquired from the completed hard-copy training evaluations provided to participants at the end of each SBEP training. Data were analyzed to identify specific trainings and their relative success.

Surveys. The two surveys queried SBO clients and SBEP statewide directors and staff. The SBO survey inquired into perceived training needs. The SBEP director's survey gathered information to establish the types of training opportunities other programs were affording their client businesses. The rationale for the director's survey was to identify potential training opportunities, which might be implemented within the region.

The pilot tested surveys contained multiple choice, yes/no, fill in, open-ended, and Likert scale questions. The consultant provided for survey data management through procurement of a subcontract with an independent research platform. The listed surveys were created within the software and subsequently administered via email to identified participants.

To establish the respondent pools for both surveys, email lists were generated using names from both regional and statewide SBEP databases. These lists included both past training attendees, active and closed case SBEP clients for a period of 24 months, and the directors and staff of all state SBEP programs. To answer technical data management questions, and streamline the use of data, the consultant engaged the resources of an SBEP state-employed data analyst.

The survey's face validity was supported through discussions with directors of SBEP programs to explore potential questions and subsequently evaluate them, using discreet pilot-testing questions. Additionally, examination of current literature on SBO training needs was considered for the purposes of survey validity.

Interviews. Interviews with 15 regional SBO owners were conducted. Participants were chosen based on their availability, and their engagement of the SBEP program over the 24-month period. Although the entrepreneurs were exceedingly busy, they enthusiastically participated. To accommodate participant needs, interviews were conducted by varying means and locales (i.e., via telephone, at the SBEP, or at interviewee's places of business). Protocol notes were taken during the interviews, and the sessions were recorded for transcription.

The procedure for refinement of the interview protocol was based on the process described by Castillo-Montoya (2016) for qualitative research. The protocol included question types regarding what training or other programs participants believed would be most supportive and help ensure their success as SBOs, what they would be willing to pay for training, and the format with which they would like to see training disseminated. To ensure the richest possible data were gathered, a more naturalistic approach (Creswell, 2015) was permitted. This approach included additional questions, which arose organically. The interviews' transcription data were coded for themes and subsequently analyzed and presented within the interview data analysis section of the Phase III interim report.

Phases III and IV: Data Analysis and Final Reporting

Phase III involved the analysis and interpretation of collected data and the reporting of results. Data analysis was undertaken using quantitative and qualitative approaches that adhered to analysis best practices, as characterized by Creswell (2015) and Sleezer, Russ-Eft, and Gupta (2014). Data analysis and interpretation summaries were presented in the form of narrative discussion.

Given the data collection methods and instruments, descriptive statistics (Reviere, 2013) were used to express the survey's quantitative data results. Initial analyses activities included the provision of online spreadsheets, by the contracted survey research platform, listing the quantitative survey items for which data were gathered. Results were broken out by frequency of response, percentage, and central tendency (Sleezer, Russ-Eft, & Gupta, 2014) for the Likert scale. Ultimately, quantitative data were narratively discussed/summarized, and also expressed in frequency distribution charts/tables within the final reporting document.

Qualitative data (survey fill-in questions and interviews) were analyzed based on content analysis (Russ-Eft & Preskill, 2009). Data were first organized by coding for themes within the responses of the current dataset. Response categories emerged organically from the data. Responses were then classified into meaningful, labeled, and relevant groups. Responses with two or more like replies were discussed within reporting.

Deliverables

The assessment's deliverables consisted of interim reports: *Phase I, assessment planning; Phase II, data gathering; Phase III, data analysis; and Phase IV, final assessment report*. In terms of these written deliverables, the Phase I report documented (a) the needs assessment tools and described their pilot tests; (b) the meeting for confirmation of finalized tools; and (c) how data were to be collected, managed, and organized for analysis. The Phase II report documented how data were collected, monitored, and organized for analysis. The Phase III report analyzed data and identified training considerations. The Phase IV report was the finalized assessment document, which was the consolidation of the three previous reports. An executive summary (Creswell, 2015) of the Phase IV report was also prepared.

Additionally, to assist with data interpretation and integration, interim reporting presentations were delivered to the primary stakeholders at the end of each phase. At the culmination of the assessment, a final project presentation was convened for all stakeholder groups.

Needs Assessment Results

The following section will examine the outcomes of the assessment. The section also discusses the consultant's recommendations.

Findings of Survey and Interview Data

The statewide SBEP holds standards for training success as the following: 80% of training attendees classify either a 4 or 5 out of 5 on a Likert scale rating for specific training evaluation response items. Past trainings were rated high and all but one item on the surveys met this goal. It is noteworthy, however, that there was a consistent and general downward trend in positive responses toward the program's past training offerings, the most noteworthy being a 13% decline in the belief that workshops met training expectations.

The majority of survey respondents who had previous SBEP training expressed that it had been of value to their business endeavor. There were, however, a considerable number of SBO clients who valued small business training but had not yet availed themselves of the service. Of those who received small business training, the training they had received was characterized as fragmented.

Survey respondents clearly stated the trainings believed to be most valuable. At the top of their list was marketing training, with accounting, business-plan training, and employee issues following closely.

In terms of training formats, the overwhelming majority of respondents chose synchronous classroom as their most desirable training delivery method. However, this manner of training delivery was listed as inconvenient during daytime business hours.

Nontraining service provision was characterized by identified differences between services rendered and those classified as most desired/helpful. The most identified SBEP service provided to SBOs was general small business advising. Conversely, the services identified as being most helpful included, in ranked order: marketing support, business/financial plan support, and general business advising.

Within the interview data, marketing again emerged as the most strongly represented theme. It ranked highest both in terms of past positive training experiences and desire for additional training support.

Surprisingly, interbusiness networking was also a well-represented theme of the interviews. The opportunity to connect with other small businesses, while receiving training, was deemed invaluable.

Summary

The assessment was designed to capture regional entrepreneurs' needs and desires, which it clearly did. There were strongly voiced indications of SBOs' training and other needs. Ultimately, only a small proportion of respondents had obtained comprehensive small business training. This fact bolstered the case for an existing unmet training need, which informed needed training changes. The gathered information motivated primary stakeholders to institute additional strategic training options and provide requested nontraining support.

Given the fragmented nature of SBOs' previous entrepreneurial training, and that marketing education was considered the most valuable, a comprehensive small business management program with a core concentration on small business marketing strategies was encouraged and ultimately implemented. Additionally, synchronous in-person evening and weekend classes and independent-study computer training became course delivery options employed by the SBEP.

Given that entrepreneurial competition was high, the most intriguing finding was the desire for networking between SBOs. This was accommodated with multiple networking activities being integrated into training curriculum.

Influences

Influences impacting the assessment included the context within which the SBEP existed and under which the assessment was conducted (i.e., the bureaucracy of the state agency and the community college). While these influences did not bear excessively on the conduct of the assessment, they had implications for the implementation of findings. Both the collective SBEP state programs and community college had specific regulations regarding training programs that did not always coincide. When working with multiple organizations, such factors are important considerations.

Challenges and Limitations

While entrepreneurs were enthusiastic about participation in the assessment, securing engagement from these stakeholders was at times difficult. Scheduling was a common challenge with many respondents. This challenge was accommodated through flexibility by both the evaluator and participants.

An addendum to the initial proposal expanded the role of the consultant. Instead of reporting data analysis results only, the consultant was asked to form opinions on programmatic improvements. Primary stakeholders viewed the constraining of the consultant's role to solely reporting results as limiting, so the scope was expanded to include data conclusions. Funding the additional tasks was a concern. Ultimately the consultant agreed to absorb these fees.

The state's economy and implementation of the recommendations presented another issue of the assessment. While most of the United States enjoyed relief from the economic downturn of the past decade, the local region was slower to recover. As a result, many businesses had very limited training budgets. Some could ill afford even a reduced cost for additional training. This factor had to be weighed and creative solutions found when designing new training options. One implemented idea was to reduce the number of trainings offered in a marketing education series, while increasing the amount of information presented during each session. This reduced the costs for deploying trainers.

The major project limitation occurred during the implementation of results. It became difficult for the SBEP to create new training programs that met expressed needs while simultaneously adhering to state and college requirements. Ultimately, there was a reconciliation of these concerns through adjusting certain of the identified training needs to fit within existing state and college curriculums.

To ensure future training meets client needs, additional research is indicated. Considerations for this work might include the reasons why the SBEP's overall training rating has declined over the past 2 years; beyond cost, why those who value entrepreneurial training are not availing themselves of it; and how SBO training offerings might become less fragmented and more comprehensive. Additionally, since it was the first of its kind, this assessment's processes might provide a template for future assessments of training need for statewide SBOs.

When exploring the question of what might have been done to enhance the assessment's procedures, the inclusion of further statistical testing for the questionnaire would have been useful (e.g., Cronbach's alpha, factor analyses). Doing so would have complemented and enhanced the other implemented validity and reliability tests.

Given that the assessment's stakeholders lacked comfort with advanced statistical analyses, simple charts and graphs were used to communicate the assessment's results. For more sophisticated audiences, exploring the question of what more advanced analyses could have been implemented might be useful. As noted by Russ-Eft and Preskill (2009), "Advanced analysis procedures may also produce insights into complex relationships among variables that would not otherwise be apparent" (p. 361).

DISCUSSION QUESTIONS

1. In addition to those listed, what do you see as major challenges and limitations of the needs assessment? How were these addressed?

2. What additional procedures might be used to "validate" the questionnaire?

3. The analyst was asked to expand her role in the assessment. Discuss the benefits and the problems of expanding the role of the analyst from that of reporting results to include offering opinions on the results.

4. What other data sources, either in lieu of or in addition to the existing sources, might have been useful in this assessment? What are the advantages and limitations of using multiple data sources?

5. Beyond written reporting, what data dissemination techniques might have been used to inform stakeholders?

REFERENCES

American Evaluation Association. (2013). *American Evaluation Association guiding principles for evaluators.* Retrieved from http://www.eval.org/p/cm/ld/fid=51.

Castillo-Montoya, M. (2016). Preparing for interview research: The interview protocol refinement framework. *The Qualitative Report, 21*(5), 811–831. Retrieved from http://nsuworks.nova.edu/tqr/vol21/iss5/2.

Creswell, J. (2015). *Educational research: Planning, conducting, and evaluating quantitative and qualitative research.* Upper Saddle River, NJ: Pearson.

Jones, C., & English, J. (2004). A contemporary approach to entrepreneurship education. *Education and Training, 46*(8/9), 416–423. https://doi .org/10.1108/00400910410569533

Katz, J. (2007). Education and training in entrepreneurship. In R. Pritchard (Eds.), *The psychology of entrepreneurship* (pp. 209–235). Mahwah, NJ: Lawrence Erlbaum.

Lans, T., Hulsink, W., Baert, H., & Mulder, M. (2008). Entrepreneurship education and training in a small business context: Insights from the competence-based approach. *Journal of Enterprise Culture, 16*(4), 363–383. http//doi.org/10.1142/ S0218495808000193

Northwest State Employment Department. (2016). *Quality information, informed choices* [Data file].

Reviere, R. (2013). *Needs assessment: A creative and practical guide for social scientists.* New York, NY: Routledge.

Russ-Eft, D., & Preskill, H. (2009). *Evaluation in organizations: A systematic approach to enhancing learning, performance, and change* (2nd ed.). New York, NY: Basic Books.

Sleezer, C. M., Russ-Eft, D. F., & Gupta, K. (2014). *A practical guide to needs assessment* (3rd ed.). San Francisco, CA: Wiley & ASTD.

United States Census Bureau. (2015). *Statistics for all U.S. firms by industry, gender, ethnicity and race for the U.S., states, metro areas, counties, and places: 2012* [Data file].

United States Small Business Administration. (2013). *Survival rates and firm age* [Data file].

United States Small Business Administration. (2015). *Frequently asked questions about small businesses.*

United States Small Business Administration Office of Advocacy. (2014). *Firm size data* [Data file].

Vehovar, V., Toepoel, V., & Steinmetz, S. (2016). Non-probability sampling. In C. Wolf, D. Joye, T. W. Smith, & Y.-C. Fu (Eds.), *The SAGE handbook of survey methodology* (pp. 329–334). London, England: Sage.

Job and Task Analysis

"Its purpose is to determine responsibilities and tasks necessary to perform a job."

(Sleezer, Russ-Eft, & Gupta, 2014, p. 31)

CHAPTER

8

Enterprise-wide Job Task Analysis in a Large Organization

Tim McGonigle

Abstract

This case study describes an enterprise-wide job analysis of over 600 roles in a government organization. The study applied a customized job analysis method to collect and analyze occupational information from across the organization to create profiles describing critical tasks, knowledges, and credentials for up to five career levels within each role. These profiles underlie an online career development portal that current and potential employees use to investigate customized career paths through the organization. Below is an overview of the case.

Where the Needs Assessment Was Conducted	Who Conducted the Needs Assessment	Focus of Needs Assessment	How Data Were Collected	How Data Were Analyzed
U.S. government agency that had dispersed sites	A consulting company	Constructed and validated over 600 role profiles that each included data for up to five career levels; provided career development information for roles filled by over 90% of organization's workforce	Background information on each role (e.g., position descriptions, vacancy announcements, and official titling and job grading standards), information from a Department of Labor database, feedback from subject matter experts (SMEs)	Content-analyzed documents; created draft profiles for SME review and feedback

Background

At its core, job analysis is the systematic study of work and worker requirements (Brannick, Levine, & Morgeson, 2007; Harvey, 1991; Sanchez & Levine, 2001). The job analysis process identifies (a) critical duties and tasks that employees must perform in the job; (b) the human capabilities (e.g., knowledges, skills, and abilities [KSAs]) required to perform these duties and tasks; and (c) contextual factors associated with the job or role (e.g., use of tools and technology, physical demands, environmental factors, interpersonal and group interactions). Organizations use job analysis information to establish human resource tools, such as employee selection, promotion, or certification assessments; training and career development programs; and workforce planning and performance management systems. Well-designed job analysis studies follow professional guidelines and procedures, including the *Principles for the Validation and Use of Personnel Selection Procedures* (Society for Industrial and Organizational Psychology, 2003), the *Standards for Educational and Psychological Testing* (American Educational Research Association, American Psychological Association, & National Council on Measurement in Education, 2014), and the *Uniform Guidelines on Employee Selection Procedures* (Equal Employment Opportunity Commission, Civil Service Commission, Department of Labor, & Department of Justice, 1978).

Within these guidelines, numerous approaches to job task analysis exist, and the choice between them should be driven by the intended use of the job analysis data. For example, a credentialing program might choose a task-analysis-oriented approach to collect detailed information on the tasks that job incumbents must be able to perform, while an organization developing a new performance management system might choose a worker-oriented approach to job analysis that identifies the KSAs needed to perform the job effectively. In the current case, a large corporate university needed to develop an organization-wide career map, which necessitated an approach to job analysis that identified both detailed information about the unique tasks and KSAs required in over 600 roles and an overarching taxonomy of information that applied across roles to support career exploration. To accomplish this goal accurately and efficiently, the organization implemented a hybrid approach to job analysis that included both task-oriented (Harvey, 1991) and worker-oriented (Sanchez & Levine, 2001) methods. The approach chosen for this study aligns closely with the process described in *A Practical Guide to Needs Assessment* (Sleezer, Russ-Eft, & Gupta, 2014). Both approaches start with a planning phase, involve conducting a workshop with subject matter experts (SMEs) to identify and refine critical components of the job, and result in training or other human resources recommendations.

The purpose of this study was to conduct an organization-wide job analysis for a large public-sector organization so that current and potential employees could create and explore customized career paths throughout the organization. As organizations face increasing competition for high-performing employees, career path exploration tools such as this have emerged as a key human resources tool for attracting and retaining staff, because they allow employees to see how their personal KSAs can be applied in the organization (Carter, Cook, & Dorsey, 2011).

Profile of the Organization

The sponsoring organization was a very large federal government agency that provides a wide range of services, including health care and benefits. Operating in locations across the United States, the organization employed workers in the full spectrum of blue- and white-collar occupations. As part of a larger transformation initiative, the organization wished to improve its ability to attract and retain high-performing employees by providing transparent occupational information that could allow motivated employees to see where they fit into the organization.

Preassessment Information

Prior to the assessment, the organization faced significant recruitment and retention problems, especially losing qualified candidates who had reached "dead ends" in their career paths and believed that they had limited opportunity to develop and advance. When it was available, existing career planning information only showed progression within a job series (e.g., financial management) to a terminal point within the job series itself. The organization wanted to provide a customizable career exploration tool that employees could use to find, and prepare for, new roles in the organization. Providing this information required thorough occupational information collected through a job analysis. The dean of the organization's corporate university requested that we perform this study in response to these issues and approved our proposed methods.

Needs Assessment Process

Most approaches to job analysis rely heavily on interviews, surveys, and focus groups with SMEs. The best SMEs are often those employees who are most critical to the organization and who have the least time to participate in the job analysis process. To minimize the burden on SMEs and because the scope of this study was so broad, essentially requiring over 600 separate job analyses, the project team developed a streamlined job analysis process that required SME input at only the most critical points. The resulting process involved four phases, which the project team conducted for each job family.

Phase I: Planning

To begin the process, the project director and the project sponsor organized the 600 roles into 55 related job families. Each role reflected a core set of responsibilities performed by employees in multiple individual positions that may have had distinct job titles. These job families provided a higher-order organizing structure for the study that aligned with government-wide job classification standards. It also guided the recruitment of SMEs to participate in the job analysis process. The project sponsor prioritized each job family's participation in the process based on (a) amount of relevant work previously conducted, (b) availability of SMEs, and (c) percent of the workforce assigned to each family. The project director identified a point of contact within each job family who was responsible for identifying SMEs to participate in the job analysis process and, ultimately, to approve the results of their work. The project director assigned a team to each job family, which typically consisted of a team lead and two trained job analysts.

Phase II: Analysis

This section describes the process used to analyze the job analysis information. The analysis process included the following steps: (a) gather background information, (b) develop overall role descriptions and career level duties, (c) identify critical areas of knowledge, (d) link role profiles to O*NET occupations, (e) identify methods for acquiring the necessary KSAs, and (f) ensure quality control.

Gather Background Information

For each job family, trained job analysts on the project team (i.e., not job incumbents) collected background information on each role, which typically included position descriptions, vacancy announcements, and official titling and job grading standards. The job analysts used this information to create draft profiles for each of the identified roles within a job family. The role profiles included an overall role description, a short description of each career level (i.e., entry, mid, senior, supervisor, manager) within the role, the major duties performed in the role, the 10 most critical areas of knowledge for performing the duties, and representative methods for acquiring the necessary KSAs (e.g., training courses, on-the-job experiences, education). To maintain consistency across roles, job families, and analysts, the project team used a spreadsheet-based analysis guide as a template for creating the draft profile. Analysts populated this guide with the draft profile and identified the source of each component of the draft profile to keep track of information used to populate each of these data fields.

Develop Overall Role Descriptions and Career Level Duties

Analysts content analyzed the identified documents to construct a general description of each role. Because these descriptions addressed the overall role, analysts reviewed at least three vacancy announcements per career level and selected duties that appeared in multiple vacancy announcements at multiple levels. Then, using the same data sources, analysts selected the three most critical duties for each career level within the role to define the differences in responsibility by career level.

Identify Critical Areas of Knowledge

Next, analysts identified up to 10 specialized knowledges (e.g., "knowledge of graphic design principles") for each role that applied across career levels to document the capabilities necessary to perform the identified duties. The project team limited this analysis to the 10 most critical knowledges so that (a) the analysis could be completed for all 600 roles in a reasonable amount of time and (b) the ultimate users of the information were not overwhelmed with information when exploring career paths.

To identify critical knowledges, analysts identified common themes in each role's duties and inferred the knowledge required to perform them. For example, if a role required the incumbent to write a press release, an analyst might infer that the incumbent would need "knowledge of AP writing style" or "knowledge of messaging strategy principles." To distinguish between career levels, analysts assigned a minimum proficiency rating to each specialized knowledge for each career level using a 5-point scale (1 = *basic knowledge* to 5 = *expert knowledge*) that included behavioral anchors for each scale point.

Link Role Profiles to O*NET Occupations

The previous steps resulted in detailed information about the unique requirements for each role. This information was critical for learning about, and preparing for, potential roles in the organization. However, career exploration tools also required an overarching taxonomy of occupational information to support career exploration. Therefore, analysts also linked each draft profile to the relevant Occupational Information Network (O*NET) (Peterson, Mumford, Borman, Jeanneret, & Fleishman, 1999) occupational profile. O*NET provided profiles of 1,110 occupational titles using a standardized set of duties and KSAs, including 41 work activities/duties (e.g., selling or influencing others), 33 knowledge areas (e.g., biology), 35 skill areas (e.g., equipment maintenance), and 52 abilities (e.g., near vision). The O*NET Information Center conducts regular surveys of job incumbents to update each occupational profile. As part of this process, O*NET analysts assess the reliability of the survey ratings to ensure the profiles are accurate and complete. After linking the custom-developed role profiles to these O*NET profiles, the analysts built an algorithm to calculate the similarity of each role to all other roles. This algorithm identified other roles that require similar KSAs to those required for each user's current role, thereby facilitating career exploration.

Identify Methods for Acquiring the Necessary KSAs

Because the purpose of this project was to provide career development guidance, analysts also identified representative methods by which each KSA could be developed. In this step, analysts first identified any formal education, licensure, or certification requirements necessary for entry to the role as required by published job-grading standards. Next, analysts mapped the identified specialized knowledges to training courses available through the corporate university.

Finally, analysts drafted on-the-job developmental experiences for each specialized knowledge at each rating level, typically by referring to information in the position descriptions and vacancy announcements about the duties performed in the role and what kinds of experiences job seekers or incumbents could perform to progress to the next career level. On-the-job experiences were activities an employee could perform in their current role to prepare for a future role.

Ensure Quality Control

Before presenting the draft role profiles to SMEs, the project team conducted a two-level quality assurance (QA) review to identify and fix (a) spelling and grammar errors, (b) unclear content, and (c) style and other compliance issues.

Phase III: Validation Workshop

Next, the project team conducted a workshop with SMEs to review, update, and validate the role profile. Prior to the in-person workshop, SMEs took part in a 1-hour online orientation session that described the overall project objectives, the data collection efforts, and the expectations for the workshop. This allowed the SMEs to understand the purpose and expectations of the workshop prior to their arrival. At the workshop, SMEs first reviewed the roles to be validated during the workshop. SMEs could recommend removing roles that were not relevant or adding positions that were missing. After the SMEs agreed on the roles, the workshop facilitator presented each element of the role profile. SMEs could suggest revisions to any element of the role profile, including the addition of new information and the deletion or editing of existing information. SMEs reached agreement on each modification before proceeding. Generally, SMEs made more edits to the specialized knowledges than to the role descriptions and career level duties. Finally, SMEs reviewed the on-the-job developmental experiences. Because the draft experiences were linked to the specialized knowledges, SMEs often had to make significant edits to the experience description if they modified the associated specialized knowledge. To ensure that the SMEs shared a common understanding of the information in the role profiles, the workshop facilitator led the SMEs through a discussion of each profile until they reached agreement on the final content.

Phase IV: Finalize Content

Following the workshop, the analyst compiled the output from the workshop and made the necessary edits. After the project team completed a second QA review for grammar, spelling, formatting, and clarity, SMEs had an opportunity to review the updated role profiles and suggest any final modifications before the dean reviewed and approved the profiles. The project team uploaded approved role profiles into the career exploration tools.

Timeline

Over the course of this study, the project team conducted over 200 work-shops during a 2-year period. The project team typically worked with each job family for approximately 4 months. Delays in identifying SMEs, scheduling and conducting validation workshops, and gaining final approval occasionally extended this timeline for specific job families. In most cases, the project team completed the analysis phase in 6 to 8 weeks.

Results of the Needs Assessment

Ultimately, the project team constructed and validated over 600 role profiles, and each included data for up to five career levels and provided career develop-ment information for roles filled by over 90% of the organization's workforce. The role profiles populated a suite of human resources tools that (a) matched users to roles based on the similarity of their current role requirements to all other roles, (b) identified career path(s) that bridge the gap between employees' current and goal roles, and (c) provided detailed data about each role and rec-ommended training and development to support employees as they considered various career paths. These tools also linked to other systems that helped users build resumes for, and apply to, jobs in their chosen career paths. The overall objective of this project was to support the organization's strategic transformation by improving its ability to attract and retain a high-performing workforce. To this end, the website hosting these tools attracted over 2.5 million site visits, resulting in over 70,000 job candidates and over 500,000 career development activities by current employees.

Influences

Conducting an enterprise-wide job analysis required the project team to modify several aspects of the traditional job analysis process. While these modifications allowed the project team to complete the study accurately and quickly, several factors influenced the performance of the project team.

The decision to have the project team develop complete draft versions of the role profiles prior to involving SMEs was a critical component of the methodology. While this saved time and reduced the SME's workload, it did not always result in accurate profiles. In some cases, available background information on a role was outdated or incomplete. As a result, the analysts could not develop an accurate draft role profile. In these cases, the project team scheduled additional time with the SMEs to jointly develop the role profile during the workshop. In other cases, the analyst had access to sufficient data to develop a draft profile, but the SMEs participating in the validation workshop did not agree on the content of the profile during the validation workshop. To resolve these disagreements, the analyst described the origin of the data in question, such as the specific position descriptions or vacancy announcements that the analyst had used to create the draft. Then, the analyst facilitated a discussion between the SMEs to identify potential resolutions to the disagreement. With few exceptions, the SMEs ultimately came to agreement. When the SMEs could not resolve the issue during the workshop, the project team identified a "super SME" who could.

Job analysis of public-sector positions required familiarity with federal human resources regulations, terminology, and culture. The project's team members all had significant experience working with government job analysis data and organizations, thereby minimizing the effect of this factor on the study.

Issues and Challenges

The size and scope of this study presented several challenges. Enterprise-wide job analysis required input from SMEs representing all parts of the organization. The sponsoring organization for this study was both geographically and organizationally dispersed, and organizational stakeholders were not accustomed to working across boundaries on projects like this. As a result, the project team initially had difficulty getting stakeholders from across the organization to collaborate. During the first phase of this study, the project team and the dean identified strategies for improving collaboration, including demonstrating the value of the study to the organization and minimizing the organization's workload to develop the tool. Ultimately, this approach convinced organizational stakeholders of the study's value, and they helped the project team access the resources (i.e., documentation and SMEs) required to complete the study.

Despite stakeholder support for the project, gaining sufficient SME participation remained a challenge throughout the duration of the study. The best SMEs were critical to the organization and managers were often reluctant to make them available for activities like job analysis workshops. In addition, the organization discouraged travel, which further inhibited access to SMEs. The project team addressed this challenge through the design of the methods. Specifically, project team analysts developed draft role profiles for SMEs to review, update, and validate, thereby reducing SME time commitment. A traditional job analysis method, in which facilitators elicit tasks and KSAs from SMEs during a workshop, would have required 3 to 5 days of SME involvement per job family. For most job families, the method used in this study required no more than 1 day of SME involvement. In addition, the project team used communication technology, such as WebEx, to minimize, and in some cases eliminate, the need for SMEs to travel to the workshop site.

While the complete project team, which consisted of a project director, two team leads, and eight job analysts, experienced both planned and unplanned turnover, the turnover had little effect on the project team's performance. When a team lead left the project, for example, one of the job analysts became a team lead.

Finally, the study produced large amounts of complex occupational data. Ultimately, the project team created over 3,000 unique profiles (600 roles with 5 career levels each) containing hundreds of variables each. The project team used a series of customized tools to manage the data during the course of the study. Analysts created draft profiles in a spreadsheet-based workbook and used the same workbook to facilitate the SME validation workshops. After SMEs validated the role profiles, analysts uploaded the finalized role profiles into a database that software developers used to populate the career development tools. The project team implemented standardized tools, style guides, and QA procedures throughout the profile development and validation process to maintain the quality of the data.

DISCUSSION QUESTIONS

1. What would you do differently if the purpose of the job task analysis were different (e.g., workforce planning or performance management)?

2. What would you differently if conducting this project for a smaller organization?

3. How would you modify the methods if you had a shorter timeline?

4. How would you modify the methods if you had a longer timeline?

5. How could you demonstrate the value of the project?

6. How would you maintain the accuracy of the job analysis data over time?

REFERENCES

American Educational Research Association, American Psychological Association, & National Council on Measurement in Education. (2014). *Standards for educational and psychological testing.* Washington, DC: Author.

Brannick, M. T., Levine, E. L., & Morgeson, F. P. (2007). *Job and work analysis: Methods, research, and applications for human resource management.* Thousand Oaks, CA: Sage.

Carter, G. W., Cook, K. W., & Dorsey, D. W. (2011). *Career paths: Charting courses to success for organizations and their employees.* Hoboken, NJ: Wiley-Blackwell.

Equal Employment Opportunity Commission, Civil Service Commission, Department of Labor, and Department of Justice. (1978). Uniform Guidelines on Employee Selection Procedures. *Federal Register, 43,* 38290–38215.

Harvey, R. J. (1991). Job analysis. In M. D. Dunnette & L. M. Hough (Eds.), *Handbook of industrial and organizational psychology* (Vol. 2, pp. 71–163). Palo Alto, CA: Consulting Psychologists Press.

Peterson, N. G., Mumford, M. D., Borman, W. C., Jeanneret, P. R., & Fleishman, E. A. (1999). *An occupational information system for the 21st century: The development of O*NET.* Washington, DC: American Psychological Association.

Sanchez, J. I., & Levine, E. L. (2001). The analysis of work in the 20th and 21st centuries. In N. Anderson, D. S. Ones, H. K. Sinangil, & C. Viswesvaran (Eds.), *Handbook of industrial, work and organizational psychology* (Vol. 1, pp. 71–89). Thousand Oaks, CA: Sage.

Sleezer, C. M., Russ-Eft, D. F., & Gupta, K. (2014). *A practical guide to needs assessment* (3rd ed.). San Francisco, CA: Wiley & ASTD.

Society for Industrial and Organizational Psychology. (2003). *Principles for the validation and use of personnel selection procedures* (4th ed.). Bowling Green, OH: Author.

Competency Assessments

"Its purpose is to identify knowledge, skills, and attitudes for superior . . . performance."

(Sleezer, Russ-Eft, & Gupta, 2014, p. 31)

9

Assessing Needs for a PhD Study Program in Human Resource Development and Organization Development

A Case Study Focused on Quality Development in an Outcome-Based Education Approach

Dawisa Sritanyarat

Abstract

This needs assessment was performed as a significant part of conducting a quality development and assessment for a PhD program. The context of the needs assessment was a higher education institution. The results were used to improve the learning outcomes of the program in developing graduates. Specifically, they were used as an input for teaching and learning design and program revision. Below is an overview of the case.

Where the Needs Assessment Was Conducted	Who Conducted the Needs Assessment	Focus of Needs Assessment	How Data Were Collected	How Data Were Analyzed
Human Resource and Organization Development PhD Program for the National Institute for Development Administration in Bangkok, Thailand	Steering team, comprised of the PhD program director, deputy dean for planning and development, and program coordinator	Focused on identifying expected learning outcomes for the human resource and organization development (HROD) program (doctoral degree) that were suitable for the labor market and related stakeholders, such as potential students, current students, alumni, and so on	Qualitative and quantitative data: a workshop among teaching staff, review by external experts, a workshop with alumni and employers, an open-ended survey of the program's visiting scholars, an online Likert survey of current students, alumni, and prospective students	HROD teaching staff workshop data were analyzed using content analysis, coding, and analyzing data; Likert survey analyzed using descriptive statistics

Background

....

This needs assessment was conducted in an institution of higher education, the National Institute of Development Administration (NIDA). It has the unique purpose of offering only master's and doctoral programs. The institution had adopted the quality development concept called the ASEAN University Network Quality Assurance (AUN-QA) that mandated developing a management system for every program offered by the institution. This AUN-QA system required each program to be designed and revised in response to the needs of the labor market and the stakeholders.

This AUN-QA assessment was of the Doctor of Philosophy Program in Human Resource and Organization Development (HROD). This program was established in 2010. Nine cohorts of doctoral students, with each cohort having 4 to 10 students, had completed, or were in the process of completing, study in this program. The program was designed to prepare high-level professionals, such as corporate consultants, researchers, and academicians, to become leaders in the field of HROD and to be able to

1) Strategically synthesize multiple bodies of knowledge in HROD from interdisciplinary perspectives

2) Creatively construct new knowledge and critically analyze the existing ideas via scholarly research and theory building

3) Ethically transform knowledge to present the obtained knowledge in practical and effective forms via means of publication, teaching, and implementation (Graduate School of Human Resources Development, 2018, p. 7)

This program was well established and has been successful in terms of the quality of graduates and the satisfaction of graduates. However, there was a need for continuous improvement to effectively sustain the program. The AUN-QA was applied to this program in response to the policy of the university. The program director volunteered to participate in the AUN-QA system as he recognized the importance of systematically improving the program.

Apart from management's decision, it was agreed by all faculty members involved that the social context of the program and the needs of the program's stakeholders had been shifting. The school wanted to be certain about those needs to be able to revise and develop the program to attract applicants and to produce high-quality graduates who would contribute to the society. In conclusion, the motivation for this needs assessment was both internal and external. However, the AUN-QA system accelerated the motivation.

When the program's curriculum was designed, opinions from scholars in the field of HROD were collected and interpreted as an input for curriculum development. This time, a needs assessment was required again to verify the fit of this program to needs of multiple stakeholders. According to the AUN-QA system, a program should be able to identify its expected learning outcomes (ELOs) that are suitable for the labor market (ASEAN University Network, 2015). Those who were associated with the HROD program wanted to be certain that the ELOs represented the needs of multiple stakeholders to ensure effectiveness of the program in producing competent graduates for the labor market. The ELOs were the core of teaching and learning design, students' assessment design, as well as extracurricular activities and students' supports design. Therefore, the needs assessment was extremely important. Achieving the needs of stakeholders could enhance the effectiveness of program design and implementation. In other words, the ELOs were set as the result of this needs assessment, and going forward, they would provide a foundation for the entire program.

To understand the case of this needs analysis clearly, it is important to understand the AUN-QA system. The ASEAN University Network is a nongovernmental organization. The secretariat office is in Bangkok, Thailand. It currently includes almost a hundred institutional members, which are higher education institutions in ASEAN countries (ASEAN University Network, 2015). This quality assurance system consists of 11 main criteria (ASEAN University Network, 2015). The system focuses on how the study programs are administered. Basically, the focus of the AUN-QA system is not on program content, but on the process and system of operating the program. This system is not only a guideline, but also an assessment to grant a certification. This certification verifies that the assessed program could perform according to the criteria at the adequate level. In other words, the AUN-QA system does not seek excellence to grant its certificate. It simply looks for adequate quality.

The PhD Program in HROD needed this certificate to (a) fulfill the requirement from NIDA, (b) enhance an opportunity for students and faculty members to participate in exchanges within ASEAN countries, and (c) fulfill the quality improvement of the program to ensure the effectiveness and sustainability of the program. To succeed in this system, the program had to be managed systematically. Moreover, the self-assessment report that provided a written account of what had been done had to be written. Finally, the on-site assessment by the AUN-QA assessors had to be completed.

Since 2016, the PhD Program in HROD had operated with a vision of achieving AUN-QA certification. The program director had been assigned to work with the deputy dean for planning and development, and the assistant to NIDA's president for quality development to verify the management system of this PhD Program, as well as to improve the quality of some processes in its routine operation. This team could be considered as a supporting factor for the needs assessment. However, because the ELOs provided the center of the study program, other improvements could not be done systematically without having solid ELOs. Consequently, it was undeniable that the needs assessment was critical.

Despite the dedication and willingness of the steering team and the sense of urgency felt by management, problems in needs assessment seemed to be just around the corner. The biggest problem was data and information. The team faced a lack of usable information to perform the needs assessment. There were incomplete raw data. Most of the data were in bits and pieces, which could not be used as an input for a needs assessment that met the requirement of the AUN-QA. Second, when the team reached out for support from the Planning Division of the University, hoping that they had a source of information, it was found that the Planning Division collected all data in a school-based format. It was not possible for the team to extract the data for the PhD program. After all the attempts, the team concluded that the existing data were not available for this needs assessment.

Profile of the Organization

The PhD program mentioned in this case existed under the Graduate School of Human Resource Development (SHRD). This 27-year-old graduate school could be considered a small-sized organization. It had 17 faculty members and 17 support staff members, and it operated under a governmental higher education institution along with 11 other schools. This graduate school functioned as a part of NIDA. It was called an institute, rather than university, for the royal establishment by His Majesty the King Rama 9, and it was established to be a higher education institution with the focus on research and education to promote the national development administration. For 52 years, NIDA has been operating as a public university. However, NIDA currently was underway to changing its status to an autonomous university, due to the government policy. The whole institution had almost 200 faculty members and almost 500 support staff members (Graduate School of HRD, 2018). Compared to a manufacturing company, the 11 schools operated as production lines, sharing the supporting functions, such as human resources, information technology, and so on. The needs assessment task mainly fell to the responsibility of the SHRD. The steering team was appointed from a group of faculty members and support staff members. This team held full responsibility in decision making and completing the requirements of AUN-QA.

To understand more about the SHRD, it is important to note that this school could be considered as a small-size organization. Even though it was operating under NIDA, the dean of the school had a certain level of autonomy in decision making and managing human resources of the school. One strength of this small organization was that faculty members and support staff members worked closely, having good relationships at work. However, as with many other educational organizations, the management positions of the school were term based. Those who were in the management positions were elected by the faculty members and volunteered to serve the school. In this case, position power was not as clear as it was for the permanent positions. It was also because of the culture of respecting opinions and academic freedom of all members. This has never been considered as a weakness. It has been agreed upon that this was a strength of this school.

Preassessment Information

The AUN-QA system was enforced by the institution yet implemented by the school. This AUN-QA effort led the HROD program and the SHRD school to the urgency for the needs assessment. The PhD program director was appointed to lead the steering team, with the support from the deputy dean for planning and development. The program coordinator, who was a support staff, was also assigned to this project. The focus of the assessment was on the needs of current students, alumni, current and potential employers, teaching staff (both in-house and international), the institution, and the office of higher education commission. These groups of stakeholders were identified by the AUN-QA criteria to be significant in the needs assessment effort. This needs assessment effort was done to reach the ELOs, which could serve the needs of stakeholders. These ELOs were the heart of managing this study program. The needs assessment process and results need to be transparent to serve the above-mentioned purpose.

One important issue in completing this task was that the needs assessment was an add-on task for every team member. The steering team was not hired only for this task. They had other job duties to fulfill. This was an extra task for everyone.

Another key issue was that some data were collected by the Planning Department of NIDA. The school and the program were not able to participate in that data collection process. Being an end user of the system did not allow the steering team to control the way data were collected and analyzed.

The second issue seemed to be a bigger concern than the first one. The voluntary spirit of the steering committee members was noticed. However, their ability to manage time for this task was still challenging. Moreover, the data collection seemed to be an issue as well.

Needs Assessment Process

The approach of the needs assessment was related to the competency-based needs assessment (Sleezer, Russ-Eft, & Gupta, 2014). However, the expected results of this needs assessment would be more than a set of competencies. Competencies needed to be translated into actions that PhD graduates could perform. The concept of Bloom's Taxonomy was suggested by the AUN-QA system. Data were collected, analyzed, and interpreted both quantitatively and qualitatively, as described below.

This needs assessment was a long process. It started with a workshop among teaching staff of the HROD PhD program. All teaching staff members were asked to reflect on their experiences teaching in the program and their expectations toward their students and graduates. The steering team facilitated this workshop. The content of the workshop was analyzed using the content analysis approach. Six main themes emerged, with 21 subthemes. By the time the workshop was over, the steering team felt it was very successful. A conclusion was reached, and everyone seemed to agree with that conclusion. That appeared to be a great sign of cooperation in the AUN-QA process.

Unfortunately, the perception was not completely true. When the steering team took the results of that workshop to be ELOs of the program, problems came from everywhere. Six main themes with 21 subthemes were too numerous to manage. Those themes were impossible to measure. This might have occurred due to different perceptions about this needs assessment among teaching staff. Those ELOs were set for top students, not for qualified students. Not every student in this program could achieve the identified ELOs. That was a big issue. The ELOs should be the minimum qualifying standard for every graduate, which the program can guarantee to employers that the program would deliver.

This result was understandable to a certain extent. The teaching staff was hoping for the best from their students. They had good intentions to produce graduates with great quality. Therefore, they provided such information and opinions. Last, but most importantly, the teaching staff, by the time of the workshop, did not take the ELOs seriously. They were willing to provide their opinions; however, they did not foresee themselves operating by these ELOs. They had not thought about the situation where they needed to use these ELOs in planning and revising their courses. That was when the steering team realized that the ELOs that they had obtained were not practical.

Even though the workshop did not produce the results that the steering team had hoped, it raised the teaching staff's sense of participation in the AUN-QA process. It also reduced the degree of resisting the system. Conducting this workshop had shown respect for the academic freedom of the teaching staff. It was not a forced-thinking process. Therefore, teaching staff did not feel offended. It might, however, have resulted in many subthemes. Yet, the outcome-based education concept of the AUN-QA was well-taken by the teaching staff.

Even though the results from the workshop were not completely usable, they were taken as an input for the next step. Those drafted ELOs were taken into consideration by the PhD Program Committee. This was when the ELOs were revised to be simpler and more concrete and more measurable. The results of this stage were reported in the SHRD meeting and were approved. Despite the approval from the SHRD meeting, these ELOs needed to be verified by external parties. The goal of this step was to verify the practicality of the ELOs. AUN-QA experts who were experienced in AUN-QA assessment and consultation were invited to give recommendations. Again, the ELOs were revised to be simpler and more concrete. This stage was a wake-up call for the steering team. The team learned that they needed to be aware of their perspective and that of others. What they considered concrete might still be abstract for others who were not experts in the HROD field.

After the external opinion stage, six main themes emerged with eight sub-themes. However, as the experts were not the experts in the HROD field, they gave opinions from the perspective of AUN-QA. Another workshop with the alumni and employers was conducted to put final touches on the ELOs. The steering team hoped to use this workshop to make the ELOs easier to understand and communicate to all stakeholders. Moreover, this was to gain the confidence that these ELOs really responded to the needs of those who joined this program and those who would hire them. It was also to make sure that these ELOs reflected the key strengths of graduates of this program. After the workshop, slight changes in the word selections were made by the steering team. Concurrently with the workshop, an open-ended survey was sent to visiting professors who cotaught in this program. The results of all workshop and open-ended survey responses were interpreted by the steering team using a coding process to form themes. Themes were used in confirming and revising the ELOs. They were reported in the results of the needs assessment as well.

The steering team was delighted by the results of the workshop and open-ended survey. They found that the ELOs were ready for the last stage of needs assessment. It could be said that the steering team considered that the ELOs had reached a stage of saturation. The final stage was a quantitative data collection and analysis. The ELOs were transformed into an online survey distributed to about 300 individuals who were current students, alumni, and prospective students. The survey asked for stakeholders' opinion on how important each ELO was for graduates from this program. A Likert-typed survey was used. Scores ranged from one, which meant that ELO was not important at all, to five, which meant that ELO was significantly important. There were about 120 respondents in total. The number of respondents might seem small. However, the steering team was not concerned, as they did not expect the PhD program to include as large a group of stakeholders as the master's programs did. The data were inter-preted in a basic technique, by examining demographic data and using descrip-tive statistics. The average score of each ELO was calculated. This was not only a data collection, but also a channel of communication. All stakeholders were informed indirectly by this survey about the focus and aims of this PhD pro-gram. This by-product was revealed a bit after the needs assessment. When the program opened for application in the year after, fewer applicants were surprised by the expectations of the teaching staff and the requirements of the program.

In conclusion, this needs assessment started with qualitative processes, then ended with a quantitative process. It began with the data from internal opinions, then moved outward to collecting external opinions. The needs assessment pro-cess and results were transparent to stakeholders knowledgeable in the field. Both internal and external opinions were taken in the process to ensure that the emerg-ing ELOs were useful in managing this PhD program, and were not self serving.

Results of the Needs Assessment

The results of this needs assessment were summarized as ELOs of the PhD program. This set of ELOs was used as a goal of the program. ELOs were taken as an input of the design of teaching methods and evaluation of each course. They would also be an input for program revision. Table 9.1 shows the results of the needs assessment presented in the form of ELOs for the HROD program.

Apart from getting the ELOs, the steering team also learned about the percep-tions of stakeholders. The workshops and the open-ended survey with different groups of stakeholders revealed that employers, alumni, and visiting professors agreed with the ELOs. Table 9.2 contains examples of their contribution.

These opinions were valuable in revising the ELOs. Moreover, it was found from the quantitative survey results that every ELO was agreed upon and expected

Table 9.1 Themes and Subthemes of ELOs	
ELO Themes	**Subthemes**
1. Worldwide Perspective	Integrate the international knowledge with the local wisdom to cope with critical organizational and/or social issues.
2. Initiative and Open-Mindedness	Analyze information to provide suggestions to enhance values for stakeholders in creative and/or innovative ways.
	Demonstrate and build awareness of diversity, multiculturalism, and social justice with open-mindedness.

3. Sustainable Leadership	Propose changes through the research and practices for the benefit of present and future of stakeholders.
4. Human Intelligence	Acquire and apply professional knowledge and skills to drive an organization and/or society humanly with integrity.
5. Ethics and Morality	Demonstrate the main ethical issues and principles used when conducting research and practicing human resources profession.
6. Scholar Instinct	Display academic intuition to identify important issues, research problems, and critique existing knowledge.
	Conduct research to respond and make suggestions to those issues and problems and/or fill in knowledge gaps.

Table 9.2 Examples of Keywords of the Qualitative Data

ELO Themes	Subthemes
Worldwide Perspective	International and Local Wisdom Global Mindset
Initiative and Open-Mindedness	Open-Mindedness Innovation Working Well in Diversities Managing Conflict and Change
Sustainable Leadership	Initiating Change for Sustainable Development Utilizing Entrepreneurial Stance Contributing to the Long-Term Viability of the Organization
Human Intelligence	Concern for Human Well-Being Ability to Implement HR System Fostering Professional Development and Advancement of All Staff
Ethics and Morality	Integrity and Ethics Ethics, Integrity, and Integration
Scholar Instinct	International and Local Wisdom Participation in International Academic Conferences Supporting Decision Making by Managing Information Resources

by all stakeholders, except the Scholar Instinct. Scholar Instinct was rated as moderately important by prospective students. This told the program committee to communicate more about the essence of the PhD program: that being scholar was important and cannot be omitted in this level of education. The steering team confirmed that Scholar Instinct was not included in a mindset of HROD practitioners by analyzing the HR professional competency model of the Thailand Human Resource Certification Institution (Thailand HRCI, 2018). Most of students and prospective students of this program were practitioners; therefore, it was not a complete surprise that they did not find Scholar Instinct important. However, it was the program's responsibility to communicate with students and to ensure that all graduates were prepared to hold the Scholar Instinct.

Influences

The most powerful influence was the organization's culture, as well as the individual opinions regarding the AUN-QA. The AUN-QA system was new to all members of the school, as well as the whole institution. Different groups of stakeholders viewed benefits of the AUN-QA differently. Some valued it, while others rejected it. Consequently, the cooperation level in the needs assessment was different from different groups. Furthermore, staff's perception about quality assurance system has never been admirable. Consequently, most of the staff members rejected this system too. Anything related to this system was perceived as a threat and extra burden.

Culture, in this case, played a significant role in success or failure of the needs assessment. Considering the background of SHRD mentioned earlier, it should be noted that the people responsible for this needs assessment had insufficient power to influence important stakeholders. This is a great example of the power issue in a needs assessment effort. Even for the steering team, which was assigned full authority, a command and control approach could not be used in the context of higher education institutions such as SHRD and NIDA. Successfully conducting this needs assessment required empathy, communication, and respect for all the stakeholders as well as understanding the bigger picture and adroitly implementing organization change.

Issues and Challenges

One important issue faced by the team was collaboration; something needed to be done for the success of the needs assessment. Initially, few faculty members and support staff members understood and bought into the AUN-QA system. When people did not see the importance and significance of this system, they also did not clearly understand the AUN-QA criteria, nor the working systems. In these cases, needs were very difficult to collect. The top management of NIDA had to provide training and communicate several times with faculty members and support staff about benefits of the system, the AUN-QA criteria, and the process to develop the NIDA's work system to be compatible with the AUN-QA system.

Another collaboration issue was that participants in the focus groups did not fully engage in the discussion. They also provided limited information. Respondents in the survey efforts were very difficult to reach. Limited responses were returned. Even though some of stakeholders were willing to participate in the needs assessment, their busy schedule prohibited them from fully participating. The steering team needed to handle this issue, as they had closer relationships with the program's stakeholders than the top management did. Continuous communication was practiced throughout the needs assessment. Reaching out to all stakeholders was the key to success in getting their feedback.

Another issue was that the existing information system was not supportive of this needs assessment. Without the understanding about the AUN-QA system, not many staff members of the school and the institution took this AUN-QA effort into their routine operations. Moreover, the existing system did not fully support the needs assessment as mentioned earlier. The institution had a regular survey system, which could have contributed to this needs assessment; unfortunately, the questions in the survey did not directly relate to the needs to be collected. Moreover, the survey system was not designed to allow the classification of data by the study program; rather, data were collected by schools. There were many times that the steering committee needed to pull raw data from the data mine and re-analyze those data. Again, the top management had to play a big part. All related parties were called into multiple extensive meetings. The survey system was revised to serve the needs analysis. It took almost 2 years to re-adjust the whole system to support the needs assessment as a part of the AUN-QA system.

In conclusion, key success factors in handling challenges of this needs assessment were (a) top management support and dedication in making changes, (b) understanding of related parties both internal and external, and (c) dedication and persistence of the steering team. Without these three factors, the needs assessment could not be done as effectively as it was in this case.

DISCUSSION QUESTIONS

The questions are about four aspects of this needs assessment.

1. How should involvement in a competency-based needs assessment be promoted among all stakeholders: students, faculty members, support staff, employers, and alumni? Would there be other ways to promote collaboration?

2. How should the data collection system be developed to be concise, practical, and sustainable? This question is extremely important as this system requires an ongoing needs assessment. A user-friendly system is needed. Related parties should not shoulder a big burden of extra work.

3. What could be considered as key threats of this needs assessment? How could the steering team handle them?

4. In higher education institutions, faculty members normally have an academic freedom, which leads to their equal voice. Even the management team does not have absolute command and control over everyone in every matter. There is beauty in that. However, that structure can cause time and resource constraints in planning a needs assessment. How should a needs assessment be planned and performed in a respectful manner to faculty members to earn collaboration, while maintaining efficiency in terms of time and resources, as well as producing desirable results?

REFERENCES

ASEAN University Network. (2015). *Guild to AUN-QA assessment at programme level version 3.0*. Bangkok, Thailand: ASEAN University Network.

Graduate School of HRD, National Institute of Development Administration. (2018). *Self-assessment report*. Bangkok, Thailand: National Institute of Development Administration.

Sleezer, C. M., Russ-Eft, D., & Gupta, K. (2014). *A practical guide to needs assessment* (3rd ed.). San Francisco, CA: Wiley & ASTD.

Thailand HRCI. (2018). *คุณวุฒิวิชาชีพสาขาบริหารงานบุคคล* [Human resource management professional qualification]. Retrieved from http://www.pmat.or.th/hrci/index.php/qualification.

Strategic Assessments

"Its purpose is to examine existing problems or address new and future needs within the context of the organization's or the community's business strategy."

(Sleezer, Russ-Eft, & Gupta, 2014, p. 32)

10

Comprehensive Needs Assessment and Asset/Capacity Building

The Case of the Westington Schools

James W. Altschuld and Molly Engle

Abstract

A middle-class, suburban school district was growing rapidly with an overcrowded single high school. Space was tight; students, faculty, and staff were physically uncomfortable. The situation would worsen with time. Negative results from a detailed architectural review commissioned by the school board were the impetus for an in-depth investigation of needs and assets. The board thought it would be best to look at current educational programs and their strengths, what future-oriented programs might be and might require, and resources potentially available in the system and community. Results from that study led to the planning of future directions. The procedures for collecting information were extensive and lengthy, carefully designed to involve local groups and individuals in unique ways, and they could generalize to similar as well as diverse districts across the country. Below is an overview of this case.

Where the Case Was Conducted	Who Conducted It	Its Focus	How Data Were Collected	How Data Were Analyzed
Middle-class suburban school district and community	External consultants in conjunction with internal district staff	Planning the future direction of the schools in the Westinghouse Schools, a rapidly growing community	Architectural study, demographic analysis, literature review, benchmarking, facilitated group meetings	Descriptive statistics, thematic analysis of group meetings

Background

High school is a key point in transitioning from the early teens to adulthood. It is where friendships and memories are made. It defines who we are and is an expression of community values. This would be true for most school districts. Thus, when Westington's sole high school exceeded capacity and could no longer accommodate educational programs and the physical needs of those working or matriculating there, it was a major concern for everyone in the community (Altschuld, 2015a).

At the start of this needs assessment, the high school had more than 3,000 students and was projected to rise to more than 5,000 in a decade. The school building was not suitable for expansion given that it was over 60 years old and had many prior additions (some not well thought out). The school simply could not be expanded due to factors of cost, what would have to be done, building regulations, etc. The idea to enlarge and/or alter the structure was abandoned after the Board had a detailed architectural analysis performed. The findings afforded the district and community an opening to take a broad look at educational needs, resources, and assets in regard to the future, which is not often done by schools. Physical concerns were the initial drivers for a needs assessment, but what happened went well beyond just the building limitations morphing into a large-scale community-involved endeavor.

Profile of the Organization

The suburban community had a city population of 16,500 with 6,000–7,000 K–12 students, and with surrounding areas to be served, the effective sizes were closer to 35,000 and 12,000, respectively. The schools were well respected throughout the central part of the state for their very successful graduates. The population was primarily White, with less than 10% students of color (Asians were the main part of the latter group).

Because of new housing being developed in the city and the service area (which was the district's educational responsibility), the school numbers were rising quickly. The suburb ceded a tax-rich site to its large nearby metropolitan neighbor in exchange for preserving school district boundaries. When this first occurred (about 10 years earlier), not much was going on in the service area but that began to change and enrollment growth was causing problems.

The local situation was evolving from a small village and village-like educational-family mentality on the outskirts of a major urban center to a much larger one, bursting at the seams and causing disruption to usual ways of operating. Westington was caught somewhat by surprise; it was a sleepy little place for much of its history. Now everything was in a state of flux; teachers needed to be hired, additional space was required, and there were busing and transportation problems. Administrators for the increasing population had to be brought on board, as well as other changes. The issue was how to cope thoughtfully with what was happening. Fortunately, the district staff, school board, and community were forward thinking, and a consensus emerged to conduct an in-depth strategic needs assessment (Sleezer, Russ-Eft, & Gupta, 2014) for information and insight prior to moving forward. Identification of assets was an integral part of the assessment.

Preassessment Information

This school district had accurate records/data about students (demographics), homes in the community, and areas under construction (what was to be built in terms of single-family dwellings, apartments, condos, their potential costs, and economics related to new residents). A sense of what existed and what was anticipated was clear (the need was obvious). Initially, as noted, the idea was to expand the high school from approximately 3,000 students (perhaps the largest in a heavily populated state) to a mega status of some 5,000. Therefore, the starting point was to look at the building and what would be required to modernize and expand it.

The school board hired an established firm (one familiar with the local environment) for a detailed and substantial feasibility review including facilities, parking, how increasing size would impact traffic, electrical outlets, and so forth. A sampling of what was found included the following:

- It would be very to extremely expensive to bring the building up to current standards and building codes, especially if major alterations were to be made.

- Flow and movement patterns were convoluted and could not be easily corrected without tearing down portions of the building, partly a result of earlier alterations (teachers had hall traffic monitoring duties as part of regular teaching assignments to ensure orderly change of classes).

- Electrical costs for a completely up-to-date structure would be sizable and almost prohibitive.

- Even if the school could be enlarged, it would cause other unintended problems but ones that would occur nevertheless (see the next three points).

- Many more parking spaces would be needed for staff and students who drove to school; what was in place was grossly inadequate.

- As a direct effect of more cars and increased size, traffic on the main artery (a key east–west road in front of the school) and side streets would be affected in dire ways.

- East–west traffic flow would be dramatically slowed in the morning, and evening rush hours with both periods significantly elongated— traffics jams could be foreseen, causing much exasperation.

- Taking all factors into account, the conclusion was that, at best, the building should be razed and a new one built if it was desirable to go with just one high school.

- Better yet, it was suggested to seriously consider constructing one to two new buildings in other locations in the district as a better way to utilize community resources.

The findings, which were communicated via local news outlets, were an eye opener (a shocking one) in terms of likely negative outcomes. They were on the front pages of the papers. Articles, replete with detailed artists' renderings of what confronted Westington, conveyed the circumstances in a clear and straightforward manner. The embedded drawings visually demonstrated the dilemma confronting the educational system, the Board, and of course, the entire community (with emphasis on the latter). To their credit, a "throw your hands up" attitude was not the mindset of the leadership of the school system, school staff, or the overall community. Instead, the needs assessment and asset identification strategy outlined in succeeding sections was pursued.

Some preliminary comments about the principles underlying what was done warrant explication. First, open and frequent communication with the public was consistent throughout the needs assessment and determination of assets. Doing so enhanced the transparency of all activities to concerned stakeholders. This was accomplished by "osmosis," a process quietly pursued so that it became second nature to what was being undertaken and embedded in activities.

Second, the process was predicated on the heavy involvement of the community and being thoughtful about obtaining and incorporating the ideas of Westington residents into it. Third, although externally guided, school staff and community members were integral to implementing procedures. They were existing and accessible assets, generally low in costs, and presented other advantages as evident in the description of procedures. Fourth, the process would take time, a patient attitude, and a willingness on the part of the school board to commit the resources to make the large-scale endeavor happen. Lastly, the importance of these principles is to be stressed for other school districts or settings that would like to adapt what Westington had implemented. If not followed to a high degree or fine-tuned/adapted to fit other local circumstances, what resulted for this school district would not be as successful in different locations.

Needs Assessment and Asset/Capacity Building Process

After realizing the implications of the architectural report provided to the Westington district, the school board, staff, and others strongly felt that a guiding, working committee of teachers, educational administrators, and individuals from the community would be needed. The committee's responsibilities included setting the tone for future needs assessment and asset determination activities; scheduling community meetings; maintaining records of what was taking place; communicating with the public and keeping it involved in the process. Into the mix was brought an individual who had previous experience in public policy and community work. She was a faculty member at a large state university in the nearby metropolitan area, a parent of children attending or who had attended the district's schools, and was recognized as a person who could help in shaping what might be done in a positive manner. A "Godsend" if there ever was one, and she ultimately was a key force in creating the conditions for enabling the earlier highlighted, guiding points to become a reality.

She was particularly adept at organizing and at ease and natural in including others in assessing needs and finding out about resources. She made it inviting and appear seamless, although much effort occurred beneath the surface to make it look that way. Without her presence and steady hand, the procedures would not have been nearly as effective. The value of this leadership cannot be underestimated; it is an essential, a *sine qua non* condition. Time and resources invested in finding a person with relevant qualifications are critical for endeavors like this.

Tables 10.1–10.3 depict what was carried out over time. They do not contain a complete listing of all activities, and the chronological order is an approximation; rather, each table represents the highlights, an overview, of what Westington did. A lot of things had to take place to breathe life into this needs assessment, to set the stage for what could come from it, and there were overlaps in the activities and when they happened.

Table 10.1 Phase I—Beginning Key Activities in the Needs Assessment and Asset/Capacity-Building Study

Activity	Description	Advantages	Fit to Needs Assessment/Asset Process
Architectural Study	Standard ways of conducting such analyses; extensive quantitative data produced	Wealth of useful information, no substitute for it (see previous text)	Results were compelling, and from them, comprehensible diagrams were created that forthrightly illustrated problems. Need was in *what was there now and what an increasing population would require.*
Demographic Analysis	From school data bases and knowledge of what was going on in the community	Like the architectural study, no substitute for this information	Readily grasped data tables made the need clear; population growth would overwhelm the schools.

Table 10.2 Phase II—Interim Undertakings in the Needs Assessment and Asset/Capacity-Building Study

Activity	Description	Advantages	Fit to Needs Assessment/ Asset Process
Research the literature for trends in education	Under the aegis of the working committee, teachers, staff, and administrators reviewed literature; requires time.	Process engages many individuals in the system. Good way to start, takes advantage of what exists.	Framework/ideas from the working committee guided the activity for examining the *what should or could be*. Relied on that committee for direction and pulling findings together.
Search for systems in similar situations for benchmarking	Similar to above understandings of how others have dealt with similar issues.	Excellent idea, would identify sites for benchmarking and visitation. Avoids reinventing the wheel.	Tied to the framework of guiding committee. Led to a sample of sites to be visited by small district teams. Lists of what to do positively, pitfalls to avoid.
Preliminary search for new types of buildings (how they might be arranged, kinds of equipment, etc.)	Partly embedded in some prior activities.	Before formulating district plans, this would lead to imaginative ways of thinking.	Possible examples of different physical facilities.
Merge collected information into fact sheets and scenarios for future-focused discussions in small community meetings	Working group collated information into fact sheets/future-oriented scenarios for meetings. Short, thought-provoking, meaningful input was assembled for the next step, large community groups.	Summarized information, easily worked with and digested. Many small groups convened to openly review what had been found. community input encouraged, recorded, analyzed in regard to needs, assets, next steps, and so on.	Good preparation for working with the community, opening up to its perceptions and input. Meetings were started by school staff, but moved quickly into free flowing discussion.

Table 10.3 Phase III—**Concluding Events** in the Needs Assessment and Asset/Capacity Building Study

Activity	Description	Advantages	Fit to Needs Assessment/ Asset Process
Training teams to lead large community discussions of emergent directions for the district	Develop training for two-person teams (teacher, community member) to conduct large face-to-face meetings. Training prior to the meetings being held.	Puts meeting facilitators on same footing and page. Makes certain that community is involved in how the meetings are to be run and is welcoming of open commentary.	Ensured that the voice of the people was heard, good for NA and prominent. In asset determination (Altschuld, 2015b). Training leadership was well thought out and appreciated by all.
Large-scale meetings	Via flyers to homes, publicity, meetings were promoted. Over 20 get-togethers, more than 1000 people attended. Attendees voted on various program options at the end.	Show of support for the community, it could see its input in proposed options. Since community facilitators were not from the schools, attendees were encouraged to express thoughts about needs, assets, concerns, etc.	Just a continuation of the foundation of the study. Notable, in light of what had happened with a previous school levy (see final event).
Final event	After all information was pulled together, a bond issue for a new high school was successful.	Without the study, this outcome was in doubt, and prior levy had failed.	Community via vote and involvement was a full partner in the process.

A cursory review of the tables reveals that community involvement was planned and integral to this investigation. Communication was frequent via flyers sent to homes or through newspaper articles, often accompanied by illustrations and easily understood diagrams conveying the nature of problems the school district was facing. Television interviews were conducted with the working (guiding) committee. Its leader and teacher members did a very good job of explaining activities. Throughout the work, the openness of the process was emphasized as was the community's role in it.

Comments that arose during meetings in Phases II (interim undertakings) and III (concluding events) are interesting to note. Some were appreciative of the quality of the education delivered by the school system, and others were favorable in regard to the nature of the community and what was liked about living in it. Some constituents provided overall positive views of the schools and how the composition of them differed from other locations. (All of the above were assets, strengths.) And, as expected, a number of individuals noted that there would be costs to home and property owners if new buildings would be required.

Discussions in the large meetings (Table 10.3) were respectful, which is not surprising since the meeting facilitators were trained about the importance of tone: a positive, open, and encouraging one. Standard procedures for working with groups were employed. Once participants were welcomed, the facilitators briefly (5 minutes or so) described what the district had done to learn about the emerging problem. After that, the floor was open for the comments and thoughts of attendees. The patterns that were observed were verbally summarized with the proviso that the group agreed that the summary was representative of the discourse. This type of strategy was used for the rest of the meeting, which was gently moved into options for next steps for Westington. Occasionally, if some attendees were not responding, the facilitators encouraged them to do so.

For the most part, 2 hours or a little longer were needed, but some conversations continued beyond the allotted time necessitating up to 3 hours (usually in the evenings from 7–10 p.m.). The concluding activity was ranking by anonymous ballot of four proposed options depicted in Venn and/or simple diagrams (see Results). Keep in mind that the needs assessment and identification of resources procedures were viewed from an open, inclusive stance from the very beginning. Because of that and the extensive communication, the approximately 1,000 total people who attended did the ranking task with awareness and knowledge. They were not uninformed.

The nature of the comments received is suggestive that the approach of the working (guiding) team was successful. For example, a number of unanticipated thoughts were raised such as if two or three high schools were envisioned might there be a loss to educational programs at each site and whether somewhat smaller schools might lead to more limited advanced course offerings and less richness in educational programming, and as a consequence, there could be negative effects on students. One surprising thing that came up, and perhaps a further unobtrusive measure of the openness of the meetings, was a concern about athletics. Two years prior to the needs assessment and assets study, the district won the championship in the top division in state football, no small achievement and one that instilled community pride. With more than one high school, there would probably be a dilution in strength as was readily acknowledged by the meeting facilitators.

When taken in their entirety, the discussions were an indication of how well this part of the process worked. They showed that the community had been engaged and was considering what should be, not just now but in the future. Everything from the rich exchanges could not be addressed in the single issue that was put on the ballot subsequently, but what community members said was summarized and fed back to the educational system for consideration at a later time.

In addition, notice that assets were cited in the comments and certainly were in evidence in the data. They dealt with community perceptions of the quality of the education children were receiving, the flexibility of school offerings, the ways in which the schools handled problems, the community involvement efforts, and the active engagement of Westington citizens in soliciting their opinions and perceptions. In the large meetings, such views as voiced by some in attendance demonstrated how the working committee deeply valued the guiding principles that drove the needs assessment and asset/capacity-building effort from the very beginning. The committee's actions clearly adhered to the principles, even though they would be time consuming relative to gathering information and carrying out the full investigation. Given what resulted, the overall approach was worth the price (in the judgment of this case's authors).

Results

Transparency and communication to the community via its inclusion during the entire effort was a major outcome. That was seen in the courteous discourse at the community meetings, even for those who might be opposed to voting for a new school or schools.

The district staff and school board learned about preferences for new educational programs, in terms of what might appeal to the community and be supported financially through a future bond initiative. The straw polls at the end of the large Phase III meetings provided input for future educational programming and the basis for a bond issue for a new high school. In the end-of-session polls, participants reviewed and rank-ordered clever, Venn-type diagrams depicting options for what the schools might do as they moved forward. For example, if three schools were a desired choice, it was easy to depict by circles the uniqueness of each school and where advantage could be taken of overlapping curricular programs. The old admonition that a picture is worth a thousand words rings particularly true.

The results, which were tabulated and incorporated into the bond issue, were strongly in favor of a configuration of multiple schools that included possible ways educational programs might be implemented across them. The issue handily passed. Without patience in pursuing a systematic needs assessment and asset path, it is suspected that much more resistance would have been encountered.

Influences

A single new high school or multiple ones is a large multimillion-dollar investment; its effects on a community would persist for many years and should not be underestimated. Given that, some perceived influences are

- A middle- to upper-middle-class suburb with many college-educated individuals (some from a large nearby university) and mid-level business managers may be more attuned to this kind of endeavor than communities with considerably less resources

- A smaller town/community mentality

- A school board with the resources to underwrite such an effort and a total educational system that is fully committed to it

- A patient community (one with the vision that not rushing to judgment is a virtue—often a commodity in short supply) and a transparent open community presence in the process

Issues and Challenges

Many factors must align for success to be achieved. The right leadership, as noted previously, was needed for this case. A receptive educational environment with resources has to be there. If not, the project probably will not realize the outcomes seen in this case. The nature of the community involved is another major issue to be considered. Communities have unique features and commonalities. How that notion comes into play was observed by Balogh, Whitelaw, and Thompson (2008) in a study of four small towns in the United Kingdom. A major finding was that some communities are more sophisticated and better suited for positively utilizing results. They have had more experience with needs and asset assessments than others. A similar idea with regard to community readiness was described by Donnermayer, Plested, Edwards, Oetting, and Littlethunder (1997). What these two sets of authors observed may be applicable here, given the nature of the community that participated in this study.

DISCUSSION QUESTIONS

1. Small-group meetings, while costly and time consuming to implement and analyze, embed ownership in the process. How could this be done less expensively without compromising quality? What are other ways for creating ownership, including their strengths and weaknesses?

2. Could surveys and electronic means be used in place of a number of community meetings? What could be gained and lost by doing so?

3. What other techniques could help in making such endeavors more economically feasible?

4. Lots of people (the working committee, teachers, volunteers, administrators, others) were part of this study. Should students have been included through classes and/or special projects, and in what ways?

5. Reams of qualitative and quantitative data lead to a quandary. How should they be assembled and put together so that community and decision-making groups get a handle on meaning? Can decision-making groups digest all facets of what has been learned in a reasonable manner, and come to thoughtful conclusions for next steps? (Good approaches for assisting individuals and groups in their deliberations about needs and assets is complex in the best of circumstances and even more so when a lot of information has been generated.)

6. How could the procedures used in this case be ratcheted up for a much bigger community? What accommodations would have to be made, and how could they be implemented in a cost-efficient manner?

7. Given that benchmarking with districts facing similar growth to that of the Westington was valuable, what should be specifically asked of other sites (what worked, pitfalls to avoid, what assets were available to them, what key events stood out, how were snags in the process handled, etc.)?

8. While education was the focus here, the process is useful for other foci, such as public health, social problems, and community development. Parts of it might apply to such settings and what adaptations or adjustments might be made for them (Engle & Altschuld, 2014)?

REFERENCES

Altschuld, J. W. (2015a). Steps 5–8, Completing the hybrid process. *Bridging the gap between asset/capacity building and needs assessment: Concepts and practical applications.* (Chapter 5, pp. 105–134). Thousand Oaks, CA: Sage.

Altschuld, J. W. (2015b). Step 4 in the hybrid framework. *Bridging the gap between asset/capacity building and needs assessment: Concepts and practical applications.* (Chapter 4, pp. 81–104). Thousand Oaks, CA: Sage.

Balogh, R., Whitelaw, S., & Thompson, J. (2008). Rapid needs appraisal in the modern NHS: Potential and dilemmas. *Critical Public Health, 18*(2), 233–244. doi:10.1080/09581590701377010

Donnermayer, J. V., Plested, B. A., Edwards, R. W., Oetting, G., & Littlethunder, I. (1997). Community readiness and prevention programs. *Journal of the Community Development Society, 28*(1), 65–83. doi:10.1080/15575339709489795

Engle, M., & Altschuld, J. W. (2014, Winter). Needs assessment: Trends and toward the future. *New Directions for Evaluation, 144,* 33–45. https://doi.org/10.1002/ev.20101

Sleezer, C. M., Russ-Eft, D. F., & Gupta, K. (2014). *A practical guide to needs assessment* (3rd ed.). San Francisco, CA: Wiley & ASTD.

A Strategic Multiyear Needs Assessment

Leadership Development for a Global Firm

N. Anand Chandrasekar and Heather Champion

Abstract

An organization-wide leadership needs assessment was carried out at A for Apparel (a pseudonym), a leading textile manufacturing group in a South Asian country that supplied apparel to many of the world's premium clothing brands. Facing intense competition, A for Apparel chose to invest in the leadership development across the enterprise to prepare itself for the future. Using a combination of surveys, interviews, and focus groups, the needs assessment process identified the business challenges, the culture of the company, the leadership skills important for success, and the skill gaps amongst its leaders. Below is an overview of the case.

Where the Needs Assessment Was Conducted	Who Conducted the Needs Assessment	Focus of Needs Assessment	How Data Were Collected	How Data Were Analyzed
Leading textile manufacturing group in a South Asian country	Staff of a nonprofit organization focused on leadership education and research	Focused on identifying business challenges, culture of the company, leadership skills for success, and skill gaps of leaders	Combination of surveys, interviews, and focus groups	1st Year: Qualitative analysis of interviews and focus groups. 2nd Year: Survey data were organized into profiles on success, leadership, leadership gap, leadership attention index, and potential challenges. Qualitative data were analyzed into categories of challenges faced, profile of effective leader; sustaining the learning; indicators of impact. 3rd Year: Incidents around collaboration and change were reported.

Background

Apparel manufacturing is the largest manufacturing industry in this South Asian country, and it has created millions of jobs, especially for women. The Center for Creative Leadership was approached by A for Apparel, one of the leading apparel manufacturing groups headquartered in a South Asian country. They had expanded rapidly, employing over 40,000 workers across 30 factories, and they were facing intense competition in the South Asia region.

The region was home to multiple large apparel manufacturers, and the company sought to differentiate itself from its competitors. As a group, while the organization was performing well, the individual business units were at different stages of development and performance. To grow the organization as a whole, the entire group was going through a massive reorganization. The owners of the company were keen on developing the talent in the company since it was vital to provide them an edge in a highly competitive business environment.

To identify and target the greatest needs of the organization and its leaders and to design the most effective leadership development solutions, we conducted a leadership needs assessment. This case study describes the tools, the process, and the impact of the leadership needs assessment.

Profile of the Organization

A for Apparel is a very large, family-owned, and export-oriented apparel manufacturing company headquartered in a South Asian country. Besides its main manufacturing centers in the country where it is headquartered, it has operations in other Asian countries and in the United States. In addition to a corporate office, the group is organized into individual business units that produce different types of textiles and apparel. Through its business units, it supplies apparel to many of the world's premium clothing brands. The apparel includes casuals, active sportswear, lingerie, sleepwear, and lounge wear.

As the first step to talent development, the company engaged consultants to develop a vision, values, and leadership competency framework. With the vision, values, and leadership development framework in place, the company approached the Center for Creative Leadership (CCL) for leadership development solutions.

With the strong belief that leadership development was essential to its success, A for Apparel was interested in engaging almost all its leaders across multiple business units and offering development across all leader levels—from the board of directors, to the first-level managers. Given the wide and deep scope of work, the developmental initiatives were spread over multiple years. The leadership needs assessment that supplemented the leadership development initiatives were also spread over multiple years. The process focused on assessing the needs of both individual leaders and the context and culture of the organization.

Needs Assessment Process

In this section, we describe the multiyear engagement with specific reference to the needs assessment process. To do so, for every year of engagement with the client, we will describe in brief the goals of the needs assessment, the tools used, the output, and the impact of the needs assessment. Table 11.1 provides an overview of the 3 years of the needs assessment in terms of the goals, the process, and the output and impact. The details are described in the subsections below.

Year 1 Goals

Given that we had just begun working with the company and that they were in the process of undergoing a massive structural reorganization, the needs assessment in the 1st year aimed at gaining an understanding of the ecosystem surrounding the company's operations, the impact of the restructuring, and its current leadership development initiatives. We were specifically interested in developing an understanding of

a. The goals of the company

b. The external and internal challenges that the company faced

c. The company's present culture and the culture that it desired to develop

d. The current leadership development initiatives the company was utilizing

e. The current strengths and developmental needs of the company's leadership

Year 1 Process

To meet Year 1 goals, faculty from CCL held one-on-one and group conversations with the owners, the board of directors, and the CEOs of several business units and members of the corporate functions. During these conversations, some of the following questions were asked:

1. What aspect of the culture at A for Apparel should never change?

2. What aspect of the culture at A for Apparel must change?

3. Which aspects of change are met with the most resistance?

Table 11.1 An Overview of Needs Assessment at A for Apparel

	Needs Assessment Goals	Needs Assessment Process	Needs Assessment Output	Needs Assessment Impact
Year 1	Develop an understanding of • The company's ecosystem • The company's current and desired culture • Current leadership development initiatives • Strengths and development needs of the top leadership (CEO, CEO 1)	Conversations with board of directors and the executive teams of top business units	Themes indicating • Company culture • Business and leadership challenges • Effect of reorganization on alignment • Developmental areas for leaders	Design of business unit specific leadership development programs targeting the CEO and CEO 1 and CEO 2 levels
Year 2	Develop a deeper and nuanced understanding of leadership development needs of the company, its business units, and groups within the company. Understand the impact of past year's leadership development initiatives.	Leadership Gap Indicator survey among all people managers. Interviews with members of the board, the CEOs, and the functional leaders of biggest business units in the group. Focus groups with leaders at same/similar organizational levels of the biggest companies in the group.	Quantitative Output: Leadership Gap Indicator survey report with data broken out by business unit, function, and organization level. The data indicated with competencies were most in need of development. Qualitative Output: Verbatim quotes and examples of challenges faced, profile of effective leader, suggestions for sustaining the learning, and indicators of impact.	Identification of four specific competencies for development. Design and delivery of leadership development initiatives targeted to develop the identified four competencies.

(Continued)

(Continued)

| **Year 3** | Gather examples of successful and unsuccessful examples of change and collaboration at A for Apparel. | Email answers to three questions. | Collaborating behaviors. Change behaviors. Stories of successful and unsuccessful incidents of collaboration and change. Factors that aided successful collaboration and change efforts. Factors that derailed collaboration and change efforts. |

Source: Adapted from Leslie, J. B., Chandrasekar, A., & Barts, D. (2015). *Leadership gap indicator.* Greensboro, NC: Center for Creative Leadership.

4. What are the expectations of the transformation initiative that is underway?

5. With respect to the reorganization:

    a) How has your job changed or been affected by the new structure?

    b) How do you see your role on your respective leadership team?

    c) What questions do you still have relative to the new structure? Where do you need more clarity?

    d) Where do you see potential inefficiencies?

    e) What do you recommend?

Year 1 Output and Impact

The output of these conversations were summarized in text form. These notes were read by CCL faculty and led to the design and delivery of business unit specific leadership development programs for the CEO and CEO 1 level of the key business units. In addition to attending leadership development programs as an intact team, the CEOs also attended CCL's Leadership at the Peak program, a leadership development program specially designed for C-suite leaders.

Year 2 Goals

After a year of working with A for Apparel, both CCL and the human resource team at A for Apparel felt the need for a deeper and nuanced understanding of the needs of the company. There was also a need to understand the impact of the development initiatives undertaken in the past year, where it had helped, and what more needed to be done to enable the company's success. In other words, the needs assessment in the 2nd year was both a needs assessment and an evaluation of the impact of the past year's work.

Year 2 Process

To meet the Year 2 goals, a Leadership Gap Indicator survey (LGI) (Leslie, Chandrasekar, & Barts, 2005) was launched. The LGI is a tool for assessing managers' views about their leadership development needs. Managers assess the relative importance of select leadership competencies for success now and in the future and rate their peer group's ability to perform on these competencies. Gaps are exposed when these data reveal a deficit between managers' current and desired state of leadership capability.

The 25 competencies chosen to be included in the LGI represented A for Apparel's leadership competency framework and were organized into nine clusters. The LGI survey was rolled out to every people manager across all group companies, with the exception of first-line supervisors. The survey was positioned as an opportunity for the employees to make their voices heard and to offer their opinions in the company's transformation. Weekly reminders were sent by the survey administrators to those who had not completed the survey, resulting in the extremely high response rate of 87%.

Almost 2,000 managers/leaders completed the survey. They came from three different countries in South Asia. Respondents were 77% male. They were employed in 21 different group companies, across nine functions and eight organizational levels.

As stated, the second goal of the needs assessment was to understand the impact of the past years' initiatives. Fifteen focus groups were conducted with leaders of similar organizational levels from seven of the biggest companies in the group. Individual interviews were conducted with members of the Board, the CEOs, and the functional leaders of the biggest companies in the group. These interviews and focus groups sought to understand:

- Changes in business strategy and new challenges faced.

- Aspects of culture that support and detract from achieving the strategy.

- Perspectives on how leaders were applying their learning from leadership development initiatives.

- Aids and barriers to applying the leadership learning.

- Suggestions that they had for sustaining the leadership learning.

Year 2 Output

The output from the quantitative information obtained from CCI's LGI was organized into five sections as follows:

1. *Success Profile*: Which leadership competencies are critical for success in your organization?

2. *Leadership Profile*: How strong are your managers in these critical competencies?

3. *Leadership Gap Profile*: How aligned are your managers' strengths with what is considered important?

Every leadership competency was classified as being:

- On Track (OT): Competencies that are considered strengths and are important
- Key Gaps (GAP): Competencies that are not considered strengths but are important
- Reserves (R): Competencies that are not considered strengths and are less important
- Over Investments (OI): Competencies that are considered strengths but less important

4. *Leadership Attention Index*: Where should your organization focus its leadership development efforts?

5. *Potential Challenges*: What factors may lead to the derailment of leaders in your organization?

In addition to an overall LGI report for the entire group, specific LGI reports were generated for each of the 21 business units, seven functional units, and five organizational levels.

The individual business and functional unit reports were shared with the respective heads, giving them information to make decisions about the needs that were specific to their units.

Year 2 Output

An overall report that compared the LGI findings across multiple business units, functions, and organization levels was also generated. This allowed the decisions makers to determine, at a glance, the strengths and developmental needs across all groups being compared, as well as determining unique development needs of a particular group. An example of the output by organization level is shown in Figure 11.1.

Figure 11.1 Comparison of Leadership Development Needs Across Five Organization Levels—A Sample Output

LGI Competency	Level 1	Level 2	Level 3	Level 4	Level 5
Being a quick learner	GAP	GAP	GAP	R	OT
Change management	OI	OI	OT	OT	OI
Decisiveness	GAP	GAP	GAP	R	GAP
Strategic perspective	R	R	R	R	R
Strategic planning	OT	OT	R	R	OT
Building collaborative relationships	GAP	OT	R	OT	GAP
Compassion & sensitivity	OI	R	OI	OI	R
Confronting problem employees	OT	OT	OT	OI	OT
Employee development	R	OI	OI	OT	R
Inspiring commitment	R	R	GAP	GAP	OT
Leading employees	R	OT	OT	OT	R
Participative management	R	R	R	R	R

Legend: OT, On track; GAP, Key gaps; R, Reserves; OI, Over investments.

The findings of the interviews and focus groups were themed and presented under four categories: challenges faced, profile of effective leader, sustaining the learning, and indicators of impact. Table 11.2 provides an overview of how the outputs were organized.

In addition to providing verbatim quotes from the interviews and focus groups, we also provided a summary interpreting the findings, and recommendations on areas of focus for the transformation initiatives.

Year 2 Impact

As a result of the deep and wide needs assessment done in the 2nd year, A for Apparel was able to identify four specific areas of leadership development for their managers. Targeted leadership development initiatives were designed to develop the capacity of the leadership in these specific areas. The needs assessment also created an opportunity for the top leadership team to come together, discuss areas of alignment, areas of misalignment, and make adjustments to their evolving organizational structure.

Table 11.2	Organization of Needs Analysis Qualitative Output
Challenges Faced	• What would you identify as significant challenges that <business unit> faces at this time? • What are challenges that leaders at your level face in <business unit>?
Profile of Effective Leader	• What qualities/behaviors do <business unit> leaders need to address these challenges? • What characteristics, skills, competencies, or behaviors make a leader at <business unit> effective?
Sustaining the Learning	• How can we support <business unit> leaders to consistently demonstrate the desired leadership behaviors? • Think of the leadership development efforts over the last 2 years (CCL Training, e-learning). What would help you to better apply the learning?
Indicators of Impact	• When these leadership development initiatives are successful . . . (complete the sentence).

Year 3 Goals

Considering the wide and deep needs assessment that was conducted in the 2nd year, we considered going for a more targeted needs analysis in the 3rd year. By the start of the 3rd year, the organizational transformation initiatives on two of the four areas identified had touched a majority of leaders at A for Apparel. The two areas on which the initiatives had progressed most were on enhancing collaboration and on managing change. The faculty delivering the leadership programs were interested in using examples of how collaboration and change were happening at A for Apparel, so that the leaders would be able to relate better. The goal of the needs assessment in the 3rd year targeted gathering examples of successful and unsuccessful change and collaboration efforts within A for Apparel.

Year 3 Process

Toward achieving the Year 3 goal, we surveyed a group of leaders selected by human resources and the business unit heads.

Leaders were asked to reflect on their work in their organization and

1. List actions that they or their coworkers do when they "collaborate" or when they were faced with "change"

2. Recall incidents of successful "collaboration" and "change" and relate a short story about the incident including information on what happened, the people involved in it, and specific actions that they did

3. Recall incidents of unsuccessful "collaboration" and "change" and relate a short story about the incident including information on why it was unsuccessful, and specific actions that could have made it successful

Year 3 Outcomes and Impact

Leaders shared stories of successful and unsuccessful collaboration and change efforts at A for Apparel. These powerful stories were picked up by the faculty and used in leadership development programs to illustrate areas of strength and development in an engaging manner.

Influences

Having presented a picture of the multiyear needs assessment that CCL undertook at A for Apparel, it is important to understand the influences affecting this work.

Commitment of Top Leadership Team

The commitment of the top leadership team, including the board of directors of the holding company and the leadership teams of the business units, to deep and wide transformation was a key influence in enabling CCL to conduct needs assessments over multiple years. We have encountered, in the course of our work, other organizations, where a formal needs assessment is often passed over, with one or two members of the leadership team or the HR team indicating areas for development based on their perspectives. At A for Apparel, the commitment exhibited by the top leadership team to transformation and employee development allowed us the access and the resources to conduct a deep and wide needs assessment.

The commitment was clearly exhibited in the manner in which high response rates were obtained for the LGI survey. Working together with the human resources departments, there was relentless follow-up and reminders to get leaders to fill in the survey. Given the organizational culture, it was acceptable to call up individual leaders, remind them that they had not completed, and get them to complete the survey.

The environment of being a family-owned company and having a certain level of hierarchical power structure helped the researchers gain necessary access to leaders once the initiative was signed off at higher management levels.

Creating a Sense of Inclusion With Confidentiality

The LGI survey, interviews, focus groups, and surveys were all positioned as an invitation by management to share and shape the future of the company together. This was especially true of the LGI survey. A series of teasers were sent out before the survey was actually sent out, thus creating a buzz and expectation around the survey.

All needs assessment initiatives were treated with a high level of confidentiality and no leader was individually identified in any of the reports that we delivered back to the company. In the LGI survey, leaders answered survey questions with a peer group as their reference point. This might have served to reduce individual response biases. In conducting focus groups, we ensured that all attendees were of a similar management level, allowing them to freely share their concerns without the worry of any higher authority present.

Issues and Challenges

As with many organizational interventions, this needs assessment team experienced issues and challenges.

Language

This was an issue for some leaders at the lower organization levels. The English language used in the survey was made simpler, and some phrases were substituted so that it would correctly convey the sense in more common words.

Taking an Enterprise View

The needs assessment in the 2nd year (LGI) covered all of the business units of A for Apparel. Since the LGI reports were also generated by business unit, there was a tendency among the CEOs of the respective business units to pay more attention to their particular business unit. The company owners and the board wanted the CEOs to think beyond their business unit and consider their implications for the entire enterprise. To help gain this perspective, CCL organized a 2-day session for the business unit and the functional heads. Over 2 days, they were organized into pairs, read each other's business unit/functional LGI reports in detail, and coached each other in steps that they could take to address leadership gaps in the peer's function/business unit. This helped them to look at similarities and differences in their needs and view the development plans from a more holistic enterprise-wide perspective.

DISCUSSION QUESTIONS

1. Who were the critical stakeholders needed to successfully implement this needs assessment? Does this vary depending on the approaches or methods being used? The leader level or individuals being targeted? Country or region? Functional area of the business?

2. How important was it to have support at the most senior levels?

3. What factors contributed to the successful use and application of the findings of the needs assessment?

4. How was the needs assessment in this case used to help support evaluating the impact of the initiative?

REFERENCE

Leslie, J. B., Chandrasekar, A., & Barts, D. (2015). *Leadership Gap Indicator* [Measurement instrument]. Greensboro, NC: Center for Creative Leadership.

Needs Assessment in Rural Communities

Eric Einspruch

Abstract

The Coalition works with six communities on a large, remote U.S. island. It received state funding to address behavioral health concerns, beginning with a needs assessment. Coalition staff surveyed a random sample of adults living in the six communities, supplemented by a survey of a convenience sample in one community. Respondents in each community identified what they thought was the most important problem in their community, that is, the one they thought the Coalition should work on in their community first. Below is an overview of the case.

Where the Needs Assessment Was Conducted	Who Conducted the Needs Assessment	Focus of Needs Assessment	How Data Were Collected	How Data Were Analyzed
Six communities on a large, remote U.S. island	External consultant	Identified most important behavioral health problem in each community to provide a focus for future work	Surveys (collected via interviews)	Quantitative survey data: descriptive statistics (i.e., frequency distributions); qualitative data were summarized

Background

In 2014, the Coalition received funding from the state's Department of Health and Social Services, Division of Behavioral Health, through a funding stream that supports behavioral health prevention and early intervention services. This program follows the federal Substance Abuse and Mental Health Services Administration's (US DHHS, Substance Abuse and Mental Health Services Administration

[SAMHSA], 2018) five-step Strategic Prevention Framework (SPF) process. The five steps in this process are assessment, capacity building, planning, implementation, and evaluation. As described by the state in documentation to grantees,

> A community assessment is a tool that can be used to understand a community's needs based on available resources and readiness to address community concerns, issues, problems or challenges. In short, it tells an objective story about the conditions and characteristics of a community. By collecting primary and secondary data, the tool begins to take shape and helps to describe substance use, mental health issues, and suicide within the community, as well as the impact of these behavioral health conditions, current prevention/enforcement activities already being used, and gaps in community resources. This information can be used to educate community members and stakeholders, dispel misconceptions, review current prevention efforts, and prioritize strategies to address the most pressing concerns identified during the assessment process.

The assessment step consisted of two parts: a needs assessment was conducted first, followed by a community readiness assessment based on the Colorado State University's Tri-Ethnic Center model of community readiness (Stanley, 2014). This case study focuses only on the needs assessment. The needs and readiness assessments were elements of a broader Coalition evaluation, which was primarily conducted by a team of two people. One of them was an independent program evaluator with many years of experience. The other team member was a longtime program manager, grant writer, and strategic planner who also brought experience with program evaluation. The team was supplemented by two independent program evaluators for one data collection activity. Throughout the evaluation, the evaluation team focused on building the evaluation capacity of the Coalition staff. In particular, the evaluation team worked with Coalition staff to plan and implement the various evaluation activities and to understand and interpret the evaluation results. The Coalition staff included seven members: an executive director from the fiscal agent and six liaisons (one for each Coalition community). One of these six also served as the coordinator for the Coalition.

By building evaluation capacity, the evaluation team sought to increase the Coalition's ability to use the evaluation results to facilitate ongoing program improvement and to be able to continue evaluation efforts beyond the life of the grant funding. Thus, the evaluation team led the development of the assessment process, trained Coalition staff to collect the assessment data, analyzed and reported the assessment results, and worked with Coalition staff and members to understand and interpret the assessment results. Coalition staff were community members hired part-time to work on the grant. Other Coalition members were additional community members who joined the Coalition. This may be considered an example of a strategic needs assessment, as described in Sleezer, Russ-Eft, and Gupta (2014).

Profile of the Organization

The Coalition is a small organization with representatives from six communities on a large island in a remote area of the United States. Four of the communities lie in a north–south direction, and the two of these four communities that are the farthest apart are separated by a road that is about 77 miles long and takes almost 3 hours to drive. Two of the communities lie to the east, connected to the other four by a road, part of which is dirt road rather than paved road. The road from (about) the middle of the north–south communities to the eastern-most communities is just over 50 miles long and takes almost 2 hours to drive. Some services are for a local community, while others are provided on an island-wide basis (that is, a person would travel from one community to another to receive a service that is located in only one community, but also can be provided to a member of another community). Internet is available on the island, only recently arriving in one of the communities. The Coalition's fiscal agent is a nonprofit health services organization. Coalition members represent a variety of community sectors ranging from nonprofit social services to local businesses.

Preassessment Information

The first step of the Strategic Prevention Framework process was to assess community needs. As part of completing this step, Coalition staff surveyed a random sample of adults living in the six communities served by the Coalition. A separate sample was drawn for each community, so that relevant community-specific reports could be prepared. The list of people from which the evaluation team drew the sample was compiled from sources that varied by community. The evaluation team worked closely with the Coalition to convey the importance of a complete and accurate sampling frame, random sampling of respondents from the sampling frame, and achieving a high survey completion rate among respondents, emphasizing that this level of rigor would maximize the generalizability of the results, and therefore their usefulness. This level of rigor was reasonably implemented in five of the communities. In one community, however, despite considerable efforts by Coalition staff, the participation rate was low, and the random sample had to be supplemented with a convenience sample. To improve the convenience sample, the evaluation team structured the sample so that data were collected at different times, on different days, and in different locations frequented by community members. Table 12.1 details the source of the list for the sampling frame, the number of adults in the community, the number and percent sampled, and the number and percent of those sampled who were surveyed. Note that in some communities, the staff member reviewed the relevant sample list and made changes to reflect recent movements within the community. Also, in one community many of the people who were sampled turned out no longer to be living there, so that additional people were added to the sample.

Community	Source of List of Adults in the Community	Number of Adults in the Community	Number (Percentage) Sampled	Number (Percentage of Sample) Surveyed
Community 1	City water and garbage service records, city voter list, communication between staff and community members	941	100 (11%); during the assessment, 42 people were added to the sample to replace sampled persons no longer living in the community	Twenty-three of the sampled persons plus 31 persons added as a convenience sample obtained at the local grocery store—a total of 54 persons
Community 2	Coalition staff who went from house to house and recorded the names of those over 18 years of age	237	50 (21%)	33 (66%)
Community 3	List obtained from the city, which was then updated by local community members	43	22 (51%)	14 (64%)
Community 4	City voter list supplemented by feedback from Coalition staff who worked with community members to identify and add persons not on the voter list	444	50 (11%)	22 (44%)

(*Continued*)

Community 5	Coalition staff who went from house to house and recorded the names of those over 18 years of age	73	37 (51%)	29 (78%)
Community 6	City water and garbage service records, city voter list, and communication between Coalition staff and community members	334	50 (15%)	30 (60%)

Needs Assessment Process

The needs assessment survey was administered by interview rather than as a paper-and-pen or an online survey. This format was chosen based on local understanding that community members would be far more likely to respond to this format than another format (e.g., paper-and-pen or online). The survey was developed in close collaboration with Coalition members and staff, to ensure that the questions were relevant to the community and to Coalition members' interest. The survey included questions about community strengths, behavioral health and other social problems, and perceived availability of services in the respondent's community. In general, respondents were asked to

- Name three strengths that make their community a good place to live

- Name the top two problems in their community related to alcohol and other drug use, the top two problems related to mental health, and the top two other social problems not already mentioned

- From these six problems, select the most important problem (that is, the one they think the Coalition should work on in their community first)

To elaborate on the topic that they identified as the most important problem, respondents provided their perceptions of the cause for concern about the problem, the cause of the problem, existing efforts to address the problem, strengths that contribute to solving the problem, barriers to solving the problem, and cultural values that could help address the problem. Respondents were asked to indicate, to the best of their knowledge, whether or not selected services existed in their community. From a list of 14 services, respondents were asked to indicate (one a scale of 1 to 5) for each service whether

The service is not available and it is not needed (1)

The service is not available but is needed (2)

The service is available but does not meet the level of need for the service (3)

The service is available and meets the level of need for the service (4)

Don't know (5)

Finally, respondents were asked for their perception of how ready the community was to address the problem. This latter question was not intended to be a full readiness assessment, which was conducted as a second step in the assessment process. Rather, it was intended as a supplement to the readiness assessment, providing a point of information from the random sample of adults in the community. The lead evaluator created frequency distributions for each community detailing the results of the quantitative data, and a second member of the evaluation team summarized the qualitative data (i.e., responses to open-ended questions). A community-level report was prepared for each of the six communities.

Results of the Needs Assessment

The survey results included the top priority issue identified by community members, along with related perceptions in response to the questions mentioned above. The results were consistent with a previous needs assessment conducted a few years earlier, which were already generally known by people in the community who were interested and by the evaluation team. The evaluation team prepared a report for each community, communicating the methods and results in a brief document written for a nontechnical audience. The evaluation team noted that Coalition members could use the needs assessment results as one source of information as they select the priority issue in each community to address with the grant, and that once a priority was selected, an assessment of community readiness to address the issue would be conducted as part of the grant process. The results of the needs assessment are summarized below.

Community 1

Of the 54 community members surveyed, 15 people (28%) thought that the willingness of people to help one another was a strength that made the community a good place to live. Other strengths mentioned included the small and rural nature of the community, community togetherness, outdoor activities, youth activities, the people and friendships, facilities, and the low crime rate. The results indicated that community members thought that *alcohol and other drug use* was the priority issue that the Coalition should address first. The results also detailed specific aspects of this priority that respondents believed were important. Community members who identified alcohol and other drug use as the priority issue (39% of the respondents) were concerned about the impacts on families. Respondents identified lack of activities and addiction as the main causes of alcohol and drug use in the community. To address the problem, respondents pointed to the strengths of togetherness and caring people. Respondents who identified this priority problem generally thought the problem was being poorly addressed by existing services in the community, and that their community was somewhat ready to make changes to reduce or eliminate the problem.

Community 2

Of the 33 community members surveyed, 17 people (52%) thought that the general community togetherness was a strength that made the community a good place to live. Native culture was identified as a strength by 13 respondents, and family ties were mentioned by 11 respondents. Hunting and fishing and the subsistence lifestyle were also commonly identified as strengths of the community. The results indicated that community members thought *alcohol and other drug use* was the priority that the Coalition should address first. The results also detailed specific aspects of this priority that respondents believed were important. Community members who identified alcohol and other drug use as the priority issue (88% of the respondents) were most concerned because of the presence and accessibility of alcohol and drugs, as well as the thefts related to alcohol and drug use. Respondents identified the presence of alcohol and drugs as the main cause of the issue, and most respondents thought that nothing was being done about the problem, likely because of denial of the issue. To address the problem, respondents pointed to the strengths of families, and suggested that Native activities and values could help address alcohol and drug use.

Community 3

Of the 14 community members surveyed, nine thought that community togetherness was a strength that made the community a good place to live. Other strengths commonly identified included Native culture, and the community's small size and rural location. The results indicated that community members thought that *depression and lack of activities for youth* were tied for the priority that the Coalition should address first. Those who identified these problems pointed to lack of available activities. Though some community activities did exist that addressed the problems, lack of funding was seen as an obstacle to effectively addressing the problems. Respondents indicated that Native language and art activities could contribute to addressing the problems.

Community 4

Of the 22 community members surveyed, 10 people (45%) thought that the small size of the community was a strength that made the community a good place to live. Other strengths commonly identified included community togetherness and Native culture (9 respondents each). The family-oriented quality of the community, as well as the mutual financial support that was offered among residents, were also mentioned as significant strengths of the community. The results indicated that community members thought *alcohol and other drug use* was the priority that the Coalition should address first. Community members who identified alcohol and other drug use as the priority issue (86% of the respondents) were concerned about the issue because of youth substance use and because of how normalized substance use had become in the community. Most respondents identified the causes of the problem as the availability and accessibility of alcohol and other drugs, and the normalization of substance use. Most respondents thought that nothing was currently being done in the community to address the problem, likely because of embarrassment or denial of the issue. To address the problem, respondents suggested creating more youth and culturally focused activities.

Community 5

Of the 29 community members surveyed, 15 people (52%) thought that the small and rural setting of the community was a strength that made the community a good place to live. Other strengths commonly identified included hunting and fishing, community togetherness, the general good nature of the people in the community, limited government, and the connection to the new road system. The results indicated that community members thought *alcohol and other drug use* was the priority issue that the Coalition should address first. The results also detailed specific aspects of this priority that respondents believed were important. Community members who identified alcohol and other drug use as the priority issue (69% of the respondents) thought that the availability of drugs and alcohol or a lack of individual moral values were the main causes of alcohol and drug use in the community, and most respondents thought that nothing was being done about the problem. To address the problem, respondents suggested that faith-based activities, community activities, and health education may be effective in addressing drug and alcohol use. Respondents who identified this priority problem generally thought the problem was being poorly addressed by existing services in the community, and that their community was not very ready to make changes to reduce or eliminate the problem.

Community 6

Of the 30 community members surveyed, 12 people (40%) felt that the community's friendly people provided a strength that made the community a good place to live. Other strengths commonly identified included connections among community members, practical amenities such as clinics and grocery stores, and the rural location. The small size of the community and hunting and fishing were also mentioned as strengths of the community. Less commonly identified strengths included the beautiful scenery, outdoor activities, family-oriented community, and a quality school. The results indicated that community members thought *alcohol and other drug use* was the priority that the Coalition should address first. Community members who identified alcohol and other drug use as the priority issue (50% of the respondents) thought that patterns of substance abuse were in part established when parents used substances around their children, making substances easier to access and more acceptable to use. Respondents identified physiological addiction and a lack of alternative activities as the main causes of alcohol and drug use in the community, and most respondents thought that nothing was being done about the problem. To address the problem, respondents pointed to the strengths of a caring and connected community. Respondents who identified this priority problem generally thought the problem was being poorly addressed by existing services in the community, and that their community was somewhat ready to make changes to reduce or eliminate the problem.

Influences

The communities served by the Coalition are very small, relatively far apart, and in a remote area. In addition, completing yet another survey is often not a priority of community members. Coalition staff therefore had to expend considerable effort to complete data collection. One of the influences on the assessment, which increased the interest in it being conducted, was that it was required by their grant funding. Another influence was that community members wanted to ensure that the current assessment built on an assessment that had been conducted a few years before, rather than simply repeating the earlier assessment. Finally, the evaluation team influenced the assessment by strongly encouraging that the assessment be conducted as rigorously as reasonably possible, to best ensure its generalizability and usefulness.

Issues and Challenges

The Coalition was understandably interested in building evaluation capacity so that staff could better understand evaluation and carry out evaluation activities after the end of the grant. Since Coalition staff carried out the data collection as part of an evaluation capacity building effort, they therefore had to be trained. The evaluation team provided details of the procedures for conducting the interviews and provided training via teleconference prior to beginning the assessment. Although it was challenging to deliver training via teleconference, it was, nevertheless, accomplished, and such training provided a way to overcome the challenge of local data collection when the evaluation team resided in a different area.

As noted previously, response rates to the random sample were reasonable in five of the six communities. In the sixth community, the random sample had to be supplemented with a convenience sample, representing the need to balance rigor with real-world constraints. Even though the data collection for the convenience sample was structured to improve the sample, it still had the potential disadvantages of a nonrandom sample.

DISCUSSION QUESTIONS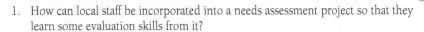

1. How can local staff be incorporated into a needs assessment project so that they learn some evaluation skills from it?

2. What are the challenges posed by having to train local staff from a distant location?

3. How do we balance striving for the greatest rigor possible with real-world constraints?

4. One of the communities supplemented the random sample with a convenience sampling method. What, if any, issues might arise with a convenience sample?

5. What might be the benefits and the challenges of having local staff undertaking the data collection?

6. How can use of the results of the needs assessment be encouraged?

REFERENCES

Sleezer, C. M., Russ-Eft, D., & Gupta, K. (2014). *A practical guide to needs assessment* (3rd ed.). San Francisco, CA: Wiley & ASTD.

Stanley, L. R. (2014). *Community readiness for community change* (2nd ed.). Fort Collins, CO: Colorado State University.

U.S. DHHS, Substance Abuse and Mental Health Services Administration. (2018). *Applying the strategic prevention framework*. Retrieved from https://www.samhsa .gov/capt/applying-strategic-prevention-framework.

13

Assessing Needs of a Community College

A Mixed Methods Case Study

P. Cristian Gugiu

The Ohio State University

Abstract

This case study focuses on the analysis and use of open-ended survey data that were collected as part of a strategic needs assessment for a community college. The needs assessment surveyed students, instructors, administrators, office staff, librarians, custodians, and security guards. These surveys netted 1,201 open-ended responses that were coded into 2,142 distinguishable statements and that were used to create eight macro values: (a) safety and security, (b) student behavior and policy, (c) quality of life, (d) health and sanitation, (e) management, (f) factors that impact student learning, (g) staff job performance, and (h) resources. These macro values were comprised of 38 subdimensions (i.e., micro values). The importance ratings provided quantitative data that were analyzed statistically. This chapter only provides findings regarding one of the macro values: that of safety and security. Below is an overview of the case.

Where the Needs Assessment Was Conducted	Who Conducted the Needs Assessment	Focus of Needs Assessment	How Data Were Collected	How Data Were Analyzed
Community college in Latin America and the Caribbean	Two external consultants who were doctoral students	Focused on determining major factors (i.e., student needs), influenced by college's actions, facilities, policies, or resources, that affected student life.	Surveys completed by 49 staff and 291 students; only 200 respondents provided responses to the open-ended inquiries.	Thematically analyzed open-ended responses; eight categories identified: (a) safety and security, (b) student behavior and policy, (c) quality of life, (d) health and sanitation, (e) management, (f) factors that impact student learning, (g) staff job performance, and (h) resources. Likert-type items were analyzed using descriptive statistics and analysis of variance to compare student and staff responses.

Background

The needs assessment literature contains few cases that describe in detail the use of statistics to analyze qualitative survey data. This case study addresses that void by describing the collection, analysis, and use of open-ended survey responses to undertake further statistical analyses. To protect confidentiality, a pseudonym (i.e., CC) replaces the name of the organization throughout the case. Note that much of the information in this case was delivered to the CC in the final report for the project.

The needs assessment was part of a larger evaluation project for the CC. A participatory evaluation methodology was used to elicit the values, standards, and grading rubric used to synthesize performance into summative evaluation conclusions. Hence, the study methods were structured to conform to the value system of the society in which the study was conducted. The evaluative methodology was contingent upon the identification of criteria or values[1] that affected the

---

[1] The terms *criteria* and *values* will be used interchangeably throughout this report to refer to the factors (representing merit, worth, or significance) that are relevant for evaluating the CC.

lives of the target population (i.e., the students and the staff). The open-ended survey data—after analysis—were used in conjunction with information from the survey's scale items and information gained from individuals to reveal problem areas within the CC; assess the impact of each value on student academic performance and quality of life; determine the extent of the concerns expressed for each value; rank each value based on stakeholder input and comparison with other values; analyze discrepancies between the concerns expressed by students and staff; and when warranted, provide suggestions for alleviating some of the problems.

Profile of the Organization

The CC was located in a country in the Latin America and the Caribbean region. It offered courses in 20 subject areas, including accounting, art and design, biology, business studies, chemistry, computing, economics, French, geography, history, information technology, law, literature, mathematics, physical education, physics, psychology, Spanish, and sociology. The CC had 1,014 students and 70 staff. The CC's top administrative official was the principal.

Preassessment Information

Globalization affects businesses and industry; it also affects educational institutions. Simply put, educational institutions must use their limited resources to deal with ever greater complexity. A strategic needs assessment can be used to examine an organization's existing performance problems (Sleezer, Russ-Eft, & Gupta, 2014).

This needs assessment was part of a larger evaluation that was conducted by two principal evaluators as part of their doctoral studies. Interview and records data were collected by a local collaborator with whom they regularly communicated. As one of its data collection methods, the needs assessment included surveys with scaled and open-ended items. This case study describes the analysis of the surveys' qualitative data and the integration of that data with the quantitative, scaled responses, and with the information contributed by individuals.

Needs Assessment Process

The evaluation team developed a survey instrument for each of the CC's following groups: students, instructors, administrators, office staff, librarians, cleaners, and security guards. The survey instruments reflected the literature and information contributed by CC decision makers. Each survey was designed to elicit the macro and micro values,[2] or factors, relevant for evaluating the CC's performance. Figure 13.1

---

[2] Micro values measure the performance of the CC on a single dimension of merit, worth, or significance, whereas macro values encompass several related micro values (Gugiu, 2007, 2011). For example, an evaluation of staff job performance (macro value) may entail examination of instructor competence, staff competence, and staff training (micro values).

A. Identify the major factors (i.e., student needs) that affect student life. Please limit this list to those factors that are directly or indirectly influenced by the CC's actions, facilities, policies, resources, etc. The list should include factors that the CC is aware of, as well as any factors that you believe the CC is largely unaware of. This list may include factors already included in this survey but is not limited to this list. *Please feel free to include any additional factors that impact student life but were not included in this survey.* Also, make sure to specify the nature of these factors and how they may impact student life.

B. Prioritize the list of factors provided above with respect to (a) the level of attention it should receive from the administration, (b) its impact on your academic performance, and (c) its impact on your quality of life in school.

Figure 13.1	Sample Items From the Student Survey Instrument	
	What is the impact of this factor on your academic performance?	What is the impact of this factor on your quality of life at school?
Rank the factors you listed above in order of the importance it should receive from the administration (i.e., which problems should they attempt to solve first).	① Almost no impact ② Very little impact ③ Slight impact	④ Moderate impact ⑤ A lot of impact ⑥ A great deal of impact
1. (Most important)	① ② ③ ④ ⑤ ⑥	① ② ③ ④ ⑤ ⑥
⋮	⋮ ⋮ ⋮ ⋮ ⋮ ⋮	⋮ ⋮ ⋮ ⋮ ⋮ ⋮
10. (Least important)	① ② ③ ④ ⑤ ⑥	① ② ③ ④ ⑤ ⑥

presents a sample of the items included in the student survey instrument. Similar items were included in the surveys administered to other key informants.

Librarians, office staff, cleaners, and security guards were asked to list in their survey the values that affected the performance of their duties. These staff were also given the opportunity to provide additional needs apart from those that affected the performance of their duties. In slight contrast, students, instructors, and administrators were specifically asked to comment on all the needs that affected the overall performance of the college.

Survey responses were collected via printed surveys since electronic means of collection were not possible. Staff responses were either anonymous or confidential depending upon whether the staff preferred to drop the survey off in a box or have their responses collected via an interview with a staff member who collaborated with the principal evaluators. Participation in the study was optional. Approval to conduct the study was obtained from the Ministry of Education, school administrators, and the student council. Student survey data were collected during class time, whereas staff survey data were collected over the course of a month.

Table 13.1 presents the survey completion rate for all the CC staff. Only 42 of the 49 staff respondents provided responses to the open-ended inquiries. This small drop in the response rate is likely due to the length of the surveys. Post-hoc analyses of demographic data between respondents and nonrespondents did not reveal any meaningful differences.

A total of 291 surveys were completed by students. However, only 200 respondents provided responses to the open-ended inquiries. According to the survey administrator, this modest response rate was due to the length of the student survey, which exceeded 40 minutes for some students. Post-hoc analyses

Table 13.1   Survey Completion for CC Staff

CC Staff	Surveys Distributed	Surveys Returned	Percent Completed
Administrators	2	2	100
Lecturers	20	17	85
Tutors	27	11	41
Librarians	7	7	100
Office Staff	5	3	60
Cleaners	4	4	100
Security Guards	5	5	100
Total	70	49	70

Table 13.2   Survey Completion for CC Students by Department

DASGS Students	Total Population	Surveys Completed	Percent Sampled
Arts and Humanities	546	152	27.8
Business and Social Science	292	85	29.1
Natural Sciences	176	54	30.7
Total	1,014	291	28.7

of demographic data between respondents and nonrespondents did not reveal any meaningful differences. Hence, the results derived from qualitative responses generalized to the entire student population with only a minor increase (1.4%) in sampling error due to the reduction in sample size for these analyses. Table 13.2 presents the completion rate of students by each of the three CC departments.

Qualitative Data Analysis

This section describes the qualitative data coding scheme and the macro- and micro-value data sources. It includes details on determining inter-rater reliability as well.

Qualitative Data Coding Scheme. A total of 1,201 open-ended responses were provided to the needs assessment surveys by 200 students and 42 staff (see Table 13.3).

Consequently, it was necessary to develop a coding rubric to reduce the qualitative data to a set of key needs that facilitated comparisons between respondents and coding categories. This rubric was developed thematically by analyzing all the open-ended responses and developing a comprehensive and reliable classification system. The resulting coding rubric consisted of eight categories (i.e., macro values): (a) safety and security, (b) student behavior and policy, (c) quality of life, (d) health and sanitation, (e) management, (f) factors that impact student learning, (g) staff job performance, and (h) resources. These macro values were comprised of 38 subdimensions (i.e., micro values). For example, the student behavior and policy macro value consisted of four micro values measuring peer pressure, student behavior, disciplinary policies and procedures, and student dress code.

Analysis of the classification power of the coding rubric revealed that the two raters (i.e., the evaluation team members) were able to successfully code

Table 13.3   Number of Open-Ended Responses to Needs Assessment Inquiries

Source	Raw Statements		Classified Needs	
	Number	Percent	Number	Percent
Students	855	71.2	1,434	66.9
Instructors	163	13.6	340	15.9
Administration	28	2.3	82	3.8
Office staff	22	1.8	41	1.9
Librarians	53	4.4	97	4.5
Cleaners	26	2.2	60	2.8
Security guards	54	4.5	88	4.1
Total	**1,201**	**100.0**	**2,142**	**100.0**

92% of all the statements into one or more micro values. Some statements were assigned multiple codes because a respondent may have listed several needs in one statement. Occasionally, however, a statement was assigned more than one code if the content embodied more than one value. This was particularly the case with resources that not only represented itself but also impacted other values. For example, the statement "*Insufficient classrooms, sometimes students have to go outside to have classes*" expressed a lack of adequate resources and also suggested that this need impacted student learning. Thus, the statement expressed two needs: one for adequate resources and the other for student learning. Fortunately, a macro-value code could be assigned to a majority of the statements for which a micro-value code could not be assigned. Consequently, over 98% of the open-ended responses were classified by the coding rubric.

Interrater agreement analyses for the 38 micro values were conducted to determine the extent to which the two raters assigned the same code(s) to open-ended statements. These analyses indicated that the coding scheme was very reliable. Examination of the phi correlations (φ) indicated that the agreement rate exceeded the generally accepted minimum standard of 0.70 for 28 of the 36 micro values. Interrater analyses of the macro-value codes also revealed very high phi correlations, ranging from 0.729 to 0.966. Therefore, the 1,201 open-ended responses were classified into 2,142 needs.

Double-counting occurs when the same datum is counted more than once. This practice has the potential to bias results by giving more weight to respondents who repeatedly complain about the same need. To reduce bias from double-counting, individual-level data in the final data set were coded so that micro-value indicators only designated whether an individual ever expressed the need, rather than the number of times they expressed it.

Table 13.3 shows that two-thirds of the classified needs were expressed by students. However, this percentage was greatly influenced by the number of students who responded to the needs assessment's open-ended survey items and the complexity of the statements they provided. For instance, although staff accounted for less than 30% of the total open-ended responses, the content of their statements tended to be richer and thus resulted in a greater number of classified needs than the statements provided by students.

Macro- and Micro-Value Data Sources. Prior to delving into the results of the open-ended survey items, it is important to note that some minor limitations were placed on some of the staff responses, but everyone was provided with the opportunity to express concern regarding any factor. The limitations that were placed were in the form of questions that directed respondents to focus their responses to the areas in which they had the most knowledge. For example, librarians were asked to comment on the factors that impacted student use of library resources, and so on.

As a result of these restrictions, it was necessary to use similar restrictions when analyzing the data. Therefore, the percentage of respondents who expressed a specific micro value was calculated by dividing the number of *eligible* individuals who expressed the micro value by the total number of *eligible* individuals. Eligibility for each micro value was determined by the evaluation team along with a key local informant and was based on whether the respondent group was believed to have the requisite knowledge to comment on the micro value. For example, only the opinions of students, instructors, and administrators were considered when calculating the percentage of individuals who expressed a concern regarding instructor competence. It was necessary to exclude from analyses the groups that were not in a position to reach an informed opinion regarding performance on the value (the instructor in this example). Including these groups in the analysis would bias the results and lead to erroneous conclusions. It should be noted that the analyses contained within this case were replicated on the full dataset (i.e., 200 students and 42 staff), and all but two of the 33 results were replicated. Therefore, the results contained herein are not due to sample selection.

Quantitative Data Analysis

This section describes the way in which the importance of each need was measured. In addition, the section offers as an example the quantitative analysis results for the macro-value safety and security needs. Also included are additional safety and security insights based on key informants and analysis of safety and security resources.

Measuring the Importance of Each Need Using Quantitative Data. Determining whether the CC should take steps to resolve a problem required knowing the areas that needed improvement and their importance. Four sets of statistics were used to estimate the impact of the expressed needs in the lives of students and staff: (a) percentage expressing a need, (b) rank level of importance, (c) rating (by students only) indicating effect on academic performance, and (d) rating (by students only) indicating effect on their quality of life.

First, the percentage of eligible individuals who expressed a need was reported for each micro value. High percentages connoted greater need than low percentages.

Second, average rank scores were provided for each macro and micro value. These scores reflected the degree of importance attributed to the value by respondents. In this instance, lower numbers represented higher importance.

The final two statistics (effect on academic performance and effect on quality of life) were only available for students. Both the academic performance and quality of life (QOL) statistics were measured using a 6-point Likert scale: 1 = "Almost no impact," 2 = "Very little impact," 3 = "Slight impact," 4 = "Moderate impact," 5 = "A lot of impact," 6 = "A great deal of impact." The academic performance statistic reflected students' perception of the degree to which the value affected their academic performance, whereas the QOL statistic reflected students' perception of the degree to which the value affected their quality of life.

A table was created for each macro value that included a summary set of statistics. Three of these statistics provided an average score for the rank, academic performance, and QOL statistics. The summary statistics could not be calculated by averaging the statistics reported for each of the micro values because an individual may have expressed a concern regarding one micro value but not the other micro values that comprise a given macro value. Hence, these summary statistics were calculated by averaging the scores for each individual who reported one or more micro values and then averaging across these individuals. Therefore, the summary statistics may appear to be slightly off but are in fact correct. The summary percentage statistic, however, represented the percentage of individuals who expressed concern regarding the performance of the CC on one or more micro values that comprise the macro value. Therefore, in many regards, this was the most crucial summary statistic. The next section offers an example of the analysis of survey results for one macro value, safety and security needs.

Example of the Initial Analysis Results for the Safety and Security Needs Macro Value. Somewhat surprisingly, only 30.4% of the key stakeholders who were consulted regarded the safety and security of persons and property to be of critical importance to the overall performance of the CC. The low level of relative importance, however, mirrored the level of importance accorded by students and staff. Although both groups assigned an average rank score of 4.0 to this macro value (see Table 13.4), this was the highest rank assigned (least important value). Students who reported safety and security concerns indicated that these concerns had a slight to a moderate impact on their academic performance and QOL, respectively. The average of the percentage of students and staff who reported a safety concern was nearly one-fifth (19.2%).

An analysis of variance (ANOVA) was conducted to determine whether the percentage of students who expressed a concern regarding safety and security was significantly different from the percentage reported by staff. When multiple statistical tests are conducted, the risk of at least one false positive p-value increases because the risk associated with each test is incurred multiple times. To control for Type I errors, a Bonferroni correction was utilized to adjust the p-value for each ANOVA. Therefore, there is a very low probability ($p < 0.05$) that a significant result from this case was in fact a false positive.

Table 13.4 Safety and Security Needs

Safety and Security	φ	Students				Staff	
		Rank	Academic	QOL	(%)	Rank	(%)
Safety and security	0.935	4.3	3.0	4.2	9.0	3.8	15.8
Safety and security (resources)[a]	0.929	4.0	2.7	4.8	3.5	3.5	18.4
Macro value	**0.966**	**4.0**	**3.0**	**4.4**	**12.0**	**4.0**	**23.8**

Statistically significant difference between students and staff needs: [a] $p < 0.05$; [b] $p < 0.01$; and [c] $p < 0.001$.

This analysis revealed a statistically significant difference between the percentage of students and staff who expressed a resource-related safety and security concern. Specifically, staff believed that there was a lack of safety- and security-related resources, $F(1, 236) = 13.46$, $p < 0.05$. Of course, these statistics communicate little about the nature of the concerns expressed. For a deeper insight, one must examine the qualitative data directly.

Additional Insights Based on Open-Ended Responses. To maintain an atmosphere conducive to student learning and the execution of staff duties, the CC must ensure the safety and security of individuals and their property. Examination of the 19 student statements revealed few details regarding the nature of their concerns. By contrast, the eight staff statements revealed that some students were aggressive, brought weapons to school, and belonged to gangs. Additionally, both students and staff expressed concerns regarding slippery stairways, absence of fire drills and safety plans, falling windowpanes, the pedestrian crossing to the CC, and the number of outside individuals permitted on the campus.

Additional Safety and Security Insights Based on Key Informants. According to several key informants, there were no written plans for dealing with natural disasters (i.e., fire, volcano eruptions, earthquakes, hurricanes) or human problems (e.g., sexual harassment, medical emergency). Instead, there was an expectation that "natural disasters will be dealt with by the National Emergency of Disaster Commission, while human problems will be handled by the Chief Education Officer." While this approach may work in the case of natural disasters or human problems that can be predicted, it falls short of ensuring student and staff safety. For example, how will unpredictable events, such as fires and earthquakes, be handled? While the CC was equipped with fire alarms, there were no plans for the following issues: (a) the procedure to evacuate each room in the school, (b) the locations where everyone would meet or where fire safety instructions would be posted, (c) the person who decided when it was safe to return to buildings, and (d) the frequency of fire drills to ensure that, in the event of an actual emergency, everyone would exit the school in an orderly manner. In the case of human problems such as medical emergencies, a safety plan should include contacting the student's parents or staff member's family, administering first aid, contacting a hospital (if necessary), transporting the individual to the hospital (if appropriate), and requiring that at least one staff completes a first-aid training program. In light of these issues, the performance of the CC on this micro value was judged to be in "need of improvement." Had a written safety plan been found to exist to deal with some of these safety concerns, particularly fire and medical emergency, we would have rated the performance of the CC much higher, potentially as high as "very good."

Analysis of Safety and Security (Resources). Ensuring an acceptable level of safety and security at CC also entailed providing adequate resources. Examination of the seven statements provided by students and the 14 statements provided by staff did not reveal a specific concern. Rather, a number of concerns were expressed, including a need for more security guards, security cameras, metal detectors, secure parking, secure filing cabinets to protect the privacy of student records, etc.

Overall Performance

Examination of the performance of the CC on the previously mentioned eight macro values indicated that the lack of adequate resources was the most critical need faced by the CC. This need was followed closely by the factors that impacted student learning macro value. However, because many of the factors that affected student learning were resources, the summary statistics for each macro value were recalculated without the influence of resources (see Table 13.5).

Removing the impact of resources from other macro values produced interesting results. The most noticeable difference occurred in the factors that impacted the student learning macro value. Exclusion of resource factors dramatically

Table 13.5　Macro-Value Summary Statistics

Macro Values	Students			Staff		
	Rank	%	Sans Resources	Rank	%	Sans Resources
Safety and security	4.0	12.0	9.0	4.0	23.8	15.8
Student behavior and policy	3.8	8.0	8.0	3.1	38.1	38.1
Quality of life	3.6	41.0	34.5	3.8	40.5	33.3
Health and sanitation	3.3	56.5	51.0	3.4	33.3	26.2
Management	3.4	33.0	33.0	2.9	59.5	59.5
Factors that impact student learning	2.5	80.0	36.5	2.4	73.8	57.1
Staff job performance	3.1	31.5	31.5	2.6	95.2	71.4
Resources	2.7	82.0	—	2.6	97.6	—

reduced the proportion of students who expressed a concern regarding this macro value. Consequently, health and sanitation needs were regarded by students as the second most important need (based on the proportion of students who expressed these needs). In contrast, staff regarded the health and sanitation macro value as the second least important need. Students viewed the macro values of quality of life, management, staff job performance, and the factors that impacted student learning to be of medium importance. Lastly, they expressed the least concerns about the macro values of safety and student behavior and policy.

Influences

This case describes a needs assessment that was part of a larger evaluation project. The analysts' knowledge and skills in evaluation affected the project. For example, their expertise in statistics enabled the evaluators to make use of these powerful tools to analyze open-ended comments, combine the analyses with data collected in other ways, and offer the CC powerful insights into student and staff perspectives.

Issues and Challenges

Collecting open-ended data yields incredibly rich data that would otherwise be missed if one relied solely on close-ended data. For example, at no point did our background literature nor intuition suggest the importance of asking about the cleanliness of bathrooms. Yet, this was one of the most frequently raised topics, particularly among female students. Had my colleague and I not included open-ended responses and relied solely on the close-ended items developed based on our literature review and desires of the client, we would have missed this (and other) important themes entirely. Furthermore, analyzing qualitative data requires considerably more effort than quantitative data. Developing the coding scheme for this study required over a month of work during which we continuously refined the scheme to improve its reliability. Reaching consensus on definitions was not always easy. A tension exists between developing too many codes versus too few. Creating a scheme with a lot of codes preserves the specificity of the raw data and reduces the number of statements relegated to the "other" category. Nevertheless, it may prevent one from seeing the forest from the trees. In contrast, having very few codes prevents one from clearly defining categories and often results in relegating codes to the "other" code when they do not fit in an existing theme. A balance must be struck between these two extremes. We chose only to create a new code if at least five individuals clearly mentioned the topic in their responses. During this process, it is important to be careful to discuss the definition of micro and macro values in general terms, rather than reference specific instances, so as to not inflate reliability.

When analyzing survey responses using statistics, one challenge is to report the results in a manner in which they can be understood by the key stakeholders, some of whom may need instruction in how to interpret the statistics. Great care should be taken to avoid overly burdening readers with technical details. For example, the original report failed to account for the ordinal nature of the survey items that were rated and simply averaged the Likert responses. This oversight was due to a lack of knowledge on the part of the author at the time. Such data should always be analyzed with Rasch modeling. However, the minutiae of this analysis would have added more confusion than information for uninitiated readers. Hence, although one should not avoid doing sophisticated analyses, one should avoid the inclusion of overly technical details in nonacademic reports.

DISCUSSION QUESTIONS

1. What steps should evaluators take to ensure that their findings have credibility with their key stakeholders?

2. How can one integrate qualitative and quantitative data to produce summative evaluation conclusions?

3. When using statistics, how can one protect against inaccurately classifying qualitative data?

REFERENCES

Gugiu, P. (2007). The logic of summative confidence. *Journal of Multi-disciplinary Evaluation, 4*(8), 1–15. Retrieved from http://journals.sfu.ca/jmde/index.php/jmde 1/article/view/64.

Gugiu, P. C. (2011). *Summative confidence* (Dissertation). Retrieved from https://Scholarworks.wmich.edu/dissertations/413.

Sleezer, C. M., Russ-Eft, D. F., & Gupta K. (2014). *A practical guide to needs assessment* (3rd ed.). San Francisco, CA: Wiley & ASTD.

14

Needs Assessment for Employee Empowerment in a Large Multinational

A Case Study

Gary N. McLean

Abstract

An existing client asked us to conduct an employee empowerment workshop based solely on observations of senior management. To determine the need for such a workshop and, if needed, its content, we conducted a literature review, a review of existing survey results, interviews, and focus groups. The survey was reviewed, edited, and distributed. We recommended executive coaching; the client opted for an extended workshop, along with peer coaching. The client did not allow follow-up of the year-long workshop to determine impact. Below is an overview of the case.

Where the Needs Assessment Was Conducted	Who Conducted the Needs Assessment	Focus of Needs Assessment	How Data Were Collected	How Data Were Analyzed
Large multinational R&D	External consultant	Determining the needs and content for a workshop on employee empowerment	A literature review, a review of existing survey results, interviews, and focus groups	Reliability using Cronbach alphas; checked for multicollinearity; ran experimental factor analysis on half of data to determine if there were subfactors; ran confirmatory factor analysis on the second half; t-tests; chi-square analysis

Background

One of our ongoing clients, a large multinational headquartered in the United States (more information is not provided to protect the required anonymity of the client), asked us to conduct a workshop for managers on employee empowerment in one of its large divisions responsible for research and development (R&D). The R&D function had not been successful going back 10 years, and senior management had decided that the problem related to micromanaging and a lack of empowerment for employees by their managers.

Preassessment Information

The company had not anticipated doing a needs assessment, as the division had conducted extensive focus groups to define empowerment prior to contacting us. Top management assumed that we would simply take their word for the solution and begin work on developing the workshop. We pushed back and indicated that, even if a workshop were the appropriate intervention, we really needed to understand what was happening, whether a lack of employee empowerment was really the issue, and what aspects of empowerment needed to be emphasized in the workshop, assuming that a workshop was appropriate.

Many years before, the division had done an employee survey that included some questions on empowerment. Further, the entire company did an annual employee survey that included a couple of survey items related to empowerment. So, we began by reviewing the related items and identifying where within the division apparent issues existed related to employee empowerment. From the few questions available, it did appear that there was a perceived issue related to empowerment based on responses to these questions. We also reviewed the outcome of the focus groups that they had conducted on defining empowerment. But we decided, in concert with senior management, that there was insufficient information to determine an appropriate intervention or to direct the development of a workshop.

After asking several questions of top management, they agreed that they had insufficient information based on the information available. They bought on to the need for additional work to determine where in the division the problems existed and what types of problems might be addressed through an intervention, whether or not that intervention was a workshop, coaching, or some other organization development intervention. They agreed to allow us to do an extensive needs assessment.

Strategic Needs Assessment Process

The strategic needs assessment (Sleezer, Russ-Eft, & Gupta, 2014) began with an extensive literature review to identify factors found in research to be related to employee empowerment, productivity, and innovation. For each factor identified, I wrote a draft item for a potential survey. A review of the existing information from the surveys and focus groups was also used to insert and modify items into the potential survey. This was followed with a number of interviews with both managers and employees. The question posed for both groups was, "What experiences have you had related to employee empowerment?" Probing questions were asked, but the interviews were completely open ended. These responses led to additional questions being drafted for the potential survey. Next, focus groups were held in four different regions using both on-site groups and the company's Telepresence system. The potential draft was updated further based on the focus-group responses.

The draft survey was then reviewed extensively for clarity, reducing redundancy, ensuring that no item contained more than one concept, keeping the wording simple, and other factors involved in good questionnaire construction. Once this process was completed, we then asked the senior management team to review the survey, providing feedback with further clarifications and adding items that they thought needed to be added. The survey was again updated, and then both face-to-face and Telepresence focus groups were asked to review the survey, item by item, with instructions to provide feedback on all of the issues related to high-quality surveys as mentioned above. Following the focus groups, the survey was again reviewed and finalized. Senior management reviewed the survey one more time and approved the finalized survey. The final survey consisted of 50 items: 20 related to general empowerment, 20 related to employee experiences with their manager, and 10 items related to empowerment by top leadership. Each item required two responses: one indicating the importance of the item and one requiring their experiences related to that item.

The survey was administered using SurveyMonkey, distributed to all employees worldwide in the division. To ensure anonymity, we were given the emails for all employees, and we sent out the survey. In that way, the company would not be able to trace the IP address of respondents, adding a measure of confidence that we meant what we said about anonymity. The response rate exceeded 90%.

Results of the Needs Assessment

The results of the survey were then treated with appropriate psychometric analyses. Reliability was determined using Cronbach alphas (it was very high, exceeding .9). We checked for multicollinearity to ensure that there was no redundancy in the items (there was none). We ran an experimental factor analysis (EFA) to determine if there were subfactors to the survey (there were). We had a sufficient number of respondents that we were able to divide our responses randomly and run the EFA on one half and then conduct a confirmatory factor analysis (CFA) on the second half. The factor analyses provided good results. The psychometrics allowed us to have high confidence in the results of the survey. We then met with subgroups of employees and managers to feed back the results. As an R&D division, many of the employees had PhDs. Unlike a normal client, this client wanted more and more statistics. In fact, it was a challenge to keep them focused on the results and not be fascinated by the statistics and wanting more and more analyses and statistical tests. At their request, additional statistics were run, and we held a final feedback session with all of the requested statistics. We had, initially, provided a rank-order list showing the difference between importance and experience. We were asked to do t-tests (which we had done for our own interest) to determine the point at which such differences were statistically different. They also asked us to do chi-square analysis to determine the impact of the demographic factors; again, we had done this for our own interest. Because of our own curiosity, we were able to provide the results of these statistical tests quickly. In my experience, this was very unusual; most clients do not want to be bombarded with statistics. The statistics were very useful in providing the desired information. They also asked for regression analysis, but on pushing them to identify the predictor and criterion variables, they gave up on this request, as did we.

The next step was to determine the intervention that would be most appropriate. In sharing the results with senior management, and based on the nature of the results, we tried to encourage them to adopt an executive coaching approach. However, senior management preferred staying with an extended workshop system that would be combined with coaching for managers who had been identified as having the greatest difficulty with employee empowerment. One of our subcontractors was selected to develop and implement the workshop over a period of a year. The results of the survey were used to determine the priority foci of the development of the workshop. Unfortunately, in spite of our counsel to administer the survey at the end of the 1-year series of workshops and coaching to determine whether there had been a change in employee empowerment within the division, senior management decided against this and relied on satisfaction feedback, not a very robust measure of a successful outcome. This measure, though, was very positive, confirming to the client our value as consultants—even though we tried to convince them not to rely on happy sheets.

Influences

There are no data to support my conclusions about the factors that influenced the processes and the outcomes of this needs assessment. The first factor I would point to is the culture of the organization. It is a top-down, hierarchical organization. So, even while the senior team was asking us to investigate employee empowerment in the department, they were, themselves, exercising top-down authority. They knew what was best. They didn't care about what the research said. They didn't care, particularly, what the consultant (me) had to share. They knew what they wanted. In my experience, this is a common phenomenon. So, the *culture* of the organization, among managers, is the first factor.

A second factor was the nature of the product produced by this organization, resulting in the employment of many PhD scientists. This did not seem to be a factor in the results of the survey, but it definitely influenced the analysis that they wanted. This was not a negative, by any means, but it was so unusual in my experience that it caught me off guard. We were readily able to respond to the request for more and more statistics, but such were not included in the initial report. It did make for a robust conversation about the data having greater sophistication in the analyses.

A third factor was the technology available to this company. Using the Telepresence to conduct focus groups was an amazing experience that allowed focus groups to be inclusive of all locations where the company did business. Given the available budget, there is no way that the needs assessment could have been conducted with input from around the world in this rich way without such technology. Another piece of technology that was very useful in the needs assessment process was the availability and flexibility of SurveyMonkey.

A fourth factor was the ongoing practice of using organization development processes. These processes created a comfort with the proposal to do a needs assessment. These processes included experience with focus groups and surveys. They provided us with existing data in the form of reports from those focus groups and surveys. Our needs assessment would have taken much longer and been less comprehensive had it not been for these preexisting data.

A final factor to highlight is the specific set of individuals involved in both the management of the department and the willingness of employees to share so openly. In spite of initial resistance to doing a needs assessment, it went forward with positive support. And the diversity of responses from focus group and survey participants allowed for strong insights into what was needed in support of employee engagement.

Issues and Challenges

It is interesting that some of the issues and challenges are related to the factors that influenced the needs assessment process. The first issue that confronted us was convincing the department management that a needs assessment was necessary. They were content to proceed directly into a workshop without doing a needs assessment, though what would be included in such a workshop was a mystery to us (and to them). We knew it was not as simple as telling the department's managers, "Empower your employees." But, until we could determine exactly where the problems were and what it was the employees desired, it was impossible to create a customized workshop. We would have had to plan it based solely on the literature, which, as it turned out, would have been very inadequate for the department. Fortunately, management was open-minded enough to hear our concerns and agree to the implementation of a needs assessment.

A second issue was employees' lack of trust in management because of their long experiences of management being top down in its decision-making processes. This issue was reflected in focus groups as they tried to determine what process would be used for the survey. Once they heard that all emails and subsequent communication would come from our company IP address, they were much more comfortable in participating.

A third issue was related to the push for more and more statistical analyses to be shared with the steering team. It proved difficult to keep them on task with the information that was being shared, rather than becoming enamored by the results of the increasingly sophisticated statistics being requested. Further, the steering team consisted of clerical employees who had no idea how to use the statistical analyses that were being presented. As a result, we needed to provide double feedback—first, in a simplified format, and second, with the more sophisticated statistics.

Language was another challenge. While the company conducted its business in English, they had employees in parts of the world in which English was not a first language. Because the company's language policy was that all business was to be conducted in English, the survey and the focus group process were conducted in English. We did try hard to keep the language of the survey relatively simple for those for whom English was not their first language. There was no pushback from any potential participants regarding the language.

Another challenge was trying to convince management to use both executive coaching and the workshop to implement the findings of the needs assessment. With this issue, we failed. We were not able to convince management to do this. However, at the end of the year-long workshop, there was a greater willingness on the part of managers to use executive coaching, and, at a modest level, it was then implemented.

A final challenge, not technically part of the needs assessment but, in our view, critical to the entire process, was our inability to convince management to repeat the survey to determine if the long series of meetings associated with the workshop had made a difference in managers' behaviors. The use of a happy sheet was so insignificant in determining if the workshop really accomplished its goal.

DISCUSSION QUESTIONS

1. How would you convince management that a needs assessment was necessary before implementing the workshop? What arguments would you make?

2. What questions would you have posed in the individual interviews and focus groups?

3. How would you have responded to the request for increasingly more sophisticated statistical analyses? Why?

4. How would you have tried to influence management to repeat the assessment tool at the end of the year-long workshop? Why would this be important?

5. What is your overall assessment of the processes used in this strategic needs assessment?

REFERENCE

Sleezer, C. M., Russ-Eft, D. F., & Gupta, K. (2014). *A practical guide to needs assessment* (3rd ed.). San Francisco, CA: Wiley & ASTD.

Diverse Students' Needs Assessment Case Study

Erich N. Pitcher

Abstract

In this case study, I describe three needs assessments conducted at a large, public university in the Pacific Northwest. The needs assessments were conducted simultaneously and in collaboration with the directors of three cultural resource centers, with the primary aim being to discern how well students' needs were met by current programs and services, as well as whether there were unmet needs among Native and Pacific Islander students, Black and African American students, and/or LGBTQ+ students. The following table provides an overview of the case.

Where the Needs Assessment Was Conducted	Who Conducted the Needs Assessment	Focus of Needs Assessment	How Data Were Collected	How Data Were Analyzed
University in northwestern United States	Faculty member	Focused on determining how well students' needs were met by current programs and services of three cultural centers	Interviews conducted with center directors; archival data (enrollment trends); a survey of students for each center	Descriptive statistics for closed-ended questions; thematic analysis for open-ended questions; reports combined text, infographics, and data tables to convey findings; organized data around strengths and areas for growth

Background

PacWest University (PWU, a pseudonym) is a large public research university with over 30,000 students (PWU, 2018a,b). PWU is a land-grant institution that emphasizes fields like agriculture, engineering, business, and science. Historically White, PWU university has intentionally sought to increase enrollments of students of color, but the institution remains nearly 80% White (PWU, 2018b). PWU enrolls very small numbers of Black and Native students, with the largest racially minoritized group being Latina/o/x, followed by Asian Americans, and then multiracial individuals (PWU, 2018b). More than 10% of students have international student status (PWU, 2018b). The institution enrolls roughly 50/50 male and female-designated students (Enrollment Report, 2018).

PWU is located within a state with a long, storied history of racist laws and practices. The state explicitly forbade Black individuals from moving to and residing within the state during its early formation (State Encyclopedia, 2018). The state also forcibly re-located Indigenous peoples onto reservations through a series of treaties in the 1850s (State Encyclopedia, 2018). In the 1920s, the state had one of the largest Ku Klux Klan chapters in the United States (State Encyclopedia, 2018). While the state is perceived to be a liberal paradise, it reflects the larger political divisions of the United States. In other words, the state is fairly politically polarized, yet one party has controlled state politics for many years. Each of these events shaped the political landscape of the university, especially the low numbers of African American and Native American students present on campus.

Profile of the Organizations Undertaking the Needs Assessment

PWU is home to seven separate cultural and resource centers: Black Cultural Center, Latinx Cultural Center, Indigenous Cultural Center, Asian and Pacific Islander Cultural Center, and Middle-Eastern Cultural Center. PWU also has a Women's Center and an LGBTQ Center. These spaces are free-standing buildings in all but one case and are located all across campus. Together, these cultural and resource centers form a diversity, equity, and inclusion unit located within the Division of Student Affairs and Services at PWU. The primary aim of these cultural and resource centers is to provide a space for students to connect with their cultural backgrounds, develop community, and provide education for the broader community (Cultural and Resource Centers [CRC] Website, 2018). As noted elsewhere, cultural centers are typically born out of student activism (Patton, 2010) and the cultural and resource centers at PWU were similarly birthed.

The larger diversity unit of which the cultural resource centers are a part has faced significance changes in staffing and structure since early 2010. As such, there was a start-up feel to the unit and a sense of chaos regarding routine procedures and decision making. This chaos is reflected in the needs assessment cases discussed below. More specifically, the need to conduct needs assessment work derived from the larger lack of focus in the unit, the perceived sense that students' needs were being unmet, and a lack of clarity about how to better meet those needs given staffing levels.

Preassessment Information

This case most closely aligns with a strategic needs assessment, as the primary aim was to identify the needs of communities served by the respective centers (Sleezer, Russ-Eft, & Gupta, 2014). A strategic needs assessment focuses on systematically identifying the needs of an organization by looking to internal and external factors that affect organizational performance. As the analyst for this needs assessment project, I was especially concerned with identifying where a center wished to be and where they presently were.

To begin to understand the organizational context, I first sought to understand the current issues and challenges facing each of the staff members. I began by interviewing each staff member about what they perceived to be the strengths and weaknesses of the unit, as well as what opportunities and threats they anticipated managing in the future. Consistently, staff within the cultural and resource centers felt that they lacked sufficient data to guide decision making for the development of programs and initiatives. Common threats included heavy workloads, organizational inequities, declining funding, and a hostile university/state/city environment. Opportunities included better partnerships, strategic use of staffing strengths, and rapport with students.

I also informally interviewed key partners across the university who routinely or seldomly worked with the diversity unit that houses the cultural and resource centers. These interviews revealed that collaboration, accountability, and consistency were challenges in partnerships. External stakeholders who partnered regularly with the diversity unit suggested that the unit lacked focus, was cumbersome to collaborate with, and often did not follow through on commitments. Key partners who should collaborate with the diversity unit, but did not, stated that the unit was inward looking in a way that did not facilitate partnerships.

Following this first round of informal interviews with internal and external stakeholders, I offered to conduct needs assessments for any center wishing to know more about their communities' needs. The Black Cultural Center, LGBTQ Center, and Indigenous Cultural Center opted to participate in conducting needs assessments. Given that the only existing assessment data and campus climate data were nearly 5 years old, there was little existing data available to inform practice. I did, however, draw on enrollment trends, which indicated that Black and Native student enrollment had declined in the previous 10 years.

Needs Assessment Process

Once the three directors of the Black Cultural Center, Indigenous Cultural Center, and LGBTQ Center agreed to participate, I developed a list of potential data collection strategies. The initial list included surveys, interviews, asset mapping, and focus groups. Given limited resources and staffing constraints, we decided to use a survey with open- and close-ended questions. If time permitted, we would engage student staff in asset mapping and then follow-up with student focus groups. Ultimately, time and staff constraints limited us to completing only the survey.

I developed an initial boilerplate survey that included questions about the level of involvement a student had with a given center, the purpose of their visits to the center, any barriers to accessing the space, and the extent to which programs offered met respondent needs. We asked a ranking-type question about the greatest stressors they faced as a student. We also asked open-ended questions that included potential programming ideas, the words one would use to describe the space to someone who had never been there, and then a series of demographic questions.

I then worked with each of the directors to tailor the boilerplate questions to the particular community that would receive the survey. In the case of the LGBTQ Resource Center, a specific question about well-being programming was added. We also added a question about whether programs challenged attendees' thinking. In the case of the Indigenous Cultural Center, we tailored questions to identify whether Pacific Islander students felt well-served by the center. For the Black Cultural Center, we did not modify the survey. The various versions of the survey were then loaded into Qualtrics for distribution.

Given that there was a defined population for the Indigenous Cultural Center and the Black Cultural Center, I requested the emails for these student populations and created distribution lists in Qualtrics. The needs assessments were completed in the fall term of 2016, so we invited any student who had been present on campus for at least one term and who selected a racial category served by the respective center to complete the survey (including students who may identify as two or more races). To further facilitate completion of the survey and sustained engagement with the student populations, we sent the survey along with invitations to various events over the course of the data collection period. Each survey was addressed to students by name, and the email text was collaboratively written by the director and me.

Given the lack of a defined population for the LGBTQ Resource Center, we collected data through social media, at large events, and by tabling in high-traffic areas on campus. The lack of a defined population made it difficult to track progress and to accurately calculate a response rate. However, we collected more surveys for the LGBTQ Resource Center than the other two centers.

Following the close of the fall term, I cleaned and began to analyze the data. I used descriptive statistics for closed ended questions and used thematic analysis for open ended questions. I then created reports that combined text, infographics, and data tables to convey to the directors the findings of our needs assessment. I organized the data around strengths and areas for growth.

Findings From Needs Assessment

For the Black Cultural Center needs assessment, we had an 11% response rate and respondents had a range of involvement with 27.3% of respondents saying they visited daily, while 33% had never visited. Barriers to visiting included lack of time/open hours, personal fears and anxieties, lack of awareness of the space, and lack of a reason to go. Respondents most often used words like welcome, safe space, and community to describe the center. A strong majority felt the space met their needs. Identified needs included difficulties with time management, inadequate financial support, lack of community in the city where the university is located, and facing difficulties in completing their academic work.

For the Indigenous Cultural Center needs assessment, we had a low response rate of 5%. Half of respondents had never been to the center, and 17% visited the center daily. Barriers to visiting included time/open hours, unclear reasons to go, and personal fears and anxieties. Respondents most often used words like home, welcome, and references to the architecture to describe the center. Respondents were more mixed in their sense that the Indigenous Cultural Center met their needs with 29% and 11%, saying the center met their needs very well or well, while 41% stated that their needs were met at an acceptable level. Identified needs included lack of time management skills, issues with mental health/well-being, difficulties completing their academic work, lack of financial support, and familial demands.

For the LGBTQ Resource Center, we cannot calculate a response rate, but 115 students responded to the survey. Roughly 45.2% of respondents had never been to the center, while 33% visited 1–2 times per month and 10.4% visited daily. Barriers to visiting the center included being too busy, distance to the center, and lack of reason to go. Respondents most often used words like safe, supportive, and community to describe the center. A majority of respondents felt their needs were met with 33% indicating they strongly agreed, 17.8% agreed, while 34.4% neither agreed nor disagreed. Identified needs included mental health/well-being, difficulties with time management, difficulties completing their academic work, and inadequate financial support.

Across all three centers, there was a pattern with some students not feeling they belonged in the space and/or that they would not be Black, Indigenous, or LGBTQ enough to feel a sense of belonging in the space. Some respondents indicated that they feared others' judgments if they entered the space. Some students described negative events or associations they held with the various spaces. Students reported fairly high needs in mental health support and financial issues and difficulties in their academic performance/time management.

After I completed my analysis, I met with each of the directors to discuss the findings and to provide direction to future potential changes. Given stressors common across all three centers and information gathered as a part of the informal interviewing, it was suggested that the centers partner with units on campus responsible for mental health services, financial aid, and the academic success support services. It was also suggested that each center work diligently to ensure that students have positive experiences in the space and to specifically train student staff on how to create an inclusive environment. A final recommendation was to hire student staff strategically to meet the diverse needs of students. For example, I suggested hiring a bubbly staff member to work the front desk and a highly academically successful student to support the academic achievement of students in the space.

Influences on the Needs Assessment Process

First, it is worth noting that these assessments are all limited given the use of a survey instrument without additional focus groups or asset mapping activities. Asset mapping and focus groups could have allowed for triangulation of the data through multiple data collection methods, provided more details about the severity of the needs (e.g., financial, time management), as well as potential solutions. Second, these centers serve populations who have been subject to varying forms of oppression. As such, it is often the case that a piece of the oppressor is planted within the oppressed group (Freire, 2012), and this ultimately influences how one perceives the cultural and resource centers. In other words, if Black students have internalized messages of anti-Blackness, invariably this influences how a student perceives the Black Cultural Center. Finally, given the limited staffing and chaotic organizational context, it is very difficult to enact sustainable change within the organization and the respective centers. There are innumerable internal and external demands placed on the staff that detract from meeting the needs of students.

Identified Issues

Within this organization there were three primary issue areas that needed to be addressed: focus of the work, management issues, and political context. These issues were identified using the needs assessment process and by conducting a series of strategic planning sessions. Related to the first point, there was a need to focus the work on the intended purpose of cultural centers, which was primarily to provide social, psychological, and intellectual support for students served by the respective centers. Secondary to that goal was providing the much-needed education for dominant groups about various racial and ethnic communities. However, within an institutional context where the mission of cultural centers shifted to being primarily about recruiting, retaining, and graduating minoritized students, the very institutionalization of cultural centers seemingly disrupted the directors' abilities to focus on the care and support of their communities.

A second issue was related to the management of the unit. The unit had significant employee turnover, faced reorganization efforts, and had significant change in the larger leadership structure. No manager can be successful in such an environment, and ultimately the lack of clarity about the focus of the work and expectations of staff made the work of serving the needs of students all the more difficult. It was also the case that the right people to make a decision were often not involved in those decisions; that lack of involvement directly affected the communities served by the centers.

Finally, the broader political context, both nationally and locally, shifted significantly with the rise of Donald Trump to the presidency. White nationalists were emboldened and mobilized once again, and this made an already challenging work context more difficult. While the campus community espoused liberal values, often the practice of those values fell short. The sense of fear among students of color, international students, and undocumented students continued to rise, while the capacity of the staff remained the same. This meant that the staff working in the centers faced a great deal of fatigue and anxiety while providing support for students.

DISCUSSION QUESTIONS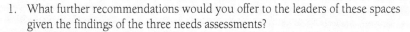

1. What further recommendations would you offer to the leaders of these spaces given the findings of the three needs assessments?

2. How might the history of the state be influencing the university? How does that history ultimately influence the needs of communities?

3. While I did not report in this chapter the demographic data from the needs assessment, those data indicated that students hold a wide array of racial, ethnic, gender, ability, and sexual identities. How would you use the demographic data collected as a part of this survey to better understand the needs of the communities served?

4. Given the success of using social media, tabling in high traffic areas, and asking people to respond at large events, would you anticipate there being a stronger response rate from Indigenous and Black students if the same strategies were pursued with those surveys?

5. Only three of the cultural centers—Black Cultural Center, Indigenous Cultural Center, and LGBTQ Resource Center—participated in the needs assessment What might be some of the reasons for a lack of participation by the other cultural centers—Latinx Cultural Center, Asian and Pacific Islander Cultural Center, Middle-Eastern Cultural Center, and Women's Center? The three participating centers identified needs concerning providing mental health support and financial issues and difficulties in their academic performance/time management. How might the results from the other centers have differed? What might be some reasons for the differences?

6. The response rate for the Indigenous Center was much lower than that for the other two centers. What might be some of the reasons for that lower response rate? What might have been done to improve the response rate? Would undertaking a "nonrespondent" survey and comparing those results been useful? Why, or why not?

REFERENCES

Cultural and Resource Centers (CRC). (2018). About us.

Freire, P. (2012). *Pedagogy of the oppressed.* (M. Ramos, Trans.). (Reprint). New York, NY: Continuum.

PacWest University (PWU). (2018a). About us.

PacWest University (PWU). (2018b). Enrollment trends, 2016–2017.

Patton, L. D. (2010). *Culture centers in higher education: Perspectives on identity, theory, and practice*. Sterling, VA: Stylus.

Sleezer, C. M., Russ-Eft, D. F., & Gupta, K. (2014). *A practical guide to needs assessment* (3rd ed.). San Francisco, CA: Wiley & ASTD.

State Encyclopedia. (2018). *Racist history of the state*.

16

Spending Other People's Money Responsibly and Strategically

Using Needs Assessment in Philanthropy

Lauren A. Silverstein

Abstract

Needs assessments are critical to philanthropy organizations that aspire to allocate dollars strategically. This case provides an example of a needs assessment conducted by a philanthropic organization to better understand a community's priorities in particular areas of giving and to inform the funding strategy. This case demonstrates the value of multiple stakeholders and data sources and, most importantly, how needs assessments can be used to answer pressing questions and make important decisions. Below is an overview of the case.

Where the Needs Assessment Was Conducted	Who Conducted the Needs Assessment	Focus of Needs Assessment	How Data Were Collected	How Data Were Analyzed
New Jersey	The philanthropic organization	Focused on understanding community's needs in five impact areas	Survey instruments administered to all executive directors and lead staff of grantee organizations; face-to-face inquiry meetings held with all executive directors of grantee organizations.	Data placemat created for each impact area. (A data placemat is a visual document [the size of a placemat] that displays themes from the collected data, typically in the form of charts and graphs.)

Background

Imagine you work for an organization that has a significant amount of money to give away to worthy community organizations and causes. A lot of work by your colleagues went into raising this money. And your donors entrust you to make wise, impactful decisions with their resources. The problem is that there are so many places to which you could give, each with a compelling story and with a need greater than you alone can fill. And everyone has his or her "favorite" organization. *How do you decide where to allocate the money? How can you be sure your decisions are informed, strategic, and made with minimal personal bias?*

A needs assessment can help you better understand the larger context of community needs. It can help you take a perspective that offers a more complete picture of the community's landscape by aggregating data from various touch points. Then, when individual proposals come in from various grantees, you will have a lens through which the proposals are contextualized and prioritized.

This case provides an example of how a needs assessment was used to make strategic decisions, in this case to specifically inform planning and allocations strategy. Readers can understand the value and necessity of multiple stakeholders and data sources for telling an accurate story. And, most importantly, readers can see how evaluation, and needs assessments specifically, were used to answer pressing questions and make important decisions.

Profile of the Organization

We are a multimillion-dollar philanthropic organization located in the United States. We allocate funds in our local community and overseas. Our mission is to care for those in need; build community and save lives, one person at a time. Our donors are generous individuals who deeply care about our mission. Our lay leadership (volunteers) make up our various decision-making committees, including many of those mentioned in this case: our allocation committees, Strategic Priorities Council, and our board of trustees (which holds all fiduciary responsibility for the organization). To best accomplish our mission, we continuously strive to learn about and respond to pressing needs.

Preassessment Information

> *"I want proof of impact. I believe my parents give much more for the 'feel good' feeling that comes along with giving, whereas I am dead-set on maximizing the impact of my philanthropic dollars."* (Goldseker & Moody, 2017)

It used to be that charities could rely solely on pulling people's heartstrings to get donations. In today's philanthropic marketplace, prospect donors want evidence that their money is meeting real needs. Increasingly, the philanthropic sector is responding to this call by creating evaluation and learning departments. In our philanthropy organization, we found that evaluation answers our donors' tough questions about where the money goes, and it helps *us* understand the community needs better so we can more effectively and strategically allocate our resources. To help determine our strategic priorities, we decided to conduct a needs assessment in our various impact areas (areas of giving). The hope was that the results from this study would lead to a more informed planning and allocations strategy.

Focus of the Needs Assessment

Our organization supports local programs that influence change in five main funding areas: (a) seniors, (b) individuals with disabilities and their families, (c) education, (d) outreach and engagement, and (e) safety net services. This needs assessment focused on understanding the needs in each of these five impact areas. If we learned from our grantees which impact areas needs were growing, where needs were urgent, and where our money could make significant impact, we could prioritize our funding in a way we had not done before.

Boundaries of the Effort

Our organization funds programs both locally and also overseas. As this was the first time an effort was conducted to better understand the needs of the community with the intention of informing the funding strategy, we decided to start locally. First, it was practically more feasible due to the proximity of our grantees to our headquarters. Second, we knew that English would be the common language and that we would not require translation services or risk misinterpretations due to language nuances.

Key Players

The key players for this needs assessment were the executive directors and lead staff of 26 community organizations that work in the space of our various impact areas (e.g., seniors, education, etc.). Most of these organizations receive allocations from us each year because their missions align with ours. Each of these individuals has "ears to the ground" on the needs in our various funding areas. In addition, our organization's Strategic Priorities Council, a high-level committee comprised of senior board leadership, was the administering body of this work. This leadership worked with our Impact Assessment Department to collect the data from our grantees, analyze the information, and then make recommendations to our board of trustees based on the findings.

Needs Assessment Process

This needs assessment utilized a strategic needs assessment approach (Sleezer, Russ-Eft, & Gupta, 2014). Given the goal of the needs assessment, the approach gathered and analyzed information from grantees. The intention of the study was to inform future strategy, in our case, the philanthropic organization's annual planning and funding strategy.

Data Collection

Data collection occurred in two ways: (a) survey instruments were administered to all executive directors and lead staff of grantee organizations; and (b) face-to-face inquiry meetings were held with all executive directors of grantee organizations.

Surveys—One per Impact Area

We asked the same questions about each impact area. Consistency was important so that we could make relative comparisons question-by-question across the five impact areas, in addition to examining each individually. The executive directors/lead staff only needed to complete a survey for the impact area(s) that their programs addressed. For example: A nursing home completed the survey questions as they related to the seniors' impact area but did not need to answer these same questions as they applied to youth education, as their agency did not have this focus. Below are the questions we asked of each impact area:

1. With respect to [insert impact area], what are the biggest problems and/or needs your organization is facing?

2. With respect to [insert impact area], what are the biggest needs the community is facing?

3. Consider your budget for [insert impact area], what are your biggest costs?

4. With respect to addressing the needs for [insert impact area], what does your organization do really well? In other words, if you were to "double down" with resources, where would the resources go the furthest in terms of supporting existing work you're already doing to address these needs?

5. What are you not doing that you want to be doing if you had more resources to address these problems? What resources would you need to do this (physical infrastructure, additional staff, training/capacity building for staff, technology infrastructure, other)?

6. What are your organization's top three strategic priorities over the next 5 years?

Face-to-Face Meetings

The purpose of the face-to-face meetings with the executive directors was to provide a mechanism to hear firsthand about each organization, and for each executive director to share additional information and details that may not have come out on the survey. Face-to-face meetings also added the "personalized element" that the survey could not.

Our organization's relationships with our grantees is important, and building in the personal interactions to our study design helped reinforce the importance of the relationship to our grantees. Furthermore, our organization's chief planning officer, and in some cases CEO, conducted these meetings, which was also a symbolic gesture of how important this study and the input from grantees were to us. In general, the face-to-face meetings were held before the survey was administered. Our chief planning officer/CEO used this meeting as an opportunity to introduce our grantees to our needs assessment initiative, explain its importance, answer their questions, assuage any concerns, and get their buy-in. See Appendix A for a list of the guiding questions used during the face-to-face conversations.

Data Analysis

Once all surveys were collected, we created a data placemat for each impact area (see Appendix B). A data placemat is a visual document (the size of a placemat) that displays themes from the collected data, typically in the form of charts and graphs (Pankaj & Emery, 2016). Most importantly, it is used as a facilitation technique to engage stakeholders in data interpretation and analysis. While it is common to engage stakeholders in gathering information, it is less common to involve them in making meaning of the data. It is here that they can provide significant, invaluable insights. This process also allows stakeholders to "co-create new knowledge with each other and with the evaluator" (p. 83).

The chief impact officer created one data placemat for each impact area and then held a meeting with members of the Strategic Priorities Committee. During the meeting, committee members reviewed the placemats and used the information to draw conclusions. By working with our impact assessment team to co-create meaning of the data, our leadership team played a role in understanding what the data meant, as opposed to having someone tell them what the data said. When it came to making recommendations, the members of the Strategic Priorities Council felt confident in their decisions, because they had seen and made meaning of the data firsthand.

In addition to analyzing the data from our partners, we analyzed the distribution of our funding among the impact areas. Seeing what percentage of our resources were currently being allocated to each impact area helped us have a better sense of how our money was being spent. With these data, we could analyze our findings against the distribution as a "check in" to see if the balance was appropriate. Finally, data from the placemats were synthesized and included in an Ears to the Ground Report, a report that specifically provides a summary of community needs and our organization's current levels of funding for each need. Reports for the impact areas that had them available were distributed to our Strategic Priorities Council, board of trustees, and also to the various grantees who work in these impact areas. Additionally, this report was shared with donors or other community members with specific interests in a particular impact area. See Appendix C for an example of an Ears to the Ground Report.

Results of the Needs Assessment

From the data placemats and face-to-face meetings, two impact areas stood out as presenting urgent, growing needs: (a) seniors and (b) individuals with disabilities and their families. Both populations were increasing in our local area. In addition, the government funding usually supporting these agencies was facing drastic cuts. Furthermore, the needs were changing from what they had been, and so agencies found themselves facing needs in areas they previously had not experienced. For example, more seniors were living longer, and they wanted to stay in their homes. Supporting programs that provided help at home to enable seniors to live safely in their homes was a growing need. Also, these seniors' children and spouses were needing increased amounts of support. Similarly, many seniors also had a disability of some sort. In addition to our programs that supported children with disabilities, the programs that primarily served seniors were also serving increasing numbers of individuals with disabilities and trying to make accommodations, so that the programs could be as inclusive as possible.

Next, when we looked at our funding distribution, we saw that Caring and Inclusion (the organization priority that included programs serving seniors and individuals with disabilities) only received 13% of our organization's allocated dollars. This percentage represented an imbalance after learning the growing needs in these areas. To that end, the Strategic Priorities Council recommended that we increase that percentage of funding to this organization priority and that programs serving seniors and individuals with disabilities receive more funds. With respect to the current funding in these areas, the council stated, "We do not believe that a spending level of just 13% is synchronous with either our community's set of values and beliefs nor is it sufficient to meet the documented growing needs for these populations over the next decade" (SPC Recommendations, 2018). Despite recommending additional dollars go directly to programs in these impact areas, the Strategic Priorities Council also recognized that our dollars alone could not help "soften the blow of the negative government funding trend" (SPC Recommendations, 2018). So, in addition to increased allocations to programs, the Strategic Priorities council also recommended providing the advocacy arm of our organization, the Community Relations Committee, with the resources it needed to better advocate on behalf of our grantees. These recommendations *were approved by our board of trustees* and resulted in a percentage change to these funding areas, as well as the addition of a part-time employee to our Community Relations Committee department to specifically work on advocacy efforts with our grantees.

Influences

"Who said no one listens?"

—*Participant in supplying data to the Strategic Priorities Council*

Systematically gathering data from our grantees to inform funding recommendations was an historic moment for our organization. The first level of influence was on the culture of our funding recommendations. Our leadership now had experience collecting data and seeing how useful it could be to inform decision making. It instilled confidence in some who were skeptical that funding decisions are popularity contests or motivated mostly by political forces. While this case study acknowledges that multiple factors go into allocations decisions, it does exemplify the addition of data and evidence as a factor considered at the decision-making table.

Upon reflection of this process, a few organizational qualities stood out as being important to achieving this influence. First, our organization has a leadership structure that is very much respected. So, when our grantmaking committees learned of the data-driven recommendations, they did not question them or pushback. The committees trusted and accepted the recommendations because they respected the leadership bodies from which they came. Second, there was transparency in the process. When the Strategic Priorities Council was created, their purpose was made clear: As the name suggests, this body was to implement a process that would set strategic priorities for our organization. Grantmaking committees understood the product of this committee's work would result in an additional factor to help shape their allocations work.

The second level of influence was on our relationships with our grantees. Grantees were used to being asked about needs and for their thoughts, and too often not feeling they were heard because they did not see any change. In this case, a clear funding decision was made because of our grantees' input.

When people see that evaluation is used for learning and strategic decision making, it is a powerful tool. When donors hear of this strategy, they also become more confident in our organization as a grantmaking organization. They can be assured we are making informed decisions and wisely investing their money where needed most.

Issues and Challenges

As always when the survey method is used as part of data collection for a needs assessment, ensuring a strong response rate can be a challenge. For us, trying to get all our grantees to complete the surveys so that we had a representative sample was an issue at times. To overcome this challenge, we used individuals who had relationships with our grantees to urge them to complete it. In most cases, the personalized outreach from a strategic individual worked. However, there were still four to five grantees who did not take the time to complete the survey and so their insights were not included in our data and the subsequent recommendations.

A second challenge pertained to the strength of some of the survey data. For example, in some cases, an organization reported they did not work in an impact area. We are not sure if this is because they really did not feel that they worked in that impact area (even though we as an organization would have classified them as working in that impact area!), or because they wanted to avoid having to complete another survey. Regardless of the reason, we did not have data from some agencies with respect to some impact areas that we believed could have provided valuable insight. Next time we undertake a data collection effort, we will have a conversation with the grantees about the impact areas we think relate to them and also more clearly define the impact areas on the survey itself.

Third, some members of the Strategic Priorities Council were also on the Boards of the grantees from whom we were collecting information. In some cases, this was productive as they had information and insights that were not available to us otherwise. In other cases, it led to clear biases when interpreting the data and making recommendations. While one can never remove all biases, the group was large enough to bring balance to decisions and ensure that no one individual's personal experience overshadowed the data.

DISCUSSION QUESTIONS

1. When collecting information from grantees for a needs assessment, would you give higher weight to a grantee due to their size, dollars they receive, nature of relationship with you/your funders, or other considerations? Or would you treat all grantees' input equally? Explain.

2. How would you respond to someone who does not "believe the data" because he or she has personal experiences with a particular grantee that did not reflect the survey data?

3. How would you respond to decision makers who do not want to use your needs assessment findings when making decisions? Instead, they trust their gut, their heart, and the collective wisdom of the group.

4. What methods should be used to communicate the results and the decisions? In what ways, if any, might such dissemination methods affect the response rates in future data collection efforts?

5. The case focused on the United States. What modifications might need to be made to undertake similar work in other countries?

REFERENCES

Goldseker, S., & Moody, M. (2017). *Generation impact: How next gen donors are revolutionizing giving*. Hoboken, NJ: Wiley.

Pankaj, V., & Emery, A. K. (2016). Data placemats: A facilitative technique designed to enhance stakeholder understanding of data. In R. S. Fierro, A. Schwartz, & D. H. Smart (Eds.), *Evaluation and facilitation. New Directions for Evaluation, 149*, 81–93. https://doi.org/10.1002/ev.20181:

Sleezer, C. M., Russ-Eft, D. F., & Gupta, K. (2014). *A practical guide to needs assessment* (3rd ed.). San Francisco, CA: Wiley & ASTD.

SPC Recommendations. (2018, January 24). Unpublished raw data.

Appendix A

Guided Conversation With Agency Executives

Strengths

- What does your organization do really well?
- What is your secret sauce?
- How much does that cost you?

Building Capacity

- To accomplish your mission, what do you need to do better? (Where are you falling short/underperforming?)
- What would it take for you to do this well?
- How much would that cost?

Anticipating

- Think about the trends in your space, the condition of your facilities, the qualifications/capacity of your staff. What will you need to be doing well in 5 years from now (i.e., what services would you need to be providing, skills utilizing, etc.)?
- How much will that cost, and what are these costs?

Sum of All Parts

- What things or activities must be done to accomplish your organization's goals or needs?
- If all of these were done, what is the probability of success? Is this OK? If not, what other activities need to be accomplished?[a]

Funding Specifically[b]

- What funding challenges and constraints do you struggle with?
- What policies or practices in grantmaking would help overcome these challenges?
- What are the top three things on your bucket list this year? Over the next 5 years?

---

[a]http://tdmaryland.org/Resources/Documents/Program%20Documents/Needs_Assessment_Questions_Managers.pdf
[b]http://realcostproject.org/

Appendix B

Data Placemat for Individuals With Disabilities and Their Families

Serving individuals with disabilities and their families

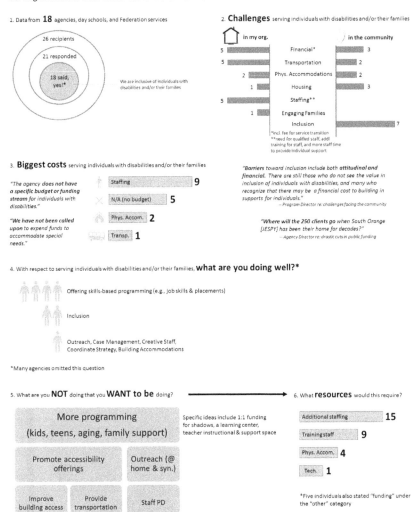

1. Data from **18** agencies, day schools, and Federation services

26 recipients
21 responded
18 said, yes!*

We are inclusive of individuals with disabilities and/or their families

2. **Challenges** serving individuals with disabilities and/or their families

	in my org.		in the community
5		Financial*	3
5		Transportation	2
2		Phys. Accommodations	2
1		Housing	3
5		Staffing**	
1		Engaging Families	
		Inclusion	7

*incl. fee for service transition
**need for qualified staff, addl training for staff, and more staff time to provide individual support

3. **Biggest costs** serving individuals with disabilities and/or their families

"The agency does not have a specific budget or funding stream for individuals with disabilities."

"We have not been called upon to expend funds to accommodate special needs."

Staffing **9**
N/A (no budget) **5**
Phys. Accom. **2**
Transp. **1**

"*Barriers toward inclusion include both attitudinal and financial. There are still those who do not see the value in inclusion of individuals with disabilities, and many who recognize that there may be a financial cost to building in supports for individuals.*"
-- Program Director re: challenges facing the community

"*Where will the 250 clients go when South Orange [JESPY] has been their home for decades?*"
-- Agency Director re: drastic cuts in public funding

4. With respect to serving individuals with disabilities and/or their families, **what are you doing well?***

Offering skills-based programming (e.g., job skills & placements)

Inclusion

Outreach, Case Management, Creative Staff, Coordinate Strategy, Building Accommodations

*Many agencies omitted this question

5. What are you **NOT** doing that you **WANT to be** doing?

More programming
(kids, teens, aging, family support)

Specific ideas include 1:1 funding for shadows, a learning center, teacher instructional & support space

Promote accessibility offerings

Outreach (@ home & syn.)

Improve building access

Provide transportation

Staff PD

6. What **resources** would this require?

Additional staffing **15**
Training staff **9**
Phys. Accom. **4**
Tech. **1**

*Five individuals also stated "funding" under the "other" category

Appendix C

Ears to the Ground Report for Individuals With Disabilities and Their Families

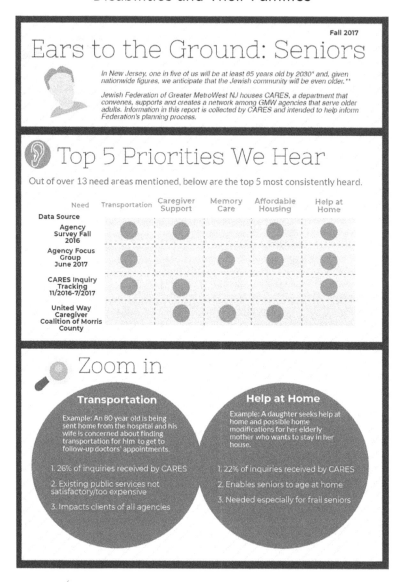

Fall 2017

Ears to the Ground: Seniors

In New Jersey, one in five of us will be at least 65 years old by 2030* and, given nationwide figures, we anticipate that the Jewish community will be even older.**

Jewish Federation of Greater MetroWest NJ houses CARES, a department that convenes, supports and creates a network among GMW agencies that serve older adults. Information in this report is collected by CARES and intended to help inform Federation's planning process.

Top 5 Priorities We Hear

Out of over 13 need areas mentioned, below are the top 5 most consistently heard.

Need / Data Source	Transportation	Caregiver Support	Memory Care	Affordable Housing	Help at Home
Agency Survey Fall 2016	●	●		●	●
Agency Focus Group June 2017	●		●	●	●
CARES Inquiry Tracking 11/2016-7/2017	●	●			●
United Way Caregiver Coalition of Morris County		●	●	●	

Zoom in

Transportation

Example: An 80 year old is being sent home from the hospital and his wife is concerned about finding transportation for him to get to follow-up doctors' appointments.

1. 26% of inquiries received by CARES

2. Existing public services not satisfactory/too expensive

3. Impacts clients of all agencies

Help at Home

Example: A daughter seeks help at home and possible home modifications for her elderly mother who wants to stay in her house.

1. 22% of inquiries received by CARES

2. Enables seniors to age at home

3. Needed especially for frail seniors

Ears to the Ground: Seniors

 Zoom in

Caregiver Support

Example: A son feels the intense responsibility of finding appropriate care for his aging parents and inquires about resources and support.

1. 22% of inquiries received by CARES

2. An emerging need as seniors live longer

3. Reliable sources of information key

Affordable Housing

Example: A disabled senior needs an affordable place to live without stairs.

1. Limited availability in Essex/Morris area

2. Especially affecting those with special needs/developmental disabilities

3. Growing gap between Medicaid & reimbursements and costs

Memory Care

Example: A daughter asks about programs for her mother who has begun having memory issues.

1. GMW agencies hearing more about prevalence of dementia in older adults

2. Two agencies recently started memory care programs to respond to demand

3. More information on dementia being requested

2017-2018 investments

Annual Campaign funds directed at seniors

Transportation
$70,000 MetroTransport (Daughters of Israel)

Help at Home
$100,000 Home Care (JFS CNJ)

Caregiver Support
$10,000 Care Consultation Program (JFS MW)

Senior Daily Activities
$23,000 YM-YWHA of Union County

Kosher Food
$187,400 Daughters of Israel

$65,000 Kosher Meals on Wheels (JFS CNJ)

Counseling & Social Work
$65,000 JFS MW (estimated 1/2 of counseling is for older adults)

Rabbinic & Pastoral Services
$130,140 Joint Chaplaincy Committee

$110,000 Daughters of Israel

Senior Support & Planning
$82,916 GMW CARES

Unrestricted funds to agencies that serve seniors

JCC of Central NJ	$79,000
JCC MetroWest	$395,500
Jespy House	$21,600
JFS MW	$342,000
JFS CNJ	$77,100
JSDD	$21,600
YM-YWHA of Union County	$112,000

Ears to the Ground: Seniors

 Suggestions for Action

1. **Area of Emphasis: Caregiver Support**
Few Federation dollars specifically support this growing need. "The Care Consultation program is one I refer to frequently. If JFS MW didn't have this program, we would be in trouble," says Marian Marlowe, CARES Program Coordinator.

2. **Area of Emphasis: Help at Home**
Nearly all of the findings in this report emerge as needs because more and more seniors want to age at home. "People are standing on their heads to stay in their homes," says Cecille Asekoff, Director of the Joint Chaplaincy Committee. Services are needed to prevent isolation and to make this wish possible and safe for these older adults (especially the frail ones) and their caregivers.

3. **Collaborative Working Groups**
Some areas of need cannot be addressed sufficiently by Federation monetarily but should be considered through collaboration and possible advocacy. CARES can convene these groups and then share additional recommendations.
First up: transportation and affordable housing.

References

*State of NJ, Dept. of Labor & Workforce Development, "Population and Labor Force Projections for New Jersey: 2010 to 2030

**A Portrait of Jewish Americans: Findings from a Pew Research Center Survey of U.S. Jews, 2013

Case Study of a Total Rewards Association's Needs Assessment

Lindsay Strack

Abstract

The focus of this case is a strategic needs assessments survey conducted by a global human resources and total rewards association. The organization underwent significant changes in 2017. With a transition in executive leadership and a renewed focus on maximizing organizational impact and value, a needs assessment survey of human resources and total rewards professionals was conducted in December 2017. The purpose was to gather actionable, quantifiable data on current challenges and to identify what those in the field need and how they prefer to be served. The results continue to propel the organization forward in paths of membership, certification, education, and research. Below is an overview of the case.

Where the Needs Assessment Was Conducted	Who Conducted the Needs Assessment	Focus of Needs Assessment	How Data Were Collected	How Data Were Analyzed
Global professional association	Staff of the professional association	Focused on determining current challenges faced by association members and identifying what members needed and how they preferred to be served	Reviewed previous member satisfaction surveys; information gathering interviews with association staff; survey questionnaire to 125,000 individuals—all known current and previous members, customers, and friends of association.	Descriptive statistics for surveys; content analysis for interviews

Background

The focus of this case is a global human resources and total rewards association (GHR&TRA). Founded in 1955, it underwent significant changes in 2017. Despite the previous 60 plus years of the business, the organization was becoming stagnant. The arrival of a new CEO resulted in a renewed organizational direction that touched virtually every aspect of the organization. With strong support from senior leadership, as well as the board of directors, these changes were necessary to ensure the organization's long-term relevance and financial success. Leadership redirected the projected lifecycle stage and moved it back on the path toward growth, into a renewal stage (see Appendix A for the Stages of Nonprofit Organization Lifecycle) (Stevens, 2002). According to the NH Center for Nonprofits (2013), leaders typically use measures of budget size, staffing numbers, or years in business to decide where an organization is in its lifecycle; however, indicators of achieving the mission or impact on its community are lower on the list. Gauges of staff size and financial health can be deceiving, even if they are measuring strong, because they do not always point to an organization achieving its mission. For the current association, stabilizing budget and staffing was critical, but also reaffirming the mission, vision, and values was necessary to bolster the member value proposition.

In early August 2017, nearly 3 months after the transition in executive leadership, the association leaders saw the beginnings of their new thinking and ideas for a path forward realized through a significant reorganization and rightsizing of staff. The decision behind the reorganization and rightsizing was based on an evaluation of the organization's structure and operating and staffing costs. The goals of the effort were to reprioritize and focus on core products and to streamline operations. The reduction in force took the association staff from 123 to 98 (a 20% reduction). The changes were implemented to allow the association to innovate with greater speed and efficiency.

At the end of 2017, the association had reorganized itself, and the bar was raised to move toward delivering exceptional content, education, and events, from content development through marketing, sales, and delivery. The organization established key priorities that would set the tone for 2018, including enhancing the member experience, providing relevant and timely content, reviving and reimagining certifications, and refocusing on global implementation. To shape efforts in delivering on those core focus areas and maximizing value of what the association offers, leadership turned to valuable stakeholders and the community to determine how best to serve the needs that were grounded in an objective perspective. To that end, the organization conducted a broad-based needs assessment survey in December 2017.

Profile of the Organization

Founded in the United States in 1955, today the nonprofit association serves total rewards professionals throughout the world who are working in organizations of all sizes and structures. Total rewards describes all the available tools used by employers to attract, motivate, and retain employees (Helios HR, 2013). The association's mission is to serve, educate, and inspire those who reward and engage the workforce, with a vision of a world of rewarded and engaged workforces. The global nonprofit association specializes in education and certification, and maximizing information sharing, knowledge creation, research, and advocacy.

Preassessment Information

To shape the association's efforts in delivering on the core focus areas and maximizing the value of what it offers, leadership understood the need to make informed decisions grounded in an objective perspective of the needs and preferences of the audiences served. According to Sleezer, Russ-Eft, and Gupta (2014), a strategic needs assessment focuses on learning and performance gaps within the context of the organization's business strategy. By this definition, the association conducted a broad-based strategic needs assessment in December 2017.

The transition in executive leadership and the renewed focus on informed decision making led to constructing a formal needs assessment survey that was grounded in the objective perspective. That is, the needs assessment survey focused on the needs and preferences of those the organization aimed to serve. With the association's priority of meeting the needs of its members and supporting change in the field, the results of this needs assessment had the ability to impact the direction and goals of the association. The assessment focused on improving the organization's value, member and customer satisfaction, and ultimately, increasing the market reach. The objective was to gather information quickly, exhausting the reach to all known current and previous members, customers, and friends of the association, as well as sweep an unfamiliar community and potential customer base. Learning from an audience unfamiliar with the association, and with membership potential, could reshape the direction and the assumptions about the products and/or services ordered or planned.

Needs Assessment Process

The idea for the assessment was initiated and led by the research team and supported by several stakeholders, including new leadership. Buy-in from new and existing leadership was easy to obtain as this was designed to test new concepts and desires of the audience, as well as to validate the current path of the organization. The research team, consisting of four team members, managed the effort of building the needs assessment survey. To start, the research team relied on previous member satisfaction surveys and information gathering interviews with the internal department leads from product management, marketing, news and publications, events and education, and certification. The survey was separated into three sections: membership, certification, and research. Each of the sections was comprised of yes/no, ranking and rating items, and open-ended questions. In an attempt to avoid respondent bias, association product labels and naming were stripped away and replaced with generic terms, such as daily news or legislative/policy updates.

The invitation to participate was communicated via email to 100,000 human resources and total rewards professionals, most of whom had been or were currently engaged with the association. The organization felt it was essential to attempt to reach an unfamiliar audience that was unbiased with the current offerings of products and services; therefore, an additional 25,000 professionals were invited to participate via an external list purchase from a marketing partner. The emailed survey invitation served as a cover letter, highlighting the importance and value of the needs assessment, in addition to survey details. The audience was targeted in three groups, with a slight variation of the marketed messages: members, nonmembers but current or previous customers, and the 25,000 unfamiliar professionals. Company e-newsletter and social media messages were used to promote the survey between the initial survey invitation email and two additional reminders, which were sent a week apart after the invitation using targeted emails to association members and nonmembers. A total of 1,233 responses were received, representing a varied mix of individual levels, generations, and expertise areas, along with a diverse organizational representation in terms of size, sector, industry, and country or countries of operation.

Results of the Needs Assessment

To provide the most reliable and accurate data, IBM'S SPSS software platform was utilized for cleaning and analysis. Records with missing information were kept as partial data, and duplicate records were removed. Descriptive statistics were used to provide an overview of the features of the data. Key findings can be found in Table 17.1.

Table 17.1 Key Findings

1. The most common challenges center around the ongoing evolution of work and workforces, and the need to plan for what these changes will mean for the future.

2. Members prioritize access to thought leaders and subject matter experts, practical resources, and education/training.

3. The profession continues to value certification and prefers programs that validate competencies through testing.

The results began informing the association's determinations around the best paths forward for membership, certification, education, and research. The association will continue to use this information to set and refine its strategic direction and guide decisions about products and services for all audiences.

Influences

Influences of internal and external organizational cultural norms and inter-office politics among staff members were at play. As a professional association in business for more than 60 years, offerings and expectations have been ingrained in members and customers; that is an external influence to which the organization was sensitive in designing the instrument. Change can often be met with resistance, and the organization did not transition without its own battle with internal stakeholders. Organization culture shifted to meet the vision of its new leaders, employee turnover occurred throughout all stages of the reorganization, and leaders needed to gain buy-in from both short- and long-term employees.

Issues and Challenges

To achieve a successful run of the needs assessment survey, it was imperative to organize the already existing information and new ideas on the horizon from all departments into a cohesive and digestible survey to be delivered to the membership at-large. Department and team meetings were held to collect information of interest and ideas to test, and then the research team crafted the questionnaire, which was reviewed and revised several times among the stakeholders. Previously, needs assessments were run as a revolving survey with segments of the membership randomly selected, as well as random sections of the survey activated to reduce respondent burden. This was the first time in the organization's history in which a needs assessment was conducted in the manner where all members were invited to participate, and the content was strategically built and vetted internally.

In an effort to streamline the process and gather data quickly, the organization decided to run the survey in its entirety to the whole member base as opposed to randomizing sections and audience segments over multiple months. This posed a challenge on the respondent side as the survey length was estimated to take an average of 30 minutes; however, we found that most participants needed about half that time to complete their submission. The organization incentivized participation from unknown respondents with a free e-book and relied on good faith from members and customers, as well as promoting the survey through various channels and with the voice of new leadership.

Currently, all association leadership and staff are committed to creating an organization that is bold, dynamic, transparent, and motivated. Understanding that the world of work is changing, the association spent the bulk of 2017 reimaging and restructuring to best deliver speedy and relevant content and education that will serve an evolving audience of rewards professionals.

DISCUSSION QUESTIONS

1. What is the importance of gaining buy-in from leadership?

2. How would you explain the transition of leadership and reason for the needs assessment in communicating to the membership?

3. How would you balance the need for timely results with the importance for best practices of data collection?

4. How could focus groups or follow-up data collection add to this needs assessment by triangulating data collection?

5. How was preliminary information collected about the situation, and how were aspects of the external environment examined?

6. Consider how revising the wording of the needs assessment survey provided a focus for change by requiring leaders and others to make ideas concrete and specific.

REFERENCES

Helios HR. (2013, November 11). A review of the components within a total rewards package. Retrieved from https://www.helioshr.com/2013/11/what-makes-up-a-great-total-rewards-package/.

NH Center for Nonprofits. (2013). Organizational life cycle stages. Retrieved from https://www.nhnonprofits.org/content/organizational-life-cycle-stages.

Sleezer, C. M., Russ-Eft, D. F., & Gupta, K. (2014). *A practical guide to needs assessment*. San Francisco, CA: Wiley & ASTD.

Stevens, S. K. (2002). *Nonprofit lifecycles: Stage-based wisdom for nonprofit capacity*. Wayzata, MN: Stagewise.

Appendix A
Nonprofit Lifecycle Stages

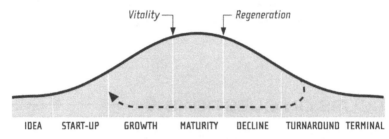

Source: Stevens, 2002

Complex Needs Assessments

"Its purpose is to assess situations that include systemic needs, as well as training needs; assess needs that are complex and require innovation."

(Sleezer, Russ-Eft, & Gupta, 2014, p. 32)

18

Needs Assessment at FMP Consulting

Louise C. Chan

Abstract

FMP Consulting was contracted to conduct job analysis and competency modeling for a federal client to improve the selection process for numerous occupations within the organization. The process included conducting a job analysis, developing and validating competency models, creating and analyzing a job analysis survey, linking job tasks to competencies, developing and validating assessment questions, and compiling all information per occupation into a master workbook. Below is an overview of the case.

Where the Needs Assessment Was Conducted	Who Conducted the Needs Assessment	Focus of Needs Assessment	How Data Were Collected	How Data Were Analyzed
U.S. federal government	FMP Consulting (consulting firm)	Conducted job analysis and competency modeling for a federal client to improve the selection process for numerous occupations within the organization	Identified key tasks from existing client documentations, drafted competencies and assessment items, conducted workshop with subject matter experts to review and validate drafted competencies and assessment items, job analysis survey	Descriptive statistics; used cut-off scores to eliminate tasks and competencies; linked tasks to competencies; developed assessment items; compiled information for each occupation into a master workbook

Background

As part of an internship with Federal Management Partners, Inc. (FMP), I assisted with the creation of competency models and assessment tools for a federal client who experienced difficulty hiring the right candidates for their positions. The selection process tended to be lengthy due to the large number of applicants and difficulty in differentiating the quality of applicants.

The goals of this project were to reduce the size of the applicant pool, identify appropriate job candidates, and provide candidates with a realistic job preview. In addition, the purpose was to identify competencies that individuals across different occupations of the agency should possess to perform successfully on the job and to assess whether candidates possessed those qualities.

Profile of the Organization

FMP Consulting is a small consulting firm that is women owned. It specializes in management and strategy consulting, such as human capital planning, human resource solutions, training and development, and organizational effectiveness. It provides tailored solutions to federal, public, and private sector clients. The federal client we worked with for this assessment employs over 10,000 individuals and has an international focus.

Preassessment Information

The federal client faced challenges in efficiently sorting through the large number of job applicants and selecting appropriately qualified candidates. As a result, they searched for a consulting firm to develop competency models and assessment tools. Because FMP has experience and expertise designing competency models for human capital projects in the federal sector, they were well-equipped to meet the client's needs.

The project team consisted of a project manager, three full-time consultants, an intern, and three subconsultants who provided assistance as needed. The members of the team had backgrounds in industrial-organizational psychology and human resources. They also had considerable experience evaluating and managing the project scope and developing an effective work team through clearly defined roles and structure.

The boundaries of this endeavor included a set budget and timeline as well as the occupations that were assessed. The client determined with which occupations in their organization they needed assistance. This helped define the scope of the project and identify deliverables to ensure the project was completed within the allocated budget and time.

Needs Assessment Process

For the selected occupations in the federal agency, FMP conducted a job analysis, created competency models, and developed assessment items to identify the necessary knowledge, skills, and abilities that individuals should possess to perform their roles successfully. This process consisted of the following steps:

Conduct Job Analysis and Competency Modeling

1. **Identify key tasks from existing client documentations and draft competencies.** From the client documentations, such as position descriptions and job announcements, and Occupational Information Network (O*NET), consultants from FMP identified tasks that were deemed essential to the position. These tasks were used to draft competencies with a competency name, definition, and behavioral indicators for proficiency levels ranging from 1 (basic) to 5 (expert). The competencies were compartmentalized into three categories: technical, core, and leadership. Similar tasks were grouped into a competency to avoid redundancy. Reducing the number of competencies helped minimize fatigue and time on the subject matter experts (SMEs) during the review process.

Over time, with more competencies created, we compiled a library of competencies that could be utilized when assessing occupations in the future. For occupations with existing competencies, each drafted competency can be compared with the one in the library and updated where necessary to reflect the successful performance of the job. New competencies, can be compared with similar existing competencies to determine appropriate proficiency levels and to incorporate new occupational information.

2. **Conduct workshop with subject matter experts to review and validate drafted competencies.** The SMEs were job incumbents and supervisors within each occupation. They were identified by the federal agency and asked to assist with the review and validation process. While five to seven SMEs are recommended in each focus group workshop, the number of SMEs is dependent on the size of the occupation and the SMEs' availability to attend the workshop.

Prior to the virtual workshop, the tasks and competencies were sent to the SMEs for review. During the workshop, the facilitator from FMP reviewed each competency along with its proficiency levels. SMEs were given the opportunity to add, edit, or remove competencies and behavioral indicators to ensure an accurate reflection of each position. After the workshop, the revised competencies were sent to the SMEs to review them once more and finalize them.

3. **Distribute job analysis survey to SMEs.** FMP created a job analysis survey using the finalized tasks and competencies. Using a Likert scale, the SMEs rated each task on its importance and frequency with which it is performed. They rated each competency on its importance and whether it was needed for job entry. The SMEs also assigned a grade level to each proficiency level of the competency.

4. **Analyze data from the job analysis survey.** After the SMEs participated in the survey, the data were collected and analyzed. A cut-off score was used to determine the tasks and competencies that were not critical to the position, which would then be eliminated.

5. **Link tasks to competencies.** FMP linked tasks to competencies to show justification that essential tasks were reflected in the competencies. Any tasks and competencies that did not meet the criticality criteria for the position, as mentioned above, were eliminated as they were shown not to be related to the job.

Develop Assessment Items

6. **Develop assessment items by grade level.** Using the results of the job analysis survey, FMP created multiple-choice assessment questions that differentiated individuals based on the technical, core, and leadership competencies. For accuracy, each competency should have at least one to two assessment questions. The responses to the questions were scored so that a qualified candidate would display mastery of the competency by receiving a higher score than a candidate who was not qualified.

7. **Conduct workshop with SMEs to review and validate assessment items.** This workshop was conducted in a similar manner as the one for competency review. The assessment items were sent to the same SMEs prior to the workshop for review. The facilitator from FMP held a workshop virtually to review and validate the assessment questions and corresponding responses. The SMEs were given the opportunity to revise the questions and responses as necessary to ensure accuracy and relevance to the position, readability to ensure a clear understanding, and variability to differentiate the applicants. After the workshop, the revised assessment items were sent to SMEs for review once more. The result of the workshop was a set of finalized assessment items for the occupation.

8. **Create a master workbook of all information.** The finalized information from each step of the process was assembled into a master workbook in Excel for the client. The client utilized the assessment items as part of their selection tool to hire candidates.

Comparison to Competency-Based Needs Assessment

The approach that FMP took in conducting job analysis and competency modeling shares similarities to competency-based needs assessment as described by Sleezer, Russ-Eft, and Gupta (2014), with the expert development and validation approach. They both utilized SMEs to refine and validate the competency model and assessment items. In addition, a competency dictionary was created to build a library of competencies and definitions, and competencies were created for each occupation.

Conversely, the approach from FMP merged the methods of job analysis and competency modeling. It utilized information gathered from job analysis to construct competency models. The SMEs were not involved in the creation of the preliminary competency draft. Moreover, the competency dictionary from FMP was not grouped into dimensions. Each competency was assessed across the five proficiency levels (i.e., basic to expert), with behavioral indicators for each level.

Results of the Needs Assessment

The client was very satisfied with the needs assessment deliverables. As a result, the original contract was extended to assess more occupations within the agency. Over a 2-year period, FMP conducted job analysis and developed competencies and assessment items for a majority of the positions within the client's organization.

Influences

Because FMP had prior experience with similar projects, there was already a well-defined structure for roles, responsibilities, and work processes. This improved efficiency in the work output as everyone clearly understood the workflow. Furthermore, FMP had a supportive culture of employees, transparent communication, and a friendly environment. This fostered collaboration, open communication, and trust among employees.

As an intern, it was important that I embraced the FMP culture and embodied their values. For example, I understood my responsibilities and referred to the project manager for questions. I checked-in regularly with the project manager to provide updates and plan ahead for the following weeks. Because of the open and collaborative culture, my team members and I felt comfortable asking one another for assistance on tasks, whether it was due to a heavy workload or difficulty with the task itself. In agreement with the client, we had a set schedule for each occupation and ensured that our work met those deadlines.

During my communications with the client, the FMP view was demonstrated through the focus group sessions I conducted. I arrived to the sessions punctually and dressed professionally. Because the sessions were held virtually, it was especially important to build rapport and communicate clearly with the SMEs. It was also important to be flexible as we worked in a dynamic environment where changes could occur anytime.

Issues and Challenges

Because it was my first time working in a consulting firm, I had to learn the processes and workflow of the organization as well as the client. In terms of communications, the focus groups were held virtually to accommodate SMEs who worked in different office locations. This presented a number of challenges. There were at times technological issues, such as background noise or difficulty accessing the conference call. It was more challenging to build rapport virtually and the lack of body language added a barrier to communication. To address this issue, the project manager sent an introduction email to the SMEs prior to the focus group. The facilitator introduced himself or herself at the beginning of the focus group and clearly explained the purpose of the project. An effort was made to increase communication during the focus group to clarify statements and check in with SMEs to ensure they were engaged and attentive.

Moreover, not every SME could attend the full duration of the focus group, if at all, due to schedule conflicts. The variability in attendance rate made it difficult to ensure a comprehensive evaluation of the competencies and assessment items. As a result, the drafted information was sent to all the SMEs for feedback before and after each focus group. That way, those who could not attend the session still had the opportunity to provide feedback.

Likewise, several job analysis surveys suffered from low response rates, which at times were due to the small number of job incumbents in the occupations. This made it challenging to gather sufficient data and assess the proficiency and importance of job tasks and competencies. While FMP had no control over the number of SMEs available for each position, we did encourage participation in the job analysis surveys by informing participants that a survey would be sent shortly after the focus group for their review, by emphasizing the value of their feedback to improve the selection process, and by sending email reminders prior to the survey due date.

Working with a federal client comes with its own set of challenges. For instance, a budget cut to the client's organization may affect their budget for our project. Thus, we had to be adaptable to changes that could occur and readjust our scope of the project as needed. The process may also be slower with a federal client (e.g., multiple people may need to review and approve documents before proceeding). It is important to manage expectations and the process, which may be different for each client.

DISCUSSION QUESTIONS

1. What are some challenges in working with a federal client rather than those in the public or private sector?

2. What would be some intrinsic and extrinsic motivation for SMEs to participate in the focus groups and job analysis surveys?

3. Because of the large applicant pool and rate of processing applications, the selection process often took longer than expected. What are the results of a long selection process?

4. Because varying levels of stakeholders were involved, how would each level (e.g., primary, secondary, and tertiary as described in Russ-Eft and Preskill, [2009] and in Russ-Eft, Sleezer, Sampson, and Leviton, [2017]) affect the project?

REFERENCES

Russ-Eft, D., & Preskill, H. (2009). *Evaluation in organizations: A systematic approach to enhancing learning, performance, and change* (2nd ed.). New York, NY: Basic Books.

Russ-Eft, D. F., Sleezer, C. M., Sampson, G., & Leviton, L. (2017). *Managing applied social research: Tools, strategies, and insights.* San Francisco, CA: Jossey-Bass.

Sleezer, C. M., Russ-Eft, D. F., & Gupta, K. (2014). *A practical guide to needs assessment* (3rd ed.). San Francisco, CA: Wiley & ASTD.

19

Readiness for Integrating Behavioral Health and Primary Care

Application of the R = MC² Framework

**Ariel M. Domlyn, Tara Kenworthy,
Jonathan P. Scaccia, and Victoria Scott**

Abstract

Organizations are complex and dynamic systems that require continuous adaptation and growth to operate effectively. These changes often involve adopting innovations (i.e., policies, programs, processes, or practices new to the setting). Understanding and measuring organizational readiness for change can increase the success of change efforts. This case study describes how readiness (motivation, general capacity, and innovation-specific capacity) was measured and utilized as part of a strategic needs assessment in a primary care practice implementing integrated care. Below is an overview of the case.

Where the Needs Assessment Was Conducted	Who Conducted the Needs Assessment	Focus of Needs Assessment	How Data Were Collected	How Data Were Analyzed
One outpatient care organization within a metropolitan area in the southeastern United States	An evaluation team was led by two community psychology professors and assisted by three graduate students from two universities. No one on the team was affiliated with the organization undergoing the needs assessment.	Assessed journey of integrating behavioral health and primary care by investigating changes in organizational readiness.	(a) The *Readiness for Integrated Care Questionnaire* (RICQ), (b) readiness score reports, (c) follow-up phone calls, and (d) qualitative interviews	Average RICQ scores and changes in scores over time; interview transcriptions analyzed by two independent coders using grounded theory and reconciliation of differences in themes

Background

Health care organizations must make continuous improvements and incorporate current science to provide quality health and human services. These improvements often involve adopting an innovation (i.e., policy, program, process, or practice new to the setting). Readiness refers to the set of conditions needed to make a change happen. In this case, we describe the use of a readiness heuristic ($R = MC^2$) as applied to an organizational assessment tool. The $R = MC^2$ model posits that the readiness of an organization to implement an innovation impacts implementation outcomes, which impact client outcomes. This case illustrates key organizational elements that influence readiness for integrating behavioral health and primary care services (i.e., "integrated care").

Implementation quality is paramount to achieving targeted outcomes (Durlak & Dupre, 2008; Fixsen et al., 2005). Quality implementation requires organizations to have adequate capacity, or the particular conditions essential to engage in a change or improvement effort. Capacity requirements can be examined across two domains: innovation specific and general (Flaspohler et al., 2008; Wandersman et al., 2008). *Innovation-specific capacities* are the knowledge, skills, and conditions needed to put a specific innovation in place. *General capacities* refer to the context and capabilities affecting an organization's overall operations.

Although capacity is a critical component of readiness, practice-based evidence in Empowerment Evaluation (Fetterman & Wandersman, 2015) has demonstrated that capacity is an insufficient condition for effective change. Organizational readiness is also contingent on the motivation of organizational staff to implement the innovation (Weiner, 2009; Weiner, Amick, & Lee, 2008). At the organizational level, *motivation* refers to the degree of interest associated with a particular objective. A low degree of motivation for change within an organization will inhibit or stunt change efforts. Akin to a three-legged stool, organizational readiness to implement an innovation requires all three legs (innovation-specific capacity, general capacity, and motivation) for the stool to stand, or to operate as intended (see Figure 19.1). Organizations must be willing (motivated) and able (capacity) to engage in the change effort. Together, these components of readiness are abbreviated as $R = MC^2$ (Readiness = **M**otivation x Innovation-Specific **C**apacity x General **C**apacity; Scaccia et al., 2015).

We have developed several guiding principles for how readiness operates in community-based settings. These principles influence the content and timing of a needs assessment process for a specific innovation.

Readiness exists on a continuum

Rather than being "ready" or "not ready," the $R = MC^2$ framework delineates distinct aspects of readiness that vary within organizations. This nuanced construct provides actionable data by identifying specific ways in which an

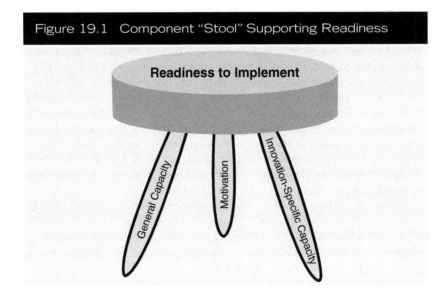

Figure 19.1   Component "Stool" Supporting Readiness

Readiness to Implement

General Capacity

Motivation

Innovation-Specific Capacity

organization's readiness may be relatively stronger or weaker. A useful readiness assessment gives a comprehensive picture of the current capabilities and motivations of an organization. To achieve this aim, each main component of readiness (general capacity, innovation-specific capacity, and motivation) includes multiple relevant subcomponents (Table 19.1; updated from Scaccia et al., 2015).

Readiness is important throughout implementation

Readiness can be relevant at the beginning during the adoption phase, for the early stages of trying an innovation out, during full-scale implementation, and when institutionalizing or sustaining an innovation (Fixsen, Naoom, Blase, & Friedman, 2005; Prasad & Ioannidis, 2014; Scott et al., 2017). An assessment of readiness provides value for planning and monitoring throughout the lifecycle of an innovation.

Readiness is dynamic

Readiness can increase or decrease in response to both planned and unplanned events. For example, readiness may decrease if a senior leader or champion leaves an organization. By understanding the specific areas in which an organization may need assistance at any given time during implementation, support providers can strategically tailor training, technical

Table 19.1 Definition of Components and Subcomponents Defining Readiness for Innovation

Motivation
Degree to which we want the innovation to happen

Relative advantage	This innovation seems better than other innovations
Compatibility	This innovation fits with how we do things
Simplicity	This innovation seems simple to use
Ability to pilot	Degree to which this innovation can be tested and experimented with
Observability	Ability to see that this innovation is leading to outcomes
Priority	Importance of this innovation compared to other things we do

Innovation-specific capacity
What is needed for this particular innovation to happen

Innovation-specific knowledge & skills	Sufficient abilities to do this innovation
Champion	A well-connected person who supports and models the innovation
Supportive Climate	Necessary supports, processes, and resources to enable this innovation
Interorganizational Relationships	Relationships between organizations that support this innovation

General capacity
Our overall functioning

Culture	Norms and values of how we do things here
Climate	The feeling of being part of this organization
Innovativeness	Openness to change in general
Resource Utilization	Ability to acquire and allocate resources including time, money, effort, and technology
Leadership	Effectiveness of our leaders
Internal Operations	Effectiveness at communication and teamwork
Staff Capacity	Having enough of the right people to get things done
Process Capacity	Ability to plan, implement, and evaluate

assistance, and quality improvement initiatives in a way that is sensitive to fluctuations in readiness.

Readiness is innovation specific

This model of readiness allows assessment of the conditions specific to an innovation. An organization may have differing degrees of readiness depending on the innovation they intend to implement. For example, an organization may have high readiness to implement an obesity prevention program, but lack readiness to do a smoking cessation program. Thus, it is important to consider the innovation-specific factors (motivation and innovation-specific capacity) of readiness to ensure quality implementation.

Preassessment Information

We now turn to how $R = MC^2$ was used within the context of a needs assessment and how these data were used to help promote change within an organization.

Most patients who experience psychological distress first seek treatment in primary care clinics (Kessler, 2012). However, primary care providers often lack adequate training to address these needs (Kathol, Butler, McAlpine, & Kane, 2010). Even though a patient may be referred to a mental health specialist, patients often do not follow through with beginning treatment (Kessler, 2012).

As part of a larger movement toward coordinated health care in the United States, integrated behavioral health and primary care settings attempt to collaboratively treat patients' physical, behavioral, and emotional problems. Integrated care happens when mental health and primary care providers collaborate as members of a patient-centered care team. Integrated care is further recognized as a promising systems-level process for reducing mental health disparities and promoting mental health equity, particularly among racial and ethnic minorities (Satcher & Rachel, 2016).

This case study describes the integrated care journey and factors affecting changes in readiness for *Sunrise Wellness*. (Sunrise Wellness is a fictional name. The clinic's name and some other factors have been changed to de-identify the organization.) Their experience provides an opportunity to understand how readiness is used as a tool for assessing needs, targeting areas for improvement, and framing support to implement an innovation with quality.

Organizational Profile

Sunrise Wellness is an outpatient care organization established in the 1980s, located within a metropolitan area in the southeastern United States. It is composed of multiple practices serving roughly 12,000 unique patients per year. Sunrise Wellness is a federally qualified heath center that serves predominantly uninsured adults, many of whom experience housing instability.

At the time of the needs assessment, the practice had been working to integrate care for 2 years, particularly at one site in the downtown area. Clinical providers at this site included three physicians, nine nurse practitioners, seven nurses, six social workers, two psychologists, one psychiatrist, and one optometrist. Previous efforts to integrate care included sending behavioral health and primary care staff to train at a regional specialty care center, using mental health screening tools for adults and children (Patient Health Questionnaire-2; Arrol et al., 2010), and establishing referral relationships with the local crisis center and hospital. Practice members had some experience with quality improvement methods, but no prior experience assessing readiness.

In 2016, Sunrise Wellness was accepted into the Integrated Care Leadership Program (ICLP), a 1-year national integrated care capacity building effort led by the Satcher Health Leadership Institute at Morehouse School of Medicine. The ICLP was designed to equip health care providers with the knowledge, skills, and resources necessary to advance integrated care within health care practices. A distinct aspect of the ICLP initiative was examining and leveraging organizational readiness for integrated care. An evaluation team, which included the authors of this chapter, worked with the ICLP implementation team to facilitate this readiness assessment and subsequent intervention process. This evaluation team, none of whom were affiliated with Sunrise Wellness, was led by two community psychology professors and assisted by three graduate students located at the University of North Carolina at Charlotte and the University of South Carolina. Under the direction of the evaluation leads, one graduate student collected and analyzed *Readiness for Integrated Care Questionnaire* (RICQ) data and created reports, and two other graduate students conducted qualitative data collection during a site visit to Sunrise Wellness. Two of these graduate students also conducted interpretive calls with the ICLP sites and all evaluation team members met in person with ICLP participants during two in-person summits. These activities were reviewed with the ICLP implementation team as part of their dynamic collaboration. The implementation team provided integrated care technical assistance and education to the sites following Wave 1 data feedback.

Needs Assessment Process

As part of a strategic needs assessment (see Sleezer, Russ-Eft, & Gupta, 2014), a readiness assessment was required for application to the ICLP. These baseline readiness data enabled the ICLP readiness team to understand variations in organizational readiness across health care practices. The readiness assessment also allowed for ongoing monitoring of each practice's weaknesses, strengths, and changing needs. This information was used to inform action plans for improving implementation of integrated care. Results from each administration, and their changes over time, were used by the ICLP implementation team to monitor areas in need of additional resources. Results were shared with participating health care practices, with an invitation for phone meetings with evaluation team members to discuss readiness data.

Primary Respondents/Informants

All staff members were eligible for contributing to the readiness assessments. A quantitative readiness tool was completed by a range of staff from Sunrise Wellness, including nurses, mental health providers, and physicians. Administrative staff did not participate. We gathered additional qualitative information from two behavioral health specialists and a psychiatrist.

Methods

The following subsections describe the data collection methods used. These include: (a) the RICQ, (b) readiness reports, (c) interpretive phone calls, and (d) qualitative interviews.

Readiness for Integrated Care Questionnaire

The RICQ, based on the $R = MC^2$ framework, was used to assess the readiness needs and resources for each practice (Scott et al., 2017). All ICLP sites completed this 82-item questionnaire online. The RICQ was based on a previous $R = MC^2$ assessment survey, which found the measure's Cronbach's alpha reliability statistics to range from .73 to .95, varying by subcomponent (Scott et al., 2016). Sunrise Wellness submitted baseline (Wave 1) data between November 2015 and March 2016, resulting in a total sample of 12 respondents from their organization. The second administration of the RICQ (Wave 2) occurred from May to July 2016, with 29 respondents from Sunrise Wellness. At the third and final wave of data collection (Wave 3) in August 2016, 22 staff members from Sunrise Wellness completed the RICQ.

Reports

Reports were created for Sunrise Wellness after each period of RICQ data collection. The reports reflected average readiness scores and (for Wave 2 and 3) changes in scores over time. The scores from all respondents at the practice were averaged for each item. The average of items within each readiness subcomponent created a subcomponent score. The appropriate subcomponents (see Table 19.1) were then averaged to create component scores for motivation, innovation-specific capacity, and general capacity. Readiness subcomponent scores that were relatively high or relatively low were highlighted to demonstrate areas of strengths and areas for improvement. On Wave 2 and 3 reports, subcomponents with significant changes from the previous wave were also highlighted in the reports.

Interpretive calls with practices

Preliminary Wave 1 results were shared with practice members during a kick-off meeting in January 2016. After each wave of data collection, 1-hour calls were scheduled with participating sites to review the practice-specific readiness scores. On these calls, the evaluation team provided practices with additional opportunities to reflect on their readiness data, ask questions, and discuss practical implications of the data. The evaluation team also provided support by assisting interpretation of the results and suggesting areas for improvement. Information gathered from these calls was relayed to ICLP staff to provide a greater sense of the strengths and challenges and issues that each practice faced.

Qualitative interviews

After the Wave 3 data collection, two evaluation team members conducted an on-site group interview at Sunrise Wellness. Two behavioral health specialists and the lead psychiatrist participated. The purpose of the visit was to understand how readiness was understood by the staff members and how the RICQ data had been used to inform action. Interview transcriptions were analyzed using grounded theory. Two coders independently analyzed interview transcriptions using grounded theory, reconciled differences in themes, then conducted member checks with the interviewees during a January 2017 in-person follow-up meeting.

Needs Assessment Results

This section integrates the quantitative and qualitative data to highlight how specific areas of the assessment were used (Figure 19.2). *Motivation* was Sunrise Wellness' strongest component across all waves. RICQ results indicated that their motivations was high due to the perceived compatibility of integrated care, the relative advantage it held over current practices, and the heightened priority of integrating behavioral health and primary care. However, this component also contained their overall lowest scoring subcomponent: simplicity.

In terms of their *general capacity,* the RICQ revealed relative strengths in leadership, organizational culture, and process capacities. The CEO of Sunrise Wellness was reported to be very supportive of the projects the clinic undertook and sought to acquire resources and trainings necessary to ensure that the staff would provide suitable patient care. He was also noted to be particularly supportive of behavioral health staff's wishes to integrate care. The strong culture of the organization indicated that Sunrise Wellness staff share a common purpose and goals for care. They also reported a strong sense of belonging and identification

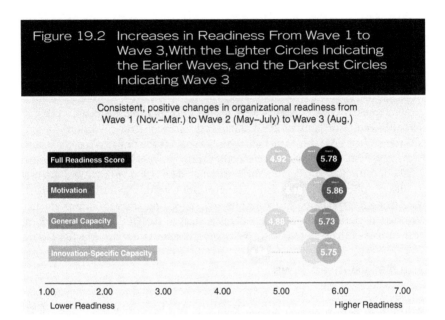

Figure 19.2 Increases in Readiness From Wave 1 to Wave 3, With the Lighter Circles Indicating the Earlier Waves, and the Darkest Circles Indicating Wave 3

Consistent, positive changes in organizational readiness from Wave 1 (Nov.–Mar.) to Wave 2 (May–July) to Wave 3 (Aug.)

Full Readiness Score   4.92   5.78

Motivation   5.86

General Capacity   4.88   5.73

Innovation-Specific Capacity   5.75

1.00   2.00   3.00   4.00   5.00   6.00   7.00
Lower Readiness   Higher Readiness

within the practice. The readiness assessment also revealed a strength in process capacities, regarding which staff felt capable of evaluating their work and developing strategic plans.

Innovation-specific capacity for Sunrise Wellness revealed the greatest growth over time from Wave 1 to Wave 3, among the three readiness components. Significant positive change was seen in the RICQ champion score from Wave 1 to Wave 2. One champion was the staff psychiatrist who instigated initial interest in integrating behavioral health and primary care and secured the support of leadership. Another champion was an early adopter physician who used the behavioral health screening and referral tools. She provided a rallying point for behavioral health staff to feel supported by the primary care branch of the clinic.

Processing of Results

Sunrise Wellness used their results from the Wave 1 readiness report to act on improving the perceived simplicity of integrating behavioral health and primary care. This simplicity score indicated that many staff felt integrated care was difficult to implement because it is perceived as a complex process. In response, behavioral health staff chose to host a retreat to discuss the innovation and address perceptions about its complexity. Strengths in leadership, culture, process capacities, and champions provided leverage for improving this relative weakness revealed by the RICQ. Leadership was supportive of the staff retreat and ensured that time was dedicated to the retreat. Conversations at the retreat were candid, indicative of their strong organizational culture, and often led by the champions.

Conversations at this retreat further revealed that perceived simplicity varied by role. Behavioral health coordinators saw integrating care as less complex than primary care providers. Using their strength in process capacities, Sunrise Wellness evaluated the effects of these clarifying conversations on readiness by requesting the Wave 3 RICQ administration to immediately follow the retreat and employing a facilitator to provide reflections on the process. Following this retreat, physician readiness scores increased. However, in qualitative interviews respondents felt that physician buy-in remained a significant barrier to full implementation. This was partly due to continued perception that integrated care is complex (as indicated by the simplicity subcomponent, which was consistently the lowest score across all administrations), and partly due to staff turnover that caused overall capacity to decline.

After a hiatus in their behavioral health task force meetings following Wave 3 data collection, Sunrise Wellness resumed their monthly meetings between behavioral health and primary care providers in November 2016 to discuss integrated care. As of January 2017, they had continued to hold monthly task force meetings. They planned to send more people for integrated care training and were working toward changing their internal operations to help smooth the path for integrated care. Qualitative interviews indicated that Sunrise Wellness planned to incorporate integrated care as part of their standard employee training for new staff, intending to mitigate issues they had with both staff turnover and perceived complexity. The experience of Sunrise Wellness suggests that RICQ is useful for both reflecting on changes in readiness as they unfold and as a tool to spark action toward improvement.

Influences

Several factors facilitated assessment efforts. Aiding the process was a preexisting agreement between evaluators and ICLP implementers that this needs assessment was a priority and would be included as a primary feature of the project. As such, evaluators oriented all clinics to the RICQ early in the process. This preexisting agreement also ensured that members of the ICLP implementation team were dedicated to conducting this process for all sites, ensuring reminders were sent and data were processed. Evaluators were also able to offer interpretation support and additional assistance upon clinics' request.

The Sunrise Wellness staff benefited from discussions with evaluators about areas for improvement in their readiness for integrated care. For example, the needs assessment identified simplicity as a lower-readiness area. By digesting this information and discussing it with other staff, the evaluation team, and ICLP coaches, Sunrise Wellness staff identified a strategy to overcome this barrier to implementation; they planned a retreat to break down the complexity of integrated care for all staff. Aiding achievement of outcomes, leadership at Sunrise Wellness sought to improve integrated care efforts and took initiative to secure resources for ongoing needs assessment. Their support ensured that RICQ data were thoughtfully processed and acted upon. Overall, staff reported that their readiness-based needs assessment allowed them to "know more now, where we're doing well and where we're not." They reported valuing the RICQ and considered continuing use of readiness assessment tools to target action.

Issues and Challenges

This readiness-based needs assessment process encountered several issues and challenges. One issue was the time dedicated to both the needs assessment and improvement activities. Sunrise Wellness staff were also treating clients and serving their community, in addition to enacting organizational changes. Another challenge was different samples at each RICQ administration. Earliest administrations included primarily behavioral health staff, whereas respondents in later waves represented a variety of positions. Leadership incentivized staff to respond to the RICQ for these later waves, which resulted in more robust data for Wave 2 and Wave 3. In addition, at times respondents did not appear to be accurate reporters of their organization's readiness. For example, physician readiness increased after the practice retreat; yet, qualitative interviews of other staff indicated that physicians remained barriers to integrated care. Staff also reported that, in hindsight, they were not as ready to integrate care as they thought they were when the ICLP began.

Specific recommendations for building readiness were not supplied by the evaluation team. After interpretive calls with readiness team members, Sunrise Wellness staff needed to identify best practices for their chosen improvement areas. The staff reported that they did not thoughtfully consider how to build their readiness. They identified simplicity as a low score and held a retreat to address this. However, they were not sure how the retreat would directly impact simplicity. While generally results showed that readiness increased after the retreat, simplicity remained the lowest score. Future work will consider more intentional methods for building readiness.

These issues highlight the importance of continued assessment of readiness, discussion surrounding results, providing clearer guidance for building readiness, and incorporating objective indicators of readiness in the future.

Reflections on the Use of Readiness

Considering readiness as a combination of general capacity, innovation-specific capacity, and motivation is a helpful lens for studying organizational conditions. Across different interventions and settings, $R = MC^2$ is a flexible heuristic useful for facilitating implementation. Although this case study describes the RICQ, an evaluator or researcher does not necessarily need a specific instrument to assess readiness. Instead, consider which current or future organizational conditions are necessary to successfully implement an innovation. By assessing these conditions per the three main $R = MC^2$ components, stakeholders can intuitively understand their organizations' needs. Engaging stakeholders in discussion about motivation and capacities meaningfully connects them to the assessment. Use of the $R = MC^2$ framework leads organizations from assessment to action and is particularly useful for program design and improvement.

DISCUSSION QUESTIONS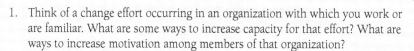

1. Think of a change effort occurring in an organization with which you work or are familiar. What are some ways to increase capacity for that effort? What are ways to increase motivation among members of that organization?

2. Consider the subcomponents in Table 19.1. Which seem most important at different points of implementation, and why?

3. Broadly, how can a needs assessment process be used as an intervention itself? How can learning about data be a stimulus for action, as was the case with Sunrise Wellness?

REFERENCES

Arroll, B., Goodyear Smith, F., Crengle, S., Gunn, J., Kerse, N., Fishman, T., . . . & Hatcher, S. (2010). Validation of PHQ-2 and PHQ-9 to screen for major depression in the primary care population. *The Annals of Family Medicine, 8*(4), 348–353. doi:10.1370/afm.1139

Durlak, J. A., & DuPre, E. P. (2008). Implementation matters: A review of research on the influence of implementation on program outcomes and the factors affecting implementation. *American Journal of Community Psychology, 41*(3/4), 327–350. doi:10.1007/s10464-008-9165-0

Fetterman, D., Kaftarian, S., & Wandersman, A. (Eds.). (2015). *Empowerment evaluation* (2nd ed.). Thousand Oaks, CA: Sage.

Fixsen, D. L., Naoom, S. F., Blase, K. A., & Friedman, R. M. (2005). *Implementation research: A synthesis of the literature.* Tampa, FL: University of South Florida, Louis de la Parte Florida Mental Health Institute, The National Implementation Research Network (FMHI Publication #231).

Flaspohler, P., Duffy, J., Wandersman, A., Stillman, L., & Maras, M. A. (2008). Unpacking prevention capacity: An intersection of research-to-practice models and community-centered models. *American Journal of Community Psychology, 41*(3/4), 182–196. doi:10.1007/s10464-008-9162-3

Kathol, R. G., Butler, M., McAlpine, D. D., & Kane, R. L. (2010). Barriers to physical and mental condition integrated service delivery. *Psychosomatic Medicine, 72*(6), 511–518. doi:10.1097/PSY.0b013e3181e2c4a0

Kessler, R. (2012). Mental health care treatment initiation when mental health services are incorporated into primary care practices. *Journal of American Board of Family Medicine, 25*(2), 225–229. doi:10.3122/jabfm.2012.02.100125

Prasad, V., & Ioannidis, J. P. (2014). Evidence-based de-implementation for contradicted, unproven, and aspiring healthcare practices. *Implementation Science, 9*(1), 1. doi:10.1186/1748-5908-9-1

Satcher, D., & Rachel, S. A. (2016). Promoting mental health equity: The role of integrated care. *Journal of Clinical Psychology in Medical Settings, 24*(3/4), 182–186. doi:10.1007/s10880-016-9465-8

Scaccia, J. P., Cook, B. S., Lamont, A., Wandersman, A., Castellow, J., Katz, J., & Beidas, R. S. (2015). A practice implementation science heuristic for organizational readiness: R = MC^2. *Journal of Community Psychology, 43*(4), 484–501. doi:10.1002/jcop.21698

Scott, V. C., Kenworthy, T., Godly-Reynolds, E., Bastien, G., Scaccia, J., McMickens, C., & Wandersman, A. (2017). The Readiness for Integrated Care Questionnaire (RICQ): An instrument to assess readiness to integrate behavioral health and primary care. *American Journal of Orthopsychiatry, 87*(5), 520–530. doi:10.1037/ort0000270

Sleezer, C. M., Russ-Eft, D., & Gupta, K. (2014). *A practical guide to needs assessment* (3rd ed.). San Francisco, CA: Wiley & ASTD.

Wandersman, A., Duffy, J., Flaspohler, P., Noonan, R., Lubell, K., Stillman, L., & Saul, J. (2008). Bridging the gap between prevention research and practice: The interactive systems framework for dissemination and implementation. *American Journal of Community Psychology, 41*(3/4), 171–181. doi:10.1007/s10464-008-9174-z

Weiner, B. J. (2009). A theory of organizational readiness for change. *Implementation Science, 4*(1), 67. doi.org: 10.1186/1748-5908-4-67

Weiner, B. J., Amick, H., & Lee, S. Y. D. (2008). Conceptualization and measurement of organizational readiness for change: A review of the literature in health services research and other fields. *Medical Care Research and Review, 65*(4), 379–436. doi:10.1177/1077558708317802

CHAPTER

20

Faculty and Student Perceptions of University Course Evaluations

Melanie Suzanne Simpson, Ginny Cockerill, Andrea Word, and Derek Koehl

Abstract

This case study details a complex needs assessment of the student course evaluation process at a public university. Analyses were conducted on course evaluation data spanning six semesters and focus group sessions with stakeholders. The assessment findings inspired an action plan to increase stakeholder engagement, support instructional practice, and better inform organizational initiatives. Below is an overview of the case.

Where the Needs Assessment Was Conducted	Who Conducted the Needs Assessment	Focus of Needs Assessment	How Data Were Collected	How Data Were Analyzed
Mid-sized, high undergraduate, higher research activity institution located in the southern United States	Internal staff and faculty with staff/ faculty from a neutral office for the focus groups	Focused on the course evaluation process to identify and address barriers to stakeholder engagement, to guide departmental and institutional support for instructional practice	Results from course evaluations for six semesters (spring 2015 through fall 2017) with both quantitative responses (Likert 4- and 5-point scales) and qualitative comments; focus groups with students and with faculty; an environmental scan of initiatives and procedures currently informing support of teaching across the institution; a review of the steps in the current evaluation process	Statistical analysis of the numeric ratings and a text analysis of the comments on student–instructor evaluations; review and analysis of focus group data

Background

Student course evaluations typically form the primary pathway that provides student feedback to faculty as they consider pedagogical and curricular changes. As Golding and Lee (2014) noted, periodic reviews of such cycles are important both to improve procedures and to determine how well the evaluations meet the stated objectives. Office of Institutional Research and Assessment (OIRA) staff collaborated with colleagues from the College of Education to conduct just such a needs assessment of the institution's course evaluations, called student–instructor evaluations (SIEs).

The organization (i.e., the university) was a regional university in the United States with seven academic colleges offering undergraduate and graduate degrees in more than 100 areas of study and serving over 9,000 students. Classified by the Carnegie Foundation for the Advancement of Teaching as a higher research activity university, the organization's dual mission was to educate through both research and teaching. The dual demands for faculty to constantly improve their teaching along with their research heightened the need for meaningful feedback and administrative support in the SIE process.

The last review of the SIE process took place in 2014 when a university-wide task force streamlined multiple college- and department-specific forms into a single form and oversaw the transition from paper to online evaluations. In 2016, SIEs were moved from another department to OIRA and the task force was reconvened to revisit the questions and recommend improvements to address the low response rates received (see Table 20.1). This task force also adjusted the Likert scale from 4 to 5 points. Based on task-force feedback, OIRA staff adjusted the distribution-reporting cycle, leveraging functions in the online software. In 2018, this new cycle had been in place for 2 full academic years and was ready for another review.

Initial analysis revealed a linear process for SIEs: They were administered to students each semester, and results were compiled and distributed to course

Table 20.1	Undergraduate Student Response Rates by Semester		
Semester	Number of Responses	Number of Students	Response Rate
Spring 2015	13,092	21,636	60.51%
Fall 2015	13,665	25,958	52.64%
Spring 2016	12,319	24,630	50.02%
Fall 2016	15,269	28,949	52.74%
Spring 2017	15,590	27,856	55.97%
Fall 2017	17,111	32,374	52.85%

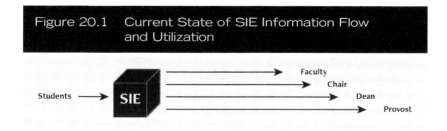

Figure 20.1   Current State of SIE Information Flow
and Utilization

faculty and the relevant academic administrators (see Figure 20.1). Because the process did not appear to inform any type of systemic improvement, key stakeholders had little impetus to engage with the process beyond the individual level. Consequently, the resulting changes were implemented sporadically across individual faculty, departments, and/or colleges.

Preassessment Information

Limited Scope

Because of the complexity inherent in any comprehensive course evaluation process, our first step was to constrain the scope of the needs assessment itself. The content of the SIE form and the policies around the process were governed by a faculty committee and not easily changed. However, OIRA staff had some leeway in implementation, such as the procedures for distributing, administering, and collecting SIEs and for reporting the results. This had historically been a linear process, as illustrated in Figure 20.1. In contrast, Figure 20.2 shows the desired state of SIE information flow and utilization, with the question mark representing aspects of the process outside the OIRA purview. Narrowing the scope of the needs assessment allowed us to focus on identifying what was needed to facilitate a cyclical instead of a linear nature. We further narrowed the focus to undergraduate courses only because graduate courses are often highly specialized and may have few students enrolled. This was seen as the first of a series of needs assessments with later efforts focusing on teaching support and professional development by other offices on campus.

Target Groups

Faculty and students comprised the core constituencies of the SIE process, and the OIRA staff managed the SIE process. Thus, any changes were anticipated to affect these three stakeholder groups. Secondary stakeholders included institutional administrators (e.g., department chairs, college deans, provost, and faculty committees).

Figure 20.2 Desired State of SIE Information Flow and Utilization

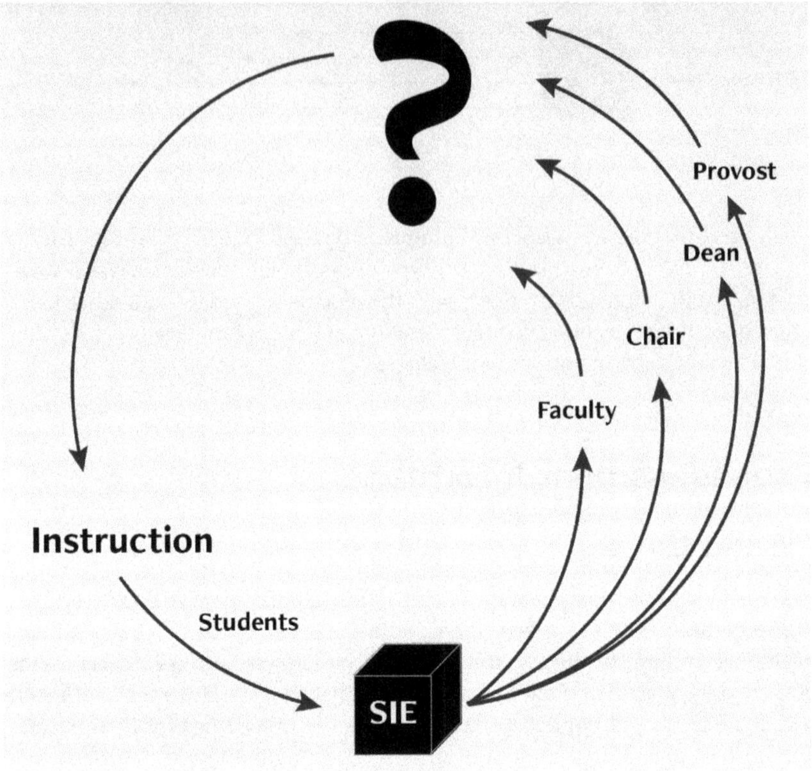

Data Sources

The initial datasets examined were the SIE results across six academic semesters, including both quantitative responses (4- and 5-point Likert scales) and qualitative responses (optional prose commentary associated with each core item and the evaluation form as a whole). Additional data were collected through focus groups with students and faculty and an environmental scan of initiatives currently informing support of teaching across the institution.

Process

This complex needs assessment approach incorporated elements of both a knowledge and skills assessment and elements of a strategic needs assessment (Sleezer, Russ-Eft, & Gupta, 2014). The knowledge and skills assessment focused on students, faculty, and administrators (students in completing their SIEs; faculty and administrators in interpreting the results). The strategic needs assessment focused on the SIE distribution and reporting process. To address the knowledge and skill components, a comprehensive analysis of the course evaluation data—statistical analysis of the numeric ratings and a text analysis of the comments—was completed to identify the kinds of information that could be gleaned from the SIE results.

Student and faculty focus groups were also convened. The student focus groups were designed to better understand the students' interpretations of each SIE rating prompt and how their perceptions of the SIE process informed their participation in it. The faculty focus groups were designed to gain insights into faculty members' assumptions about students' interpretations of SIE rating prompts and how faculty members utilized the information that they gleaned from SIE results. These data were used for a gap analysis between faculty understanding and student understanding of the survey prompts.

Further discussions on the process garnered from the two primary target groups (faculty and students) pinpointed areas underutilized in the current course evaluation process. Additional conversations with administrators and environmental scans of initiatives and policies related to decision making in the domain of teaching improvement and support were conducted as well.

Data Collection and Analysis

The course evaluation data were extracted from the course evaluation software and stripped of personal identifiers upon the collection of the data. Additional data were collected from students and faculty through focus groups regarding their perceptions of the process. After the proposed process received an internal review board (IRB) approval, faculty members and students received an email inviting their participation in the study. Faculty were sent messages through their college deans, and students received an email from the OIRA. Only students and faculty who did consented to participate in the focus group and those who were 18 years or older were allowed to participate. Ten faculty and 40 students signed up and consented to participate in the focus groups. The faculty participants included tenured, tenure-track, and clinical (nontenured) faculty from two colleges, Nursing and Science. Due to time constraints and time of year that the study was conducted, no full-time or part-time faculty from other colleges volunteered to participate; however, the faculty represented were valid across the type of faculty employed at the institution in relation to track and title.

The student participants were more representative of the undergraduate student population, with students from all four levels (freshmen, sophomores, juniors, and seniors) and from all seven academic colleges signing up to participate, although not in truly representative numbers. Fewer juniors and more seniors signed up, as well as fewer nursing students and more arts, humanities, and social sciences students, but other student groups were generally proportionally represented. Since participation was voluntary, the limited level of participation, particularly from faculty, is certainly an area that should be reexamined for future needs assessments. Because this was undertaken for the purpose of unit improvement, consent documents were signed prior to convening the focus groups. Consent documents contained (a) a summary of the needs assessment objectives; (b) a statement of the voluntary nature of the focus group and the right of all participants to exercise their consent at all times during the process; (c) notification of the possibility of publication as an outcome; (d) guarantee of anonymity with regard to all actions taken by the needs analysts; (e) statement of risks; (f) statement of benefits; and (g) contact information for the principal investigator and chair of the IRB Human Subjects Committee. During the focus group sessions, questions were asked regarding the SIE process (see Table 20.2).

Two experienced social science researchers from the university but external to OIRA facilitated the focus groups, one instructor and one staff member. OIRA wanted to mitigate sources of bias in the study and wanted the faculty and students to be able to talk freely about the SIE questions and content.

OIRA analyzed the course evaluation data starting with a meta-analysis of the numerical data. Next, to aid in the text analysis and build on the focused group feedback, the group facilitators met with representatives of the university faculty to classify the SIE questions into groups based on commonalities. The focused group facilitators organized the faculty feedback into

Table 20.2   Focus Group Questions

Faculty Questions	Student Questions
Tell us your thoughts about uses for the information you receive from the evaluations each semester.	You probably remember that you receive these evaluation forms via email and can access them through Canvas. Tell us your thoughts on the process of filling out the forms and submitting them.
Tell us about a time you have received SIE feedback and considered it in refining your instructional practice.	How do you think faculty use the evaluations?
Tell us any suggestions you might have for using evaluations at the university.	Tell us about any suggestions you might have for using evaluations here at the university.

Tell us your thoughts on the process of encouraging/reminding students to complete the forms.	You and all your fellow students complete SIE forms every semester. What would it look like if the feedback from those forms had an effect on instruction in the following semesters?

We have the core questions currently on the evaluation form at the university. We'd like to look through these and have you share any thoughts you have about the questions.

Think about evaluations you've gotten and give us examples to help us understand what each item means for you.

Tell us about how you think students understand each item.

We have a copy of the core questions currently on the evaluation form at the university. We'd like to look through these and have you share any thoughts you have about the questions.

Talk us through what each question on the SIE means to you. Think about class experiences you've had and give us examples to help us understand what each item means for you.

1) The instructor organized the course according to a syllabus.

2) The instructor followed a clear method of grading and evaluation.

3) Other course policies and procedures were clearly defined and followed.

4) The instructor effectively presented course content.

5) The instructor's teaching styles and methods promoted learning.

6) The instructor stimulated learning through questions, assignments, or exercises relevant to the course.

7) The instructor's approach made the students feel free to ask questions.

8) The instructor was available for consultation outside of class.

9) At the end of this semester, the course objectives as described in the syllabus had been accomplished.

10) The instructor graded and returned material submitted for evaluation when they said they would.

—

1) The instructor organized the course according to a syllabus.

2) The instructor followed a clear method of grading and evaluation.

3) Other course policies and procedures were clearly defined and followed.

4) The instructor effectively presented course content.

5) The instructor's teaching styles and methods promoted learning.

6) The instructor stimulated learning through questions, assignments, or exercises relevant to the course.

7) The instructor's approach made the students feel free to ask questions.

8) The instructor was available for consultation outside of class.

9) At the end of this semester, the course objectives as described in the syllabus had been accomplished.

10) The instructor graded and returned material submitted for evaluation when they said they would.

(Continued)

(Continued)

11) The instructor showed interest in student learning.	11) The instructor showed interest in student learning.
12) The instructor responded in an effective and professional manner to student comments and questions.	12) The instructor responded in an effective and professional manner to student comments and questions.
Overall, tell us your thoughts about the course evaluation process here at the university.	Overall, tell us your thoughts about the course evaluation process here at the university.

the following groups: (1) course experiences, (2) course management, and (3) student/instructor interactions. Finally, OIRA conducted the text analysis of the data. The themes that emerged from the text analysis were then paired back with the themes that were identified from the classification analysis of SIE question groupings. This process linked the numeric and textual results. The feedback from the focus groups was also analyzed to identify areas that worked or were of concern and to guide the final design of the revised reporting process.

Results

Although individual faculty were encouraged to use SIE information to improve their instruction, the results of the procedural analysis, the text analysis of SIE comments, and the stakeholder focus groups revealed little institutional guidance in translating student feedback into effective instructional changes or in identifying related resources to inform pedagogy. Placed in context of the three existing objectives for the SIE process at the university, specific needs come into focus.

Objective 1: [SIEs will] provide *productive* feedback to instructors so that faculty may improve their courses.

Results: The initial review of the SIE distribution-collection-dissemination process revealed a linear sequence with minimal, ad hoc guidance for faculty in interpreting SIE results and/or revising course content or pedagogy in response to the results. In addition, limited feedback was reported within the SIE comments, as well as by focus group participants. Faculty questioned the robustness of the feedback and reported being uncertain about how to interpret and apply the information they received to improve their instruction and courses.

Objective 2: [SIEs will] *share perspectives* on the *most or least helpful aspects* of courses so that *faculty may improve their teaching procedures.*

Results: While SIE feedback is consistently disseminated to faculty members and relevant administrators, and while student comments provided insights into students' feelings about the instruction they received, this analysis suggested that the feedback was not presented in a form that could support faculty insights into their own content and teaching within individual courses. Focus groups revealed ambiguity in the core questions and, hence, a variety of possible interpretations of the responses and associated comments. For example, when asked to paraphrase the meaning of individual SIE's items, students in the focus groups varied in their explanations and interpretations. In addition, faculty varied both from one another and from the students in their explanations of individual SIE items and questioned the extent to which their interpretations of SIE feedback aligned with students' intended meanings. Without clear guidance on interpretation of SIE results, faculty expressed uncertainty about how to use the information to guide changes in their practice.

Objective 3: [SIEs will] *share feedback* that is *an essential element in curricular planning and program review* across the institution.

Results: SIE feedback is not a consistent element in curricular planning and program review at the institutional level but is occasionally considered on an ad hoc basis across departments and colleges. The core questions shared across all units do not request information or insights that are directly relevant to program/curricular review. Although some units added questions that solicit information for such purposes, not all units have chosen to include such explicit items. Other units may have procedures for using core questions to inform program review, but those procedures were not revealed in the initial environmental scan or in focus group sessions with faculty. Because discussion of potential changes to the instrument itself was outside the scope of the current needs assessment, further investigation of procedural changes to enhance clarity in the use of SIE feedback at the curricular level is merited.

Overall Implications

Stakeholders expressed the importance of student feedback and commitments to use the SIE feedback to inform improvements in the instructional context; however, concerns about response rates, alignment of meaning, and guidance in implementing appropriate changes were all identified. Faculty expressed specific concern about the low response rates, citing their belief that dissatisfied students were more likely to respond, and so results are not truly representative. In addition, both student and faculty responses in the focus groups, and content in the comments sections on the SIEs themselves, revealed variability in the interpretations of items. Thus, both the low response rates and potential misalignment of meanings across all stakeholders must be addressed.

In the focus group sessions, students reported seeing little change based on their input; faculty reported perceiving the process as either punitive or irrelevant, depending on how significantly the results factored into their tenure and promotion process. This sentiment is not confined to this institution. Recent research, including a survey of faculty sponsored by the American Association of University Professors, was replete with accounts of faculty frustration with the prevailing course evaluation model (Vasey & Carroll, 2016). Given these broad trends, and the results of the institutional analyses, guidance and support are clearly needed to assist faculty as they incorporate SIE information into their ongoing professional development efforts.

Desired State

This needs assessment enabled OIRA staff to re-envision the SIE process as an iterative, cyclical process using the focus groups feedback to identify key stakeholder-perceived gaps that could inform improvements in the use of SIE information to improve teaching effectiveness. Specifically, the needs assessment:

- determined stakeholders' perception regarding the current effect of SIE feedback and data on course improvement;

- explored stakeholders' conceptualization of an idealized scenario in which SIE feedback and data improve courses; and

- ascertained stakeholders' perceptions regarding existing gaps or barriers preventing SIE feedback and data from facilitating course improvements.

A new model for reporting and utilizing course evaluation results is needed: one that goes beyond reporting summary scores and verbatim comments to supporting faculty in using SIE results to inform improvement within their courses (Bernstein et al., 2010). This model needs to go even further to also support administrators in interpreting results at the institutional level so that appropriate resources can be provided to support improvement of teaching practice at the institutional level (Boysen, 2016). Only then will the line become a circle where insights from course evaluations are used in making decisions to effect changes that are then evidenced in the results of future course evaluations. Clear mappings from feedback to support strategies can then inform college and university decisions to effect change in instructional support models and policies (Boysen, 2016).

While full implementation is beyond the scope of OIRA's responsibilities, this needs assessment process highlighted several areas where OIRA can help facilitate the move toward a cyclical model, as shown in Figure 20.3. The overarching insight gleaned from this needs assessment was that the current practice of providing an analysis of just the quantitative SIE results for a single semester for faculty and administrators tells only part of the story, a single data point, isolated from the greater context. A richer, fuller dataset was needed for meaningful action. Our results pointed to seven areas where improvement is needed: five slated for immediate action by OIRA and two for future consideration and collaboration. Table 20.3 breaks out each area in detail.

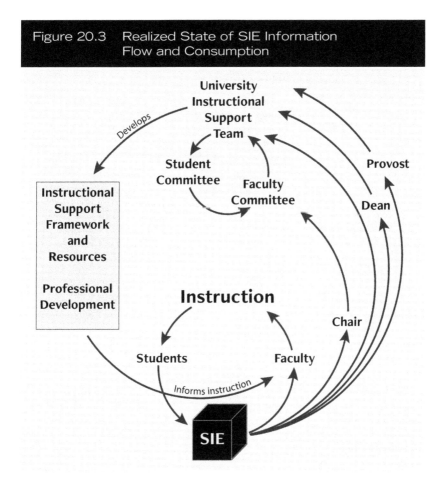

Figure 20.3 Realized State of SIE Information Flow and Consumption

Table 20.3 Areas for Improvement and Action Plans

Area for Improvement	Action Steps	Anticipated Timeline
Phase I: Immediate Action		
1. Course Context Characteristics of a specific course, which may be out of the instructor's control, can play an important role in students' expectations and perceptions. What are their motivations for taking the course (e.g., general education, major, elective)? Is this course offered online or in-person? Is it primarily a lecture course or one where more interaction is expected?	a. Add fields to the individual course report indicating the course type (lecture, lab, studio, etc.) and delivery method (traditional, hybrid, online).	Include in the next round of reports.
	b. Add the percent of students enrolled with the primary major in the college where the course is offered.	Include in the next round of reports.
	c. Offer departments the option of an additional comparison column to compare it to similar courses (e.g., Freshman Composition to other Freshman Composition courses).	Pilot with a single college in the next semester. Expand to additional colleges upon request.
2. Qualitative Analysis Student comments provide a wealth of information not currently used in a systematic or user-friendly way. Are they generally satisfied with the course, but have additional suggestions? Are there specific materials or techniques that they found beneficial or not beneficial? What experiences in this course contributed to a low rating or a high rating?	a. Add text analysis results indicating the primary themes from the comments.	Pilot with a single college in the next semester. Expand to include all colleges within 1 academic year.
	b. Expand this text analysis to allow for cross-tabulating those results with selected quantitative results for further insight.	Pilot with a single college within 1 academic year. Expand to additional colleges upon request.

3. **Trends Over Time** The students in any one section of the course represent a wide variety of needs, perceptions, and experiences that may not necessarily be indicative of all students who take that course, so making significant pedagogical or curricular change based on the feedback from a single section may not necessarily result in overall improvement. Was there something different about this group of students or about this semester that may have unduly impacted the student responses? How closely does this group of students align with the students who are likely to take this course in the future?	a. Add a new report showing the cumulative SIE results for the course and instructor disaggregated by term.	Pilot with a single college in the next round of reports. Expand to additional colleges upon request.
	b. Expand this new report to include student demographics for each course.	Pilot with a single college in the next semester. Expand to additional colleges upon request.
4. **Resources** Both students and faculty are left largely on their own in the SIE process: students in knowing what kind of feedback is helpful to faculty and faculty in knowing how to interpret student feedback. For students who want to participate fully in the process, what kind of comments are most helpful to faculty? For faculty who want to identify and implement changes, what language do students use in describing their experiences?	a. Add a link in the notification emails that goes to both faculty and students back to the available help materials.	Implement in the next semester.
	b. Expand the current help resources to include guidance for students in completing the SIEs (technical guidance and example responses).	Develop during the next academic year.
	c. Rewrite the notification emails to better guide faculty and students to the newly available materials and resources.	Implement within 1 academic year.

(Continued)

Table 20.3 (Continued)

Area for Improvement	Action Steps	Anticipated Timeline
5. Value-added faculty typically access the SIE software only to view response rates and reports. What strategies would help increase faculty familiarity with the system? Are there other resources or information that can be provided for faculty through this software?	a. Design a Class Profile template to provide basic demographic and academic preparation information to each faculty member about each section.	Develop during the next semester.
	b. Restructure the SIE data sources to include this information.	Implement during the next semester.
	c. Create and send the initial Class Profiles within 2 days of the census data.	Implement during the next academic year.

Phase II: Future Consideration

6. **Instrument Alignment** The current SIE instrument was designed 3 years ago during the transition from paper to online. How well do the existing instrument and program objectives align with the new process? What changes could be made to the ratings questions or to the open-ended questions to provide more useful information?	a. Revise as needed the SIE objectives to ensure continued alignment.	Future
	b. Request a faculty task force to review the existing instrument to identify any needed changes.	Future
7. **Organizational Integration** Although SIEs provide information that can support teaching effectiveness, there is currently no formal integration of SIE results with other institutional	a. Confer with Academic Affairs and Faculty Senate to investigate synergies among units supporting teaching and learning.	Future

initiatives that support teaching and learning. Where do SIE results confirm other observed teaching support needs? How can the OIRA collaborate with other units to share information that will enhance teaching effectiveness efforts institution-wide?	b. Work with library or other units on campus to begin developing a resource repository related to instructional effectiveness.	Future
	c. Seek guidance in establishing a task force to investigate coordination of professional development opportunities for faculty in the domain of teaching practice.	Future
	d. Include links (hopefully targeted) to the resource repository with individual reports.	Future

Influences

Although all stakeholders involved in this project were committed to academic freedom and student success, those commitments were sometimes expressed differently and often required negotiating hidden boundaries. For example, students could see SIEs as a customer satisfaction survey; faculty could see SIEs as a suggestion box; and administrators could see SIEs as a bird's eye view of trends in teaching across institutional levels. Of further concern was encouraging campus-wide discussions of teaching effectiveness without negatively impacting the role of SIEs in the promotion and tenure process.

Moreover, resources are not always available to support new initiatives. The staff member who oversees SIEs has additional responsibilities, leaving limited time available to add steps to the existing process. Moreover, faculty development opportunities have both financial implications for the overall line item budgets of institutional academic affairs, as well as workload implications for faculty, which must be considered.

Issues and Challenges

Course evaluation results can be a sensitive issue since they can have high-stakes implications for faculty who are pursuing tenure and promotion. Ensuring that all stakeholder voices are heard and valued, while maintaining a focus on the overarching goals, requires attention, diplomacy, and shared governance (Boysen, 2016). Keeping the results of the needs assessment and planned action steps focused on high-level overall improvement, rather than individual faculty performance, will be essential for long-term success. In addition, to encourage changes in teaching practice and support at the institutional level, engagement across multiple academic and nonacademic units is required. This is particularly troubling given the limited representation (only two colleges) in the faculty focus groups. Future plans will need to ensure representation from all stakeholder groups.

Motivation is the primary issue for the SIE process: Faculty who see value in the process motivate their students to participate, which in turn improves the value of the process so that it eventually becomes the cycle of improvement illustrated earlier in Figure 20.3. Phase I of the Action Plan encapsulates the changes that can be made by OIRA staff directly to begin this transformative process, and it also includes the day-to-day challenges of the additional workload within OIRA for conducting the new analysis and reporting process each semester. Future challenges will include establishing new faculty and student committees, coordinating systemic analysis of results at the institutional level, and implementing changes in teaching support and development. These challenges need to be considered in preparing for Phase II of the Action Plan and ensuring enough support to effect change in the institutional culture. SIEs at the institution should continue to be a regular and systematic piece of larger discussions centered on teaching effectiveness and faculty development that lead to improvements in student learning.

DISCUSSION QUESTIONS

1. How does the institutional context inform the choice of assessment methods in this case study? How might changes in size or organizational goals impact the approaches used in the needs assessment?

2. What is *teaching effectiveness*? How was it operationalized in this case study?

3. Why did the authors use a complex needs assessment to conduct this project?

4. What was the role of thematic analysis in understanding needs? How did qualitative information drive next steps in this case?

5. What follow-on needs assessments could expand understanding and effectiveness of the course evaluation process?

6. How did themes contribute to a design plan for improvement within teaching effectiveness?

7. How can we close the loop with a cyclical evaluation process?

8. How do evaluations help drive institutional improvements in this case?

REFERENCES

Bernstein, D., Addison, W. E., Altman, C., Hollister, D., Komarraju, M., Prieto, L., & Shore, C. (2010). Toward a scientist-educator model of teaching psychology. In D. F. Halpern (Ed.), *Undergraduate education in psychology: A blueprint for the future of the discipline* (pp. 29–45). Washington, DC: American Psychological Association.

Boysen, G. A. (2016). Using student evaluations to improve teaching: Evidence-based recommendations. *Scholarship of Teaching and Learning in Psychology, 2*(4), 273–284. doi:10.1037/stl0000069

Golding, C., & Lee, A. (2014). Evaluate to improve: Useful approaches to student evaluation. *Assessment & Evaluation in Higher Education, 41*(1), 1–14. doi.org/10.1080/02602938.2014.976810

Sleezer, C. M., Russ-Eft, D. F., & Gupta, K. (2014). *A practical guide to needs assessment* (3rd ed.). San Francisco, CA: Wiley & ASTD.

Vasey, C., & Carroll, L. (2016). How do we evaluate teaching? Findings from a survey of faculty members. *Academe, 102*(3). Retrieved from https://www.aaup.org/article/how-do-we-evaluate-teaching#.WmneIa6nGUk.

21

Orchid Candy Company

Sandra L. Williams and Kelly A. McGreevey

Abstract

Orchid is a privately owned business manufacturing nonbranded hard candy. Employees consist of both full-time and part-time English-as-a-second-language factory personnel, while management consists of a combination of third-and fourth-generation family owners. A recent critical event was the sudden death of Orchid's president. Issues include succession planning, strategic planning, leadership development, and employee engagement. This needs assessment combines initial findings with the willingness of the next generation to execute it. Below is an overview of the case.

Where the Needs Assessment Was Conducted	Who Conducted the Needs Assessment	Focus of Needs Assessment	How Data Were Collected	How Data Were Analyzed
Privately owned business in the United States	Human resource development (HRD) consultant advised two teams of graduate HRD students	Focused on issues of succession planning, strategic planning, leadership development, and employee engagement	Initial conference meeting, observational site visits, and review of archival data (such as quantitative data included financial numbers, and personnel numbers of turnover, hiring, workplace attendance, training attendance, production numbers); public data research; employee interviews; questionnaire survey of selected employees	Quantitative data analyzed using descriptive statistics; qualitative data analyzed by identifying themes then coding and categorizing the themes; data cross-case analyzed for similarity and issue identification

Background

Orchid was founded in 1928 by Jeremy Powdrey (the business name and personal names are pseudonyms). The original shop sold only seasonal candies in the local region, and the shop was open between August and December. During the 1940s, 1950s, and 1960s, Jeremy's son, Liam Powdrey, turned the seasonal business into a manufacturer of everyday candies. More recently, the third generation of Powdreys, brothers Robert and Niall Powdrey, ran the business. Under Robert and Niall's leadership, the company added additional products to the business. However, Orchid was recently rocked by the sudden and untimely death of Robert. Today, five members of the fourth generation of Powdreys take active roles in the business. Niall's three daughters include Meagan, in charge of production and purchasing; Colleen, the company's controller and manager of payroll and office staff; and Erin, the manager of Graphic Design and Customer Service. Robert's two children include Bobby, a lead sales rep, and Nora, the vice president of quality assurance, research, and development. (See Table 21.1.)

Profile of the Organization

Orchid is a for-profit, family-owned business located in a U.S. metropolitan city. It sells primarily to other candy manufacturers as a nonbranded business-to-business provider. Orchid enjoys good relationships with long-term clients and vendors. It employs 120 persons full-time and expands the employee base to over 320 during the busy season (September–October, annually).

Factory workers include candy makers, machine operators, catchers, wrappers, and bagging operators. A warehouse staff of approximately 35 conducts boxing, shipping, and receiving work. Year-round, the company runs two shifts and factory workers report to one of two production managers, Miguel Delisi or Francisco Rodriguez. Line employees are primarily of Spanish ethnicity, speaking English as a second language. The production managers communicate primarily in Spanish.

Additionally, approximately 30 employees work as office staff, speaking primarily English, and reporting to Colleen Powdrey. The company continually focuses on candy quality in order to meet the Food and Drug's Administration's food safety standards. Quality is managed by Nora, who oversees a small staff of three persons.

The general business strategy has focused on generating new business with clients to support production capacity. Orchid experienced a 3%–5% growth in revenues over the last 3 years.

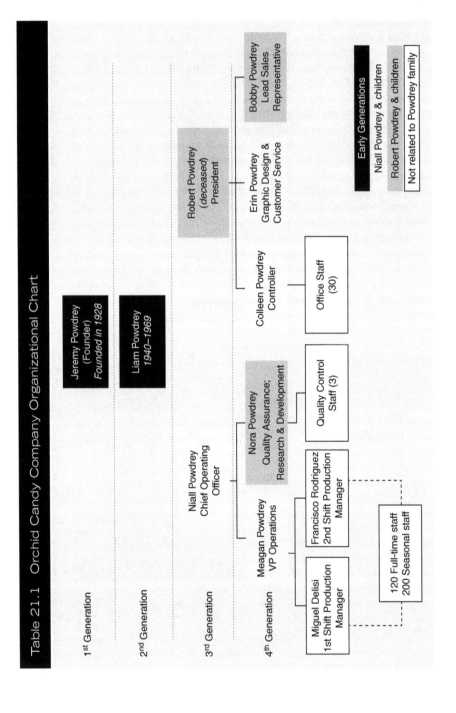

Table 21.1   Orchid Candy Company Organizational Chart

1st Generation

Jeremy Powdrey
(Founder)
Founded in 1928

2nd Generation

Liam Powdrey
1940–1969

3rd Generation

Niall Powdrey
Chief Operating
Officer

Robert Powdrey
(*deceased*)
President

4th Generation

Meagan Powdrey
VP Operations

Nora Powdrey
Quality Assurance;
Research & Development

Colleen Powdrey
Controller

Erin Powdrey
Graphic Design &
Customer Service

Bobby Powdrey
Lead Sales
Representative

Miguel Delisi
1st Shift Production
Manager

Francisco Rodriguez
2nd Shift Production
Manager

Quality Control
Staff (3)

Office Staff
(30)

120 Full-time staff
200 Seasonal staff

Early Generations

Niall Powdrey & children

Robert Powdrey & children

Not related to Powdrey family

Preassessment Information

A critical event recently occurred when Robert Powdrey, president, was suddenly stricken with a debilitating disease from which he perished within 6 short weeks. This tragedy left Niall Powdrey (age 62) as the last third-generation leader, and he stepped in to serve as both president and COO. Niall also took over Robert's former responsibilities of finance, sales, and marketing. Previously, Niall had focused on production and operations, as he can repair and operate all the factory machines. This shift in leadership responsibilities has put a strain on Niall's time and focus, causing more responsibilities to fall to fourth-generation members. As siblings and cousins, the fourth generation knows it is going to take over the entire Orchid operation soon, but this group lacks a common plan for success.

Fourth-Generation Characteristics

While all fourth-generation members have college degrees, their histories and interests vary. Meagan and Colleen grew up working in the factory. From a young age, these sisters were interested in the business and passionate about continuing the family legacy. Today, Meagan and Colleen's knowledge and experience drive the key business decisions that Orchid leaders consider. Erin also spent summers working in the factory, but she was interested in pursuing a graphic design career outside the family business. Shortly after graduating college, her uncle, Robert Powdrey, convinced her to join the company as the head of customer service and graphic design.

Robert's children never worked in the factory, but they often spent time in the office with their father. Bobby's personality made him a natural salesperson, and he is currently the lead sales representative. Nora, the youngest of the cousins, graduated from college 1 year before her father's death. She never really had an interest in working at Orchid, but a week after graduating with her bachelor's degree in chemistry, Robert asked Nora when she would be starting work. Initially, Nora reported to her father as she learned about food quality regulations. After his passing, she assumed the role of vice president of Quality Assurance and Research & Development.

This generation exhibits different work ethics and expectations of personal lifestyle. Bobby and Nora believe that Orchid should provide for their needs and the needs of their families to enjoy vacations and private schools. An avid hockey player, Nora coaches a girls' team at her alma mater. Practices are held in early afternoon at a location nearly an hour away from Orchid's headquarters. Consequently, Nora frequently leaves the office before what others might consider the "end" of the work day. Bobby works out every morning at 5:30 a.m. and goes straight to the office afterwards. It is not uncommon for Bobby to leave the office early to catch a round of golf with clients or friends.

The sibling children of Niall believe in rewarding hard work via promotion and assumption of greater responsibilities. Niall comes to work early and stays late to get the job done, a work ethic he passed on to his children. Both Meagan and Colleen are married and raising their families on dual incomes in modest suburbs near the Orchid headquarters. Erin is single and pursuing an MBA degree at night school.

Impetus for Needs Assessment

Historically, slight tension existed between the offspring of Niall and the offspring of Robert, because Robert's kids were not exposed to the business as intimately when they were growing up and claim a blended work ethic of business contribution during a nine-to-five work day, interspersed with time for attention to personal matters. Comparatively, Niall's offspring claim a work ethic of hard effort expended no matter the time of day or effort needed, with personal time frequently forfeited to Orchid's business needs. Colleen characterized this difference early in the needs assessment process as "The cousins just see different ways of contributing to Orchid. We do it in our own timeframes, with different urgency, and not always with the same result." Meagan and Colleen recently joined a Mid-Atlantic Family Business Council organization to expose themselves to current business practices, accounting services, and business law. They were the only two members of Orchid to join. Both see a long-term future for Orchid as a successful business enterprise, and they believe that pursuing that future will require significant hard work by the fourth-generation members. It was through this council that a recommendation was made for a business needs assessment at Orchid.

The focus of the needs assessment was at the organization level, including the roles of the key business leaders. All members of the fourth generation want the Orchid business to succeed, but they differ in opinions of how to achieve "success" and what success looks like. All members of the fourth generation were well aware of the needs assessment work as it was being undertaken, though none were exactly sure of what a needs assessment process entailed. The fourth-generation members all admitted that a documented business plan was not in place, the company was not skilled at employee development, and the company was in need of stronger production manager skills. While financial performance was historically good at the company, the fourth-generation members recognized that continued success could be helped with a good business plan and an assessment of business capabilities.

Needs Assessment Process

Prompted by both the executive loss and the growth expectations for the company, the needs assessment process took a combined approach of both knowledge and skill assessment of leaders, along with a strategic needs assessment of the business (Sleezer, Russ-Eft, & Gupta, 2014). Leaders were considered all Powdery family members and the two production managers. The needs assessment purposefully took an HRD focus and did not focus upon assessing mechanical efficiency, candy production, marketing efforts, or finances. Thus, while operations were reviewed, the assessment did not focus on manufacturing operations, sales operations, or quality controls. Rather, the focus remained at a holistic organizational level and took the form of an HRD consulting arrangement. Clients for the needs assessment included all members of the fourth generation and the president and COO, Niall Powdrey.

Leadership knowledge assessment involved diagnosing what the Powdrey family members understood regarding leadership of a small business and particularly talent development. This included knowledge on topics such as staffing, job responsibilities, directing others, performance appraisal, promotion, and performance management. Skill assessment involved ascertaining leadership actions (e.g., internal talent development practices, such as selecting and hiring staff, promoting employees, delegating job responsibilities, managing employee performance, and appraising employee performance).

The strategic needs assessment focused upon the strategic plans established for the future of Orchid. Strategic actions involved long-range planning activities, such as establishing a mission and vision for the business, setting business goals, establishing business objectives, tracking company progress against plans, and making adjustments in personnel and talent to meet established goals.

Needs Assessment Model and Teams

The needs assessment process followed a combination of the process consultation model (Schein, 1999), the ADDIE process (Allen, 2006), and consulting techniques proffered by Peter Block (Block, 2000). Due to various issues and a 3-month time constraint, two teams of needs assessors were simultaneously deployed to investigate issues, analyze data, and design recommendations for Orchid. Both teams had practice in diagnostic and evaluative skills but were not considered needs assessment experts.

The two teams, Team A and Team B, were similar in education and approaches to the needs assessment process, but differed demographically. Both teams consisted of three master's of human resource development (HRD) students. Demographically, Team A consisted of 66% males and 33% females, with ages ranging from 28 to 36 years. Team B was 100% female, with ages ranging from 25 to 57 years. Both teams approached the situation professionally from a Schein "helper" perspective and worked toward mutual acceptance and joint diagnosis of the issues, avoiding operating as experts or parties to a doctor–patient relationship (Schein, 1999). Neither team carried a prescribed method for issue diagnosis, data collection, or data analysis. Both teams were guided in their work by the skilled HRD consultant, who functioned in a counseling role to the teams, advising on process, but not visible to the company. All Powdrey family members were aware of the advisory role of the HRD consultant, who had been recommended by the Mid-Atlantic family business council.

With regard to professional background, Team A was comprised of persons with slightly more business experience and acumen, while Team B was comprised of persons with slightly more academic and research skills. Both teams were contracted by the HRD consultant who guided the deployment of both teams at Orchid, and the delivery of findings to Orchid management.

Data Collection

Data collection involved three phases: preliminary data gathering, examining the external environment, and examining the internal environment at Orchid. The purpose of Phase I was to develop a strong understanding of current and/or future performance needs as initially perceived by Colleen. The purpose of Phase II was to understand current and/or future external factors that could affect Orchid's performance and stability. The purpose of Phase III was to understand Orchid's operation processes, internal management roles and interests, and internal strengths and weaknesses of the company. Data-gathering methods included an initial conference meeting, observational site visits, and review of archival data, public data research, and employee interviews. In addition, a questionnaire survey was undertaken with a selected group of employees.

During Phase I, an initial group conference was held with both assessment teams and Colleen Powdrey. Colleen Powdrey outlined the company's history, described the recent demise of co-owner Robert Powdrey, explained the impact of his loss on executive responsibilities, provided a revised organization chart depicting current responsibilities, and outlined Orchid's current HRD/OD situation including her perceptions of the interests of the fourth-generation members to continue in management roles. Phase I also involved a review of the company's website, the sampling of candy products, and a review of printed company information and marketing materials. Table 21.2 provides a visual depiction of the structure and functions of key personnel within Orchid.

Phase II (understanding current and/or future external factors that could affect Orchid's performance and stability) consisted of reviewing of archival company data and public data. The archival data review developed an understanding of internal processes and written information used by the company and provided an understanding of processes and/or policies utilized by external organizations or recommended by external influencers.

The addition of external information provided further data, ensured interpretation accuracy with respect to the candy industry, and protected against personal bias and/or organizational bias. Records, documents, and databases provided the necessary data to understand Orchid's history and the marketplace

Table 21.2 Orchid Candy Company Organizational Chart at Time of Assessment

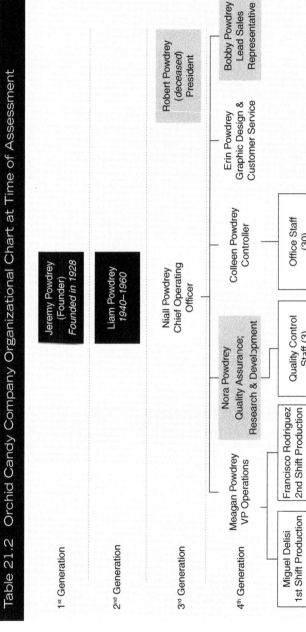

1st Generation

Jeremy Powdrey
(Founder)
Founded in 1928

2nd Generation

Liam Powdrey
1940-1960

3rd Generation

Niall Powdrey
Chief Operating
Officer

Robert Powdrey
(deceased)
President

4th Generation

Nora Powdrey
Quality Assurance;
Research & Development

Colleen Powdrey
Controller

Erin Powdrey
Graphic Design &
Customer Service

Bobby Powdrey
Lead Sales
Representative

Meagan Powdrey
VP Operations

Quality Control
Staff (3)

Office Staff
(30)

Miguel Delisi
1st Shift Production
Manager

Francisco Rodriguez
2nd Shift Production
Manager

120 Full time staff
200 Seasonal staff

Early Generations
Niall Powdrey & children
Robert Powdrey & children
Not related to Powdrey family

factors affecting Orchid. Both teams reviewed the records, documents, and databases as outlined in Table 21.3: archival data sources.

Phase III (understand Orchid's operation processes, internal management roles and interests, and internal strengths and weaknesses of the company) consisted of direct observation and employee interviews. Observation involved four private tours of Orchid's production floor, warehouse, shipping docks, executive offices, and the sample room. The research and development room (R&D Room) was not observed due to food safety issues and competitive reasons. Observations enabled a firsthand view of what was occurring between and among employees in their work environment and presented additional data that were not obtained from the preliminary conference or the archival data. Further, observations allowed for developing a holistic picture of the organization in operation, which the needs assessment meant to achieve. Phase III also involved personal interviews to collect interpretive information on the current state of business at Orchid. Individual interviews were held with eight employees, including all fourth-generation members, the president, and the two production managers.

The interviews provided interpretive information and enabled the teams to observe respondent facial expressions, tones, and nonverbal cues. A semi-structured interview design enabled the teams to ask additional questions to further explore respondents' thoughts/ideas. The semi-structured design also allowed respondents to express additional thoughts and feelings that were not initially probed. An identical instrument (interview questionnaire) was used in all eight personal interviews to ask the following:

1. Describe your role at Orchid.

2. Tell us about your educational background.

Table 21.3 Archival Data Sources

Records (Orchid)	Documents (Orchid)	Database
Exit Interview	Training Manuals • Cooking • Wrapping • Packaging • Wrappers • Machine Guard • Baggers • Steam/Hot Water Job Description • Wrappers	U.S. Census Bureau (www.census.gov) National Confectioners Association (www.candyusa.com) Illinois Department of Labor (www.illinois.gov)

3. What do you think are some of Orchid's key successes?

4. In your opinion, what are Orchid's biggest challenges?

5. How do you feel about the fourth generation taking over control of the company?

6. What is your vision for Orchid in the future?

7. What do you believe are Orchid's values?

Team Differences in Data Collection

Data collection differed between the teams. Team A established a shared email account, to which all team members had access, and centralized communications with the client. One team member was nominated to take the lead in arranging interviews, and the team committed to having at least two team members participate (either in person or by phone) in each interview. Further, interviews were recorded (with the approval of the interviewee) so the remaining team members could review the verbal data firsthand. Interviews were scheduled at the client's convenience, which resulted in some early morning and late evening meetings that minimized disruption to Orchid's regular work day.

Team A began by interviewing the vice president of operations, both production managers, and conducting two factory tours (one of each shift) to gain a stronger understanding of the business and the differences between the two shifts. As English was not his first language, Francisco requested that Meagan be present during his interview to assist with translation. Additional interviews with the remaining family members were conducted individually, with the exception of Erin and Niall, who were interviewed together. Conducting the majority of the interviews with only one client representative present at a time allowed each interviewee to speak more freely than they might have if another family member had been present. Scheduling resulted in one Team A member being able to attend all meetings, providing a consistent presence to the client in representing the team. Team A shared the notes and audio recordings of all meetings with other team members who had not been present during the discussions.

Team B focused first on the written documents provided by the company and second on the interviews and observations. For this team, interview scheduling was of less importance, and availability from a scheduling perspective led one team member to facilitate all interviews. Moreover, the team interviewed Niall, Bobby, and Nora together, which may have influenced some of their responses. Interviews were not recorded; other team members had to rely on recall and interviewer notes. Team B conducted a written survey of 19 employees, nine supervisors, and 10 factory floor workers to ask participants to rank the following on a 5-point scale of strongly disagree to strongly agree:

1. As an Orchid employee, I am confident in the judgment of senior management.

2. I share the same personal values as Orchid.

3. I could use more training to enhance my supervisory skills.

4. I am comfortable sharing my concerns with senior management.

5. As a supervisor, I am comfortable in my role.

6. I believe communication with other supervisors needs improvement.

7. I believe Orchid is a good place for personal development.

8. My daily responsibilities give me a sense of satisfaction.

The survey was written in English, and the questions were read to survey participants by a bilingual production manager. It is possible that translation or even the presence of the production manager may have influenced the responses of participants. All Orchid leaders shared an eagerness to speak about their role in the organization and their perspective on Orchid's organizational success and opportunities for improvement.

Data Analysis

Data were analyzed both quantitatively and qualitatively. Quantitative data included

- Financial numbers

- Personnel numbers (e.g., turnover, hiring, workplace attendance, and training attendance)

- Production numbers (e.g., shift output, product loss, and quality trends)

Quantitative data were analyzed using descriptive statistics to calculate percentages, averages, and ratios, and then compared to prior years, to production shifts, or to industry data to determine trends or aberrations.

Qualitative data analysis involved identifying themes and patterns in the data and then coding and categorizing the themes. Qualitative data were then cross-case analyzed for similarity and issue identification. Recurring responses and consistent patterns in each of the themed categories were identified as measures of strength or intensity.

Each type of quantitative and qualitative data was categorized into one of four sections using a SWOT analysis approach. The four sections included internal strengths, internal weaknesses, external opportunities, and external threats.

Results of Needs Assessment

Findings were categorized into themes within the SWOT analysis framework. Table 21.4 shows the strengths and weaknesses themes.

Internal Strengths

Internal strengths arose in the areas of operations, education, culture, and competitive advantage. The operations strength is based upon 89 years of business success, combined with current expertise in creating new candy recipes and products. Orchid is operationally capable of producing small batch sizes, allowing for quick changeovers of products during manufacturing. Factory workers can change-out product lines mid-shift and can perform multiple jobs on the factory floor. Operationally, Orchid is strong in serving its market niche of old-fashioned Christmas candy and in its ability to service candy sellers who are nonmanufacturing companies (i.e., private label distributors).

Education was found to be a strength at the family management level. All fourth-generation Powdrey family members have bachelor's degrees, one is actively pursuing an MBA, one has an earned MBA, and one has a master of computer science degree. In addition, both production managers have stationery engineer's licenses. These education factors serve Orchid well for complex and contrasting knowledge absorption and comprehension.

Organizational culture was found to be an internal strength. Culture was identified as a family-oriented environment where management's attitude is "care for employees and clients, alike" (Prange, 2017). This attitude fostered employee loyalty, deep job knowledge and expertise, and long-term customer relationships, the latter demonstrated through Orchid's 20- to 30-year relationships with many customers and vendors. The Orchid culture is exemplified

Table 21.4 Strengths and Weaknesses Themes

Internal Strengths	Internal Weaknesses
Operations	Operations
Education	Culture
Culture	Competitive advantage
Competitive advantage	Communication
	Planning/setting strategy
	Job profiles/responsibilities/scope

External Opportunities	External Threats
State funding for education	Imposed minimum wage
Acquisitions	Competitors
Community outreach	Food & safety regulations

by generally low employee turnover (2%–3% per year) when compared with other confection businesses. A risk-taking nature within Orchid's culture is represented in a willingness to utilize candy-making expertise to test new products and new processes. The Orchid culture carried it through economic downturns, raw material shortages (sugar embargo), and technology changes. The culture is embodied in Orchid's open-door policy regarding employee input and employee contribution.

Competitive advantage was categorized as a strength due to Orchid's expertise in rock candy manufacturing and its 55 years of candy-making experience still residing in-house. Candy expertise is recognized by outside organizations who hire Orchid personnel to lecture and teach (i.e., Niall teaches as adjunct faculty in the Department of Food Science at the University of Mid-Atlantic State). A further competitive advantage is Orchid's ability to apply its R&D expertise to develop new recipes and test new combinations of flavors and sugars in its products. This makes Orchid a fast developer of new products for the nonbranded candy market.

Internal Weaknesses

Internal weaknesses arose in the areas of operations, culture, competitive advantage, communication, planning/goals/strategies, and job profiles/responsibilities/scope.

Although manufacturing operations were considered a strength, they were also identified as a weakness. The factory was not running at capacity, and some machines had been out of production for over 6 months. Many machines had not been upgraded in nearly 70 years. In addition, the fourth-generation owners had minimal experience with plant operations, especially those on the production floor and involving machine maintenance and safety.

Culture arose as a weakness for Orchid in several areas. Orchid's family-oriented culture was exemplified by concern for employees; but simultaneously, it lacked a formal Mission or Vision statement. It also lacked formalized HR policies and structures and documented policies regarding the values upheld by the company as foundational tenets upon which workers behave.

Orchid also had no defined HR policy or structures for rewards, salary increases, promotions, titles, etc. The former president was resistant to formalizing HR policies, operations (other than the payroll function), and employee development. Orchid had no internal training programs, learning management system, or employee location on its website. Further, in one instance, a long-term employee with little managerial skill was promoted to manager, although this person's skills rested only in machine maintenance and the individual supervised no others. The production line managers operated independently of one another, and even promoted competition and skill differences between the shifts. Both production managers were resistant to suggestions for change from Meagan, the vice president of operations. It did not appear that employee workers were insubordinate in any manner; however, the lack of clarity of key values enabled the internal competition and independent behaviors to occur. Core business values, such as honesty, fairness, achievement, and concern for others (Ravlin & Meglino, 1989), were not formalized at Orchid.

Manufacturing expertise was found to be a competitive weakness. Certain manufacturing expertise within factory operations were limited to one family member, Niall Powdrey. No other Powdrey family member, nor either of the two production managers, was expert in candy manufacturing to the same extent as Niall Powdrey. Further, with the recent demise of Robert Powdrey, some expertise in customer relations and the maintenance of long-term client relationships was lost.

Communication, particularly internal communication between shifts and between production managers and the vice president of operations, arose as a weakness. Orchid experienced frequent misunderstandings between the vice president of operations, production managers, and line supervisors. Second shift managers lacked access to the vice president of operations for production guidance or decision clarification. Thus, authorized production changes did not translate to consistent implementation on the factory floor across managers and supervisors. Another communication weakness was the lack of performance feedback. Employees were not formally appraised on overall job performance and were infrequently assessed for daily task performance. Mistakes were corrected, but a formal feedback process was not in place. There was also no systematic process for understanding the development needs or learning wishes of employees.

Planning/goals/strategies were found to be an important weakness. From a business operations perspective, there existed no formal plan for revenue increases, market share growth, or the capacity expansion to support growth, although growth was identified by several individuals as a goal of the Orchid business. There was no

- Strategic business plan defining growth or targeting new customer development, sales levels, or profit margins

- Plan for the physical requirements to meet growth (i.e., plant, equipment, vehicles), formal plan for machinery maintenance

- Formal or informal plan to transfer candy manufacturing subject matter knowledge from Niall Powdrey to fourth-generation members

The lack of planning also extended into the ownership level. Orchid had no plans for family members to select or decline involvement in the candy business, or Orchid itself. The extent to which fourth-generation members truly desired to participate in the Orchid business was not extensively probed; however, findings indicated that the desire to participate was not universal. One family member confided a desire to work within a graphic design environment, which was not available at Orchid.

The fourth generation totals five cousins as potential next-generation owners/leaders of Orchid (three sibling heirs of Niall Powdrey and two sibling heirs of Robert Powdrey). The extent to which ownership shares will transfer to these five people, and in what proportions, has not been determined among family members, nor structured legally.

Overall lack of job profiles/responsibilities/scope was a fifth weakness. Job tasks, responsibilities, and expectations were not documented or described, at differentiated levels of workers or across job functions. Job descriptions did not exist for entry laborer, entry office staff, administrative assistant, specialist, team lead, shift supervisor, manager, controller, account specialist, vice president, or president. There existed very few functional depictions in written form (only one located within archival data). Thus, employees understood each other's roles only through personal familiarity, work history, and verbal job coordination. No documentation existed describing expectations, parameters, or limits to job responsibilities. Historically, the experienced workers had attempted to "help" on the manufacturing floor without proper training or expertise. The result was risk of personal injury and harm, a significant worker safety finding. Certain workers were used for finer tasks without documentation of responsibility or skill transfer. For example, only one person had expertise with the company's HVAC system, and only one other person could repair critical manufacturing machinery. A summary of Strengths and Weaknesses findings is presented in Appendix A.

Influences

Procedural influences arose within the assessing teams because not all members could be present for each site visit, interview, or plant tour. This absence issue was managed by the teams through frequent meetings and the mutual sharing of findings. Periodic joint team meetings were encouraged by the senior HRD consultant, who guided the sharing of data and communication of findings between and among team members.

No cultural or language barriers existed between the assessing teams and the family members. However, language barriers did exist in interviewing the two production managers, who were primarily Spanish speakers. To overcome this language barrier a dual-language-speaking Orchid employee was present for the production manager interviews. The language barriers may have influenced the nuances and emphases placed during conversation, and interpretation might have been influenced by selective answer formation by the interpreting employee.

Issues and Challenges

Challenges to the needs assessment of Orchid included time, client emotionality, and the psychodynamic issue of the helping relationship (Schein, 1999). Time influenced the project because needs assessment work was conducted over a hastened 3-month time horizon due to the availability of the needs assessing teams. Orchid presented a more complex situation than originally anticipated, requiring further follow-up and data collection, which necessitated longer data collection time than originally anticipated. Client availability was also tempered by time, in that business demands often superseded the needs assessment process, resulting in the cancellation of scheduled appointments and delay of interview scheduling by the client.

Client emotionality (Burke & Noumair, 2015) was a sensitive condition in this situation. The need for the assessment initially arose due to the demise of the president, a significant third-generation owner/leader. While all remaining family members agreed to conduct the needs assessment and agreed to the timeframe of this work, some were not prepared emotionally for the assessment process. The emotions of grief and loss were present at varied levels for each family member and acknowledged as such. These emotions impacted both participant willingness and personal disclosure by those still grieving. Thus, discussions, interviews, and conversations regarding growth, future plans, and business opportunities were received differently by various family members. Further, differences in reception might be due to a lack of dedication, certainty about an individual's personal future with the company, or not wanting to make commitments when major changes were imminent regarding Orchid's culture and how it conducted business.

The major psychodynamic issue of working within a helping relationship (Schein, 1999) involved the changing nature of the psychological situation in the persons seeking help, and in the interactions between the assessor consultants and the clients. The needs assessment goal was to accomplish a holistic view of the existing condition of Orchid, and to do so through a workable psychological contract in which the parties worked together through the assessment process (Schein, 1999). This was meant to include mutual diagnosing of the issues and exploration of next steps. To achieve such a contract, all parties needed to provide each other significant mutual acceptance and support. In this situation, mutual acceptance was varied among the client members, due to the emotionality still present in certain client members, as described above. This prevented the assessors from really learning about the client parties in more than a surface or impersonal nature. While the client members all readily recognized their vulnerability, and this enabled open and forthright conversations to take place, the emotionality still present due to loss caused certain client members to remain dependent upon the assessors. Some client members may have still been reacting to the shift in power, or to the unsettled nature of leadership roles. Dependency extended to the project's findings and conclusions, and negatively impacted the joint creation of solutions to findings. In this case, findings were presented to all client family members collectively, in one final meeting. The meeting garnered positive initial reactions from all family members, but ultimate issue ownership or mutual problem-solving commitment was limited.

Team Distinctions/Team Issues

The teams executed their needs assessment work slightly differently. Team A engaged in first party diagnosis from the outset. This team approached the company from a relationship-building perspective, attempting to build interpersonal comfort with each Powdrey family member. For initial data collection, Team A selected Powdrey family members with whom to conduct personal investigative interviews. Team A suggested conversations with all eight of the Orchid leaders, and Team A members made sure that at least two team members were present for each interview or site visit conducted. Team B began its diagnostic effort in research and data review including research on the industry and marketplace of Orchid products, and examination of existing documents, materials, and information supplied by the company. They became familiar with the manufacturing environment and language/jargon likely to be encountered during the on-site assessment activity. Team B members could not all be present at interviews, nor at all site visits. Both teams communicated with Powdrey family members orally and through email to familiarize the family with each team, to encourage open conversations with the team members, and to become comfortable in conversation with team members.

While the teams had different initial approaches to investigating needs at Orchid, both teams cooperated in data sharing. Conversational revelations from interviews and observations were shared between the teams. This data sharing tactic enabled both teams to be as fully informed of the situation at Orchid as possible. Teams recognized that immediate client answers or immediate data reviews could mask deeper issues. The goal was to be as helpful to Powdrey family members as possible, not for the teams to become competitive during the needs assessment process. Therefore, enough inquiries had to be made, and answers shared, to determine where help was actually needed, and that implied joint diagnosis by the teams. All team members were aware of their ignorance of the entirety of the Orchid situation due to its complexity and history.

Nevertheless, during data collection, both teams became slightly competitive with each other regarding progress, and defensive when comparing simple facts (e.g., number of interviews completed, amount of time spent meeting with Powdrey family members, number of site visits, and amount of time spent on site visits). Little competition occurred about documentation, as HRD-related documentation was minimal at Orchid, a fact that was confirmed by both teams. With little documentary evidence to analyze, the team findings from first person research (interviews, conversations, email exchanges) became important. During the joint team meetings that were held throughout the process, the HR consultant encouraged qualitative data sharing, and it did take place. By sharing data, the teams engaged in genuine mutual exploration of the situation, uncovering areas of ignorance (or assumption) by each team, such that deeper layers of reality to the Orchid situation were revealed. This tactic of multiple, mutual meetings eventually resolved the issue of team competitiveness.

Results Findings Discussion With Orchid

The results of the team findings and analyses were presented to the Powdrey family members in two formats. Each team prepared a full report of findings and recommendations, which were hard copy documents and included suggestions for follow-through by Orchid leadership. Each team also orally presented their process, findings, and preliminary recommendations to the Powdrey family members at a joint face-to-face meeting. The meeting was held off-site from the Orchid facilities to encourage a neutral hearing, uninterrupted by work tasks. Both teams made lengthy presentations (approximately 1 hour each), which involved speakers from each team. All Powdrey family members made a personal effort to be present at this meeting, and all members stayed for the entire meeting time.

Family member reactions ranged from silence to active conversation with the team members. Various family members interrupted easily for questions and clarifications. Other family members were quiet, but attentive. The team intentions were to create a dialogue with the Powdrey family as co-creators of solutions or options to the issues that had surfaced in the needs assessment process (per Schein, 1999), and this strategy was generally successful. Discussions focused upon the company and family strengths uncovered in the needs assessment process. Ideas prompting dialogue included creation of Powdrey Family Business/Succession Plan, development of a separate Orchid business plan, clarification of leadership roles and responsibilities, segregation of leadership and operational roles, and employee communication. The teams offered general recommendations of external consultants and professional experts for the family to use in execution. However, no specific "to-do" tasks, or formal "lists of steps," were recommended. This type of offering was purposeful on the part of the teams. The teams had researched outside consultants and professionals who could be of further assistance in HRD planning, legal, and strategic endeavors. At this point, the teams were attempting to encourage the Powdrey family owners to understand what possible next steps might entail and to encourage the members to address those steps. Ultimately, the actions taken by the Powdrey family as a result of the needs assessment and the findings discussion remain ongoing.

DISCUSSION QUESTIONS

1. What are the critical challenges to the leadership changes at Orchid, and why do you think so?

2. Describe what "success" from an HRD perspective should look like at a family-owned business such as Orchid. What theory supports your descriptions?

3. How did the needs assessment process address management's initial expressed desire for employee development, a business plan, and production manager skills?

4. Orchid management, including the fourth-generation members, seem to be focused upon sales and production. How can the fourth generation become engaged in the HRD practice?

5. How might the needs assessment process have been altered to address the emotional and psychodynamic issues presented?

6. As a needs assessment process, what might have been the effect of using two assessing teams? What benefits or drawbacks might have been encountered from this design?

7. What OD processes for local but continuous organizational improvement can be suggested to Orchid management?

REFERENCES

Allen, C. W. (2006). Overview and evolution of the ADDIE training system. *Advances in Developing Human Resources, 8*(4), 430–441. doi:10.1177/1523422306292942

Block, P. (2000). *Flawless consulting: A guide to getting your expertise used.* San Francisco, CA: Jossey-Bass.

Burke, W. W., & Noumair, D. A. (2015). *Organization development: A process of learning and changing.* Upper Saddle River, NJ: Pearson Education.

Prange, M. (personal communication, September 15, 2017).

Ravlin, E. C., & Meglino, B. M. (1989). The transitivity of work values: Hierarchical preference of socially desirable stimuli. *Organizational Behavior and Human Decision Processes, 44*(2), 494–508. https://doi.org/10.1016/0749-5978(89)90021-6

Schein, E. H. (1999). *Process consultation revisited: Building the helping relationship.* Reading, MA: Addison Wesley.

Sleezer, C. M., Russ-Eft, D. F., & Gupta, K. (2014). *A practical guide to needs assessment* (3rd ed.). San Francisco, CA: Wiley & ASTD.

Appendix A

Detailed Data Findings, Orchid Candy Company

Strengths	Weaknesses

• Operations
  ○ Fourth-generation ownership and management
  ○ Surviving 89 years
  ○ Very good at what it takes to make products
  ○ Small batch sizes
  ○ Changeovers between products mid-shift: capacity and skill
  ○ Niche in old-fashioned Christmas candy
  ○ Factory workers able to perform multiple jobs
  ○ Full service for nonmanufacturing companies
• Management Education
  ○ Master's Computer Science
  ○ MBA University of Phoenix (1)
  ○ BA degrees (all fourth generation)
  ○ Stationary engineer's license
• Culture
  ○ Family nature, "taking care" of employees
  ○ Loyalty, long tenure of employees
  ○ Job security
  ○ Flexible job assignments based on employee skills/interest
  ○ Open-door policy for employees with corporate office
  ○ Not afraid to test known skills by trying new products/processes
  ○ Low employee turnover
  ○ Great relationships with long-term customers and vendors
	• Operations
	  ○ Factory not running at capacity
	  ○ Wrapping machine out of production since July 2017
	  ○ Limited plant experience of fourth generation
	  ○ Some machines have not been upgraded since the 1950s
	  ○ Machines on-site not producing or operating at full capacity
	• Culture
	  ○ No defined/communicated company values
	  ○ No mission or vision statement
	  ○ No defined policy/structure for manager rewards: salary increases, promotions, titles, etc.
	  ○ Low office morale
	  ○ Line managers independent, and resistant to suggestions/change
	  ○ Limited president support for formal HR operations or HRD (employee development)
	• Competitive advantage
	  ○ Manuf. expertise is limited to very few individuals
	  ○ Recently lost 35 years of experience
	  ○ Recently lost years of client relations
	• Communication
	  ○ Second-shift line workers do not have access to managers who can make production decisions

(Continued)

(Continued)

- **Competitive Advantage**
  - Expertise in cut rock candy
  - 55 years of candy-making experience
  - HVAC system knowledge
  - Instructor—Candy School— Department of Food Science at University of Mid-Atlantic State
  - Limited types of candy in production allows for increased expertise with those candies
  - Research & Development

- Frequent miscommunication between Production VP and line managers
- Insufficient communication results in tasks not being completed 100%
- Production changes do not consistently translate to the factory floor managers or supervisors
- Lack of input from non-VPs
- No performance feedback system/process in place

- **Planning/Goals/Objectives/Strategies**
  - No preventative maintenance completed on machines
  - No marketing plan, advertising budget
  - Procedures are out-of-date
  - No strategic plan to increase growth
  - No employee development plans to transfer subject matter expert knowledge to the appropriate personnel (fourth generation or others)
  - No succession plans
  - No business/sales plan to increase revenue
  - Distribution of power "plan" not in place

- **Job profiles/responsibilities/scope**
  - Job profiles not defined, descriptions not written
  - Self-titled fourth-generation members
  - Promotion based on time with company, not abilities
  - Job task/scope/responsibilities not clear to peers at manager level and the fourth-generation peer level
  - Only one person has expertise with the HVAC system

External Opportunities	External Threats
• Grant from state possible for training ESL managers • There are some 3,200 specialty shops across the nation selling nuts and candy confections • Community—neighborhood gentrifying	• City requiring minimum wage increase—cost of labor to increase • 493 U.S. locations make nonchocolate confections selling $10 billion a year • Food & safety regulations—manager focused internally—90% focus on documentation and 10% on floor quality

Lessons Learned

What insights did you gain by reading the book's 20 needs assessment cases? This section describes some key lessons that we learned by looking over the shoulders of practitioners who successfully translated needs assessment concepts into needs assessment practice. In this chapter, you will find

- Seven key lessons
- Where we go from here

Seven Key Lessons

Compare the lessons below with the ones that you gleaned by reading the cases.

1. **Needs assessments are conducted as a normal part of community, business, association, and professional work.**

The needs assessment cases in this book were implemented to address learning and/or performance needs. Each case took place in a unique environment. The environments ranged from a therapy dog organization to multinational organizations to a community orchestra to a family-owned business to professional associations to a university department, and so on. The geographic environments of the cases also varied; they included a rural U.S. location; a Bangkok, Thailand, location; a U.S. federal government agency with many locations; multinational firms with multiple locations; and so on.

A commonality among the cases was that they challenged some thinking found in the literature about the limited use of needs assessment. Reed and Vakola (2006) summarized that thinking, stating, "Despite the seemingly universal agreement that a thorough training needs analysis should underpin all training plans and budgets the literature also acknowledges that it does not often take place and is often not done in organisations" (p. 393). It was especially interesting to read the McLean case that included "push back" by the analyst when top management wanted a workshop implemented without conducting a needs assessment. The language that McLean used in pushing back provided insights into how to successfully resist such requests.

Another commonality among the cases was that each needs assessment was implemented to inform a topic of interest to the decision maker(s) who were considering one or more future actions. Through the needs assessment processes of collecting, analyzing, and reporting stories and data, the analyst engaged those who were invested in the topic, provided a trusted communication channel, and offered insights on the "lay of the land" that could serve as the basis for action. In many instances, the analyst also built consensus for the future action (e.g., see the Altschuld and Engle case and the Chandrasekar and Champion case).

This key insight that we obtained from the various cases offered practical information for individuals and organizations that are considering whether to invest in developing needs assessment expertise. Our answer is a resounding yes. Learning how to push back effectively when decision makers want an intervention without first conducting a needs assessment may be important for professionals in real-world situations. After all, without this upfront action, the intervention will probably fail as a result of neglecting to determine exactly what the problem or need is.

2. **Needs assessments are conducted by analysts who have many backgrounds.**

The analysts' expertise in these needs assessment cases ranged from competent student (e.g., the Chan case and the Clark case) to senior professional (e.g., the Altschuld and Engle case, the McLean case, and the McGonigle case). Reviewing the cases revealed that the analyst could

- be employed by the organization where the needs assessment was conducted (e.g., the Silverstein case),

- work as an individual external consultant (e.g., the Gugiu case),

- be employed by an external consulting firm (e.g., the Chandrasekar and Champion case, which was conducted by Center for Creative Leadership employees),

- be employed by a foundation (e.g., Geary), and

- work as a team member for an external consulting firm (e.g., the Chan case and the Einspruch case).

This key insight is useful for students who are considering how to develop their own expertise and where to put that expertise to work. Clearly, individuals can begin obtaining needs assessment expertise while they are students. These experiences might be gained as a volunteer or as an intern working within the organization.

Moreover, various kinds of employment options exist for those who desire a career in conducting needs assessments. As can be seen with these cases, some of the analysts were university faculty members or employees. Others worked within the organization for which the needs assessment was being conducted. Still others worked for a consulting firm or foundation. Finally, others were self-employed as individual consultants.

3. **Needs assessments are conducted in complex environments where flexibility and patience can be required for success.**

As we mentioned earlier in this chapter, each case in the book was conducted in a unique environment. In each case, the environment affected the needs assessment process and outcomes. To make this point, consider the great variation in the five needs assessment cases that were conducted in higher education institutions (e.g., the Yonjoo, Zhu, Techawitthayachinda, and Qian case; the Sritanyarat case; the Gugiu case; the Pitcher case; and the Word, Cockerill, Koehl, and Simpson case). Thus, even though each case was conducted in a higher-education setting, the complex environment within which the case took place led to completely different approaches and outcomes.

While the cases vary greatly, a commonality across these cases—and the other cases in this book—was complexity. Needs assessments are conducted in complex, real-world environments where the actions taken during a needs assessment and as a result of a needs assessment affect real people. Such situations call for a high level of respect for all the stakeholders, as well as flexibility, appropriate transparency, and patience. Therefore, analysts adapted their actions to reflect the requirements of their specific situations. To check out exemplars in these areas, reread the Sritanyarat case and the Altschuld and Engle case. This key insight about the importance of flexibility in conducting needs assessments challenges needs assessment models that must be done in a lock-step, prescribed fashion.

4. The analysts avoided jargon in describing the needs assessments.

As you read the cases in this book, did you notice the lack of needs assessment jargon? We did. We also noticed the lack of pretentious language. The cases were written in plain English and used the language of the environment where the case was conducted.

The analysts used professional terminology only as needed to communicate the processes they used (e.g., Gugiu used the correct terminology for statistical techniques). However, there was little grandstanding in the cases. Instead, the authors described the cases using language that highlighted their expertise. Interestingly, the lack of grandstanding and the correct use of professional terminology added to our practitioners' credibility.

Did you wonder why each case mentioned the approach to needs assessment that was used in the case (i.e., knowledge and skills assessment, job and task analysis, competency analysis, strategic assessment, and complex needs assessment)? The answer: We asked authors to include this information in their case proposals, so we could organize the cases for the book. Interestingly, authors had little difficulty with this task.

This key insight highlights the importance for analysts in learning and using the language of the environment. Whether reporting the titles of decision makers, describing the issue(s) of interest, or clarifying options, the language that the analyst uses contributes to perceptions of his or her credibility. In addition, using only the professional language that was required for understanding the case added to the analyst's credibility.

5. Analysts were adept at using and explaining data collection and analysis techniques.

As discussed by Watkins, Leigh, Platt, and Kaufman (1998) and Leigh, Watkins, Platt, and Kaufman (2000), various models and approaches to needs assessments exist. Indeed, the cases presented in this book showed that many different data collection techniques were used in conducting the needs assessment cases (e.g., focus group, survey, literature review, participant observation, interview, archival data, observation). Also, many different data analysis techniques were used (e.g., triangulation, thematic analysis, constant-comparative method, content mapping, descriptive statistics).

Analysts applied their knowledge of data collection and analysis to produce data that were valid and reliable (statistics) and trustworthy (qualitative). McLean, for example, described using Cronbach alpha to determine the reliability of the items. He also checked the data for multicollinearity. What was most interesting was the random division of the sample to run exploratory factor analysis on half of the sample and to run confirmatory factor analysis on the other half of the sample. Many of the cases using qualitative methods and analyses employed thematic analysis. Domlyn, Kenworthy, Scaccia, and Scott had two independent coders analyze the interview transcriptions using grounded theory and reconciliation of differences in themes. Such applications require in-depth understanding of the data collection and analysis techniques. Furthermore, McLean's description of meeting with decision makers who asked for additional statistics highlights the importance of understanding data collection and analysis techniques well enough to be able to discuss them with others if needed.

This key insight points out the importance of learning how to conduct the many data collection and analysis techniques, so that the appropriate ones for each situation can be applied. Careful reading of the cases revealed that the different cases called for different data collection and analysis techniques. The old saying that "if one only has a hammer, then everything is a nail" applies here. Analysts need to be adept in using multiple techniques.

6. Analysts were adept at managing the needs assessment process.

Each case in this book describes the allocation of resources for needs assessment and its management. Did you notice the resource-related tips that the authors applied in their cases? Their tips included the pragmatic tip that Cumberland offered (i.e., avoid the problem of accessing interviewees by [a] requesting that the client arrange the interviews and [b] providing the client with information about the available interview dates and times). They also included Einspruch's pragmatic solution of using a teleconference to provide capacity-building training, so that members of a local community could collect data when the evaluation team resided in a different area. A more general resource-related tip was the insight that Chan offered (i.e., the importance of adapting the scope of a needs assessment project when the client organization's budget changed).

The cases in this book also provided practical information about creating needs assessment instruments. Speaking from experience, it can take hours—and even days—to create data collection and analysis instruments. Reviewing the instruments used by other analysts can provide insights into how to phrase items, to sequence them, and more. For example, check out Word, Cockerill,

Koehl, and Simpson's focus group questions and Clark's focus group protocol and resources survey.

As you read the needs assessment cases, did you recognize that some analysts made certain aspects visible? Check out

- Clark's visual representation of needs assessment findings using a two-axis matrix.

- Silverstein's use of data placemats that allowed stakeholders to co-create knowledge with each other and the evaluator. A data placemat is a visual document that displays themes from the collected data, typically in the form of charts and graphs. It is the size of a placemat.

- Silverstein's report that the chief planning officer and the CEO of the philanthropic organization held face-to-face inquiry meetings with all executive directors of grantee organizations. Such meetings with the head(s) of a philanthropic organization communicated more than information. They also communicated the importance of the grantee organizations.

- Pitcher's description of using text, infographics, and tables to report needs assessment data. Infographics represent information, data, or knowledge visually so that they can be understood quickly and clearly.

Fundamental to managing needs assessments was the analysts' understanding of the value of how knowledge could be created:

- Strack mentioned the value of collecting survey data from individuals who were unfamiliar with the association. She stated, "Learning from an audience unfamiliar with the association, and with membership potential, could reshape the direction and the assumptions about the products and/or services ordered or planned."

- Williams provided an example of a needs assessment that relied on dialogue with the clients to co-create solutions to the issues that emerged during the needs assessment.

- Star described how an addendum was added to the initial proposal for the small business needs assessment that expanded the consultant's role to include offering opinions on programmatic improvements. Given the lack of funding to implement the needs assessment recommendations, an addendum was important and enabled the development of creative solutions.

Analysts also recognized that sharing information and making the time and effort to build consensus for action was important to assessing needs. For example, Altschuld and Engle described open and frequent communication with the public that became embedded in the needs assessment activities. Sritanyarat described taking the time and effort to build consensus for action during the needs assessment. Interestingly, she described the roller coaster of needs assessment that can be experienced with its highs (when the analyst thinks people agreed with a concept) and its lows (when the analyst realized that people viewed a concept differently).

Star described a needs assessment of a grassroots, volunteer organization. At the beginning of the needs assessment some organization stakeholders did not think a needs assessment was necessary. During the needs assessment, the analyst presented at board meetings on the structure and process of the needs assessment and the support desired from participants. Also, she was accessible to stakeholders by both phone and email, which increased transparency. Interestingly, by the end of the needs assessment "those who initially questioned the process ultimately expressed gratitude for its outcome."

7. **The tensions between scientific research and pragmatic needs assessments are evident in each case.**

Rossi et al. (2004) discussed the balancing act required to negotiate the tensions between scientific research studies and pragmatic evaluations. The cases in this book reveal that many needs assessors carefully balanced and negotiated between meeting the standards of systematic research inquiry and providing practical results within contexts that had ever-changing constraints of time, resources, expectations, and stakeholders.

For example, there are tensions between rigor and practicality in such issues as the following:

- With any survey work, there are likely to be nonrespondents. Researchers are admonished to determinate the level of nonresponse, as well as the degree of nonresponse bias. But, how much effort should be devoted to that issue in a needs assessment?

- With the use of a research instrument, be it a survey or some other type of tool, the reliability and validity of the instrument should be examined. But, how important is it for the practitioner to undertake check on the reliability and validity of the instrument? To what extent is a high degree of reliability and validity of importance in a needs assessment?

- With qualitative research, researchers are admonished to utilize various approaches to enhance trustworthiness, such as member checking, triangulation, and negative case analysis. Should those approaches be employed in a needs assessment?

- Several of the needs assessment cases used an internal employee or consultant to conduct the work. This may be considered similar to the developmental evaluation approach (e.g., Patton, 2011) in which the internal employee or consultant continues to work with the organization to implement some of the recommendations. But, might this stance lead to the possibility of becoming biased or self-serving? And, would that really be a problem for the needs assessment effort?

As an exercise, select a case. Now consider how you could change the needs assessment

a) To make it more scientific and the implications of the change(s)

b) To make it more practical and the implications of the change(s)

Remember to consider the additional costs of making a case more scientific (e.g., time, resources, and so forth). And, remember to consider the additional risks (e.g., to validity and trustworthiness) by making a case more practical. The lessons learned from the needs assessment cases in this book can inform future research and practice. The next section explores both ideas.

Where We Go From Here

In Chapter 1, we defined needs assessment as "a diagnostic process that relies on data collection, collaboration, and negotiation to identify and understand gaps in learning and performance and to determine future actions" (Sleezer, Russ-Eft, & Gupta, 2014, p. 310). It seemed appropriate to use that definition to examine the gaps in needs assessment between where we are and where we want to be. First we identify some research gaps and then some practical gaps.

Some Research Gaps

The cases in the book can be thought of as examples of action research. Coghlan and Shani (2018, p. 4) defined action research as:

> An emergent inquiry process in which applied behavioral science knowledge is integrated with existing organizational knowledge and applied to address real organizational issues. It is simultaneously concerned with bringing about change in organizations, in developing self-help competencies in organizational members and in adding to scientific knowledge. Finally, it is an evolving process that is undertaken in a spirit of collaboration and co-inquiry.

In the research context, action research allows collaborative problem solving with those involved with the inquiry process and the generation of new knowledge (Coghlan & Brannick, 2001). It allows the study of a process directly as it unfolds. Such processes are similar or the same as needs assessment, as can be seen in the various cases in this book. As with action research, needs assessments apply the knowledge of social science research to solve practical organizational or community problems, and the assessments depend on a spirit of collaboration and co-inquiry. One research question might be, To what extent and in what ways are needs assessments the same or different from action research? Another research question might be, What research approaches are effective for studying needs assessment processes and the outcomes that result?

Soriano (2012) noted that the term *needs assessment* is often easier to comprehend than to apply. As was noted above, many of the book's needs assessments involved and included the participation of organization or community members in various aspects of the design, conduct, and analysis of the needs assessment work. Given the current interest in building the capacity of stakeholders to undertake needs assessments and evaluations, a research question might be, What are the knowledge and skills that stakeholders need to conduct effective needs assessments? What is the quality of stakeholder-led needs assessments, and how do these compare with expert-led needs assessments?

Lee (2018) also discussed the risks that can result from improper needs assessments. Lee stated (abstract, para. 1), "Although conducting a needs assessment has been accepted as the first step in solving performance problems, many human resource development (HRD) and training professionals find it still difficult to conduct an effective and efficient needs assessment." It would be both instructive and interesting to interview some HRD and training professionals to identify the stumbling blocks and hurdles that they have had to encounter.

Some Practitioner Implications

The needs assessment cases presented in this book provide both researchers and practitioners with ideas and models that can be adapted for use. Practitioners can examine the various cases within the five needs assessment approaches. Based on the descriptions of the data collection and analysis methods used, these practitioners can then decide whether some aspects of an approach might be useful in their own organization or situation.

In addition to examining the data collection and analysis work, practitioners should also examine the section within each case titled "Issues and Challenges." These sections identified the stumbling blocks that these experts had to face. But, most importantly, the cases described what actions the experts took to overcome the issues and challenges. Such detail may prove particularly useful for practitioners who are attempting to undertake needs assessments within complex environments.

By building on the contributions of the cases in this book and the lessons learned, needs assessment research and practice can evolve to make a better contribution to individuals, teams, organizations, and communities. We look forward to these developments—and hope that you also do!

REFERENCES

Coghlan, D., & Brannick, T. (2001). *Doing action research in your own organization.* London, England: Sage.

Coghlan, D., & Shani, A. B. (2018). *Conducting action research.* Thousand Oaks, CA: Sage.

Lee, J. (2018). Rapid needs assessment: An evidence-based model. *European Journal of Training and Development, 43* (1/2), 61–75. https://doi.org/10.1108/EJTD-08-2018-0077

Leigh, D., Watkins, R., Platt, W. A., & Kaufman, R. (2000). Alternate models of needs assessment: Selecting the right one for your organization. *Human Resource Development Quarterly, 11,* 87–93. https://doi.org/10.1002/1532-1096(200021)11:1<87:: AID-HRDQ7>3.0.CO;2-A

Patton, M. Q. (2011). *Developmental evaluation: Applying complexity concepts to enhance innovation and use.* New York, NY: Guilford Press.

Reed, J., & Vakola, M. (2006). What role can a training needs analysis play in organisational change? *Journal of Organizational Change Management, 19*(3), 393–407. doi:10.1108/09534810610668382}

Sleezer, C. M., Russ-Eft, D. F., & Gupta, K. (2014). *A practical guide to needs assessment* (3rd ed.). San Francisco, CA: Wiley & ASTD.

Soriano, F. I. (2012). *Conducting needs assessments: A multidisciplinary approach.* Thousand Oaks, CA: Sage.

Watkins, R., Leigh, D., Platt, W. A., & Kaufman, R. (1998). Needs assessment: A digest, review, and comparison of needs assessment literature. *Performance Improvement, 37*(7), 40–53. https://doi.org/10.1002/pfi.4140370711